Beginning

KENNETH BRANAGH

Beginning

St. Martin's Press
New York

Library of Congress Cataloging-in-Publication Data

Branagh, Kenneth.
    Beginning / Kenneth Branagh.
        p.   cm.
    Reprint. Previously published: New York : Norton, 1989.
    ISBN 0-312-05822-5 (paperbk.)
    1. Branagh, Kenneth.   2. Renaissance Theatre Company.
3. Actors—Great Britain—Biography.   I. Title.
[PN2598.B684A3   1991]
792'.028'092—dc20
[B]   90-28603
                                                              CIP

First published in the United States by W. W. Norton & Company, Inc.

First U.S. Paperback Edition: May 1991
10   9   8   7   6   5   4   3   2

Acknowledgements

Many thanks to my parents for their patience and help with the Belfast chapters; to Annie Wotton for her computer wizardry and her constant support; to Phyllida Law for the marvellous drawings; and to Jonathan Burnham for his expert and invaluable editorial advice.

For
Lizzie Branagh, who was there at the beginning of it all,
with love and gratitude

*'I will tell you the beginning,
and if it please your ladyships you shall see the
end,
for the best is yet to do.'*

AS YOU LIKE IT

Introduction

Beginning (bigi-nin), vbl. sb. ME. [f. as prec. + INGi.] 1.
The action or process of entering upon existence or upon
action, or of bringing into existence; commencing, orig-
ination. 2. The rudimentary stage; the earliest proceed-
ings.

As this book reveals, I have read a great number of actors' autobiog-
raphies. I've come to think of them as rather dangerous things. I'm
suspicious of talking about acting or 'life'. It seems that as soon as I
think I know something and try to describe it, it's gone. At twenty-
eight, the chances of really knowing something are slim, and the
possibility of losing what grasp you do have, great. So why write this?
Money.

In January 1988 the tiny office in my Camberwell flat was bursting
with the activities of the Renaissance Theatre Company. There was
a packed year of theatre work ahead, and little chance of earning
enough cash to remove the centre of operations from under my own
roof. I discussed the predicament with my literary agent. He and I
had both been approached by various publishers with the idea of my
writing some form of autobiography which would feature an account
of the formation of Renaissance. We decided to auction the idea, and
among the publishers who expressed an interest were Chatto &
Windus.

The deal was made, and a handsome advance was paid out. The
advance provided the funds to buy accommodation for the Company's offices, thus moving Renaissance out of my flat and bringing
me a little nearer sanity.

I had agreed to write 100,000 words. Quite what I was going to
write I wasn't sure, but I was hopeful that it would work out
somehow – a pattern that characterises much of the career described
in the pages that follow. It's an odd and difficult task to try and make
sense of one's life at twenty-eight. I've set out therefore to describe, as
far as I can understand it, the beginnings of a life and of a career.
When I read it back, this book seems merely to describe a professional journey, the arrival point of which is another beginning.

Looking back has been an instructive process for me, but for the ordinary reader, interested in actors and acting, I suspect that it will make a different kind of sense. I hope that there will be some value in the fact that this book has been written now, with all its imperfections on its head, and not in fifty years' time. It makes no claim to be a manual on acting, or a careers advice book, or a survey of the British Theatre today. It's the story of a particular talent, and how that talent was combined with a measure of ambition and some quite extraordinary professional good fortune. Above all, it describes a first stage, from which it seems too early to draw far-reaching conclusions.

This is simply what happened to me.

Home

ONE

The smell of pigs' feet boiling,
with nabs and ribs and noints,
Greeted all men-folk as they
rolled home from the joints.
Mother cut the soup-greens
whilst waiting for her sire.
Then bathed the children briskly
in a tub beside the fire.
That was Saturday night in York Street;
boyhood memories remained . . .
Saturday night in York Street
will never come again!

(From SATURDAY NIGHT IN YORK STREET, by John Campbell)

Even in the 1930s, a Saturday night in Belfast's York Street was 'a quare oul do'.

The fighting and the swearing at chucking-out time were as savage and regular as the arrival of the peelers, who gathered up the familiar faces into a packed paddy wagon and took them straight to the police station. With equal regularity, the wives would arrive the next morning at the 'polis' to say their Sunday hellos to the station officer and to bail out their hungover husbands. The rancour of the previous evening would have mysteriously disappeared and the former enemies would walk home arm-in-arm with their wives as if the combat of the previous evening had been a strange dream. The daily intimacy and neighbourliness which characterised relationships in that world returned as if by magic, and they wended, by way of a drink, back to the Belfast legend that was York Street.

At the time it was more than just a street. It constituted an area right on the docks that included names like Ship Street, Nelson Street, Pilot Street and a small network of roads and alleys that

1

collectively took their name from the main thoroughfare. The houses were battered, cramped terraces that sardined their inhabitants together for more years than the buildings can ever have been intended for. People rarely knew who owned them. Except in very few cases, it certainly wasn't the inhabitants. They paid their rent weekly – at least, that was the plan – to an agent. The mysterious landlord seldom ventured into this part of Belfast.

Rough it was, but the people who lived in and around York Street had a fierce pride in their area, and its nearness to the docks, Belfast's great heart. Everyone knew each other and York Street folk were famous in Ulster for an encyclopaedic knowledge of family affairs that stretched from street to street. This knowledge was often gained through blood ties. Large families were the norm and it was these little tribes and clans, Catholic and Protestant alike in rough segregation, that dominated the area. The Branaghs and the Harpers (my mother's family) grew up within streets of each other. Both were large Protestant families and both were ruled over by highly colourful patriarchs in the shape of my two grandfathers, who shared the same first-class York Street credentials of being universally known 'characters', hard drinking and hard up.

Alcoholism was an unfamiliar word in those days, but on a York Street drinking table Grandpa Branagh would have been in the middle and Grandpa Harper threatening the leaders. Neither of them actually found their way into the great caged Saturday night 'polis' wagon but I suspect this was only because they moved bars quickly enough.

'Speedy' Harper worked on the docks. He got his name from the pace at which he could empty cement boats, a frequent Belfast cargo. With just a sack over his head, he and his fellows ran up and down the gangplanks like ants, cement dust everywhere. The docks operated a highly discriminatory system for distributing work. There were the blue button men, the red button men and the casuals. When work was to be had, which was usually on a strictly daily basis, the stevedores would select first from the blue button men, then from the red, and then from the casuals. Much of the Saturday night bother arose from arguments about this exclusive preferential treatment. Blue and red buttons were handed down from father to son and buying or bribing your way in was very difficult. Once you were in, the difference was considerable, with a blue button man receiving as a daily wage what a casual might make for the week. In spite of being

2

a beneficiary of this local corruption, Speedy Harper seemed little better off. With his colleagues, he had the usual dockers' breakfast – an hour in the pub between 10 and 11 – and if, with his customary skill, he had emptied a cement boat by 3 pm, then the blue button benefits found their way into the bar for the rest of the day. They disappeared very quickly, commemorated only by the ever-full slate which each bar ran, and to which every York Street man inevitably became indebted.

A fearsome man in the home, dogged by injuries at work (when he was in work), Speedy Harper's volatile, alcohol-infused personality must have shuddered at the arrival of yet another addition to his large family. Frances Harper, my mother, was born on 6 September 1930. A complication after the birth ensured that some twelve days later her no doubt exhausted mother died, at the age of thirty-eight. Frances had been her eleventh child.

For a while my mother escaped the aftermath of a tragedy which was all too familiar in York Street. Her elder sisters were too young to play any maternal role, so Frances was sent to a great Aunt Alice who lived in BallyMcCarret, East Belfast, and she remained there happily until she was six. Alice, very elderly, gave her, for a brief period, some sense of what having a mother and living in a small, reasonably comfortable house might have been like. The kind, dumpy old lady doted on her, bringing her a wonderful breakfast in bed every morning – a Jaffa orange with the top cut off, full of sugar, with a spoon stuck into it. Then Aunt Alice died, and my mother's unsettled childhood took another blow. Shaken by the double loss, she returned to Belfast and a family divided by death, with a father whose drinking had intensified, and who had little sense of responsibility about the family finances.

Ship Street was a long way from Aunt Alice's, and the early disorientation had a profound effect on the six-year-old girl. There had been other deaths, all sons – Willie-John, George, Martin, who had a fall in Speedy's beloved shipyard, and Andrew, who died tragically from eating an infected banana found on a rubbish tip. The family now consisted of Charlie and James, Kathleen, Rosie and Frances. Jeanie and Sarah, the oldest girls, had left already. There were two rooms, one up one down, with a stone floor, a wooden table and a scrubbed wooden settee. It looked a bit like a butcher's shop. The girls slept together in one bed and the boys shared their bed with Speedy (something that Charlie refused to do as soon as he was able – because of the drink that reeked from his father).

Frances attended the Mariners' Public Elementary School, earning a reputation as a tearaway. Perhaps not having a mother, living with a drunken father and a measure of fierce Harper pride were the cause. In any case she was too busy rebelling to notice a rather quieter boy in the class of sixty or more, but her future husband, William Branagh, must have noticed her.

'Pop' Branagh, my father's dad, was a 'handy man' – a phrase prevalent in the folklore of the time to describe York Street men who 'dabbled' for their income. Pop could be seen at the docks some mornings (as a casual) trying for a day's work on one of the boats. But his real love was horses, and for a time he had a little yard at the back of Nelson Street where he sold hay and oats, and repaired horse-carts and bits of saddlery. Sometimes he worked as a kind of agent, buying horses for Belfast delivery men who couldn't make the trips out to the local fairs. The kids were kept off school for these missions so that they could ride or lead one of the horses back to Belfast. It was on horseback that my father first saw the Fairs at Killreigh and Ballyclare, and caught a breath of the country which had a much stronger pull for him than the brashness of docklands Belfast.

Pop and Lizzie Branagh, with five children, had fewer mouths to feed than the Harpers, but for Pop the work was even more irregular and the call of the bar just as strong. Both my parents were introduced to pubs early on with the nightly crane round the door of the public house to scream 'Tell my Da his tea's ready'. Within shouting distance of each other's homes, both Bill and Frances were aware of the cruel hold that drink had on their fathers.

At Christmas, the Da's would leave at the very last minute for the market and come back late (drunk, of course) with a chicken and some vegetables under their arms. The women in each household performed miracles, Kathleen taking the mother's role at the Harpers' and Lizzie Branagh ensuring there was at least an apple and an orange in the Christmas stocking. If she'd managed to keep the money from Pop, there would be twelve new pennies for Annie, Walter. Tommy, Lilly and Bill. For my mother, Christmas and birthdays offered much the same prospect, with perhaps fewer pennies, and more time to envy the rare child in the area (perhaps in another blue button home) who had a 'proper' present. Her dream was always to have a bicycle, a wish granted by Speedy Harper in her

4

late teens when a second-hand boneshaker was offered. Her disappointment when she talks of it is palpable even now.

My father's quiet early education at Pilot Street Elementary School was interrupted by the war. He was nine years old, and both he and Annie were evacuated to Rosharkin, in the countryside near Belfast, amid much gas-mask-issuing excitement. The sense of childhood adventure was soon shattered when Bill was placed under the demonic authority of his country schoolmaster, Mr Eaton, a Celtic Murdstone. He was now separated from both his mother and father. Pop had gone to England to work as a miner in Melton Mowbray and Lizzie was bringing up Tommy, Walter and Lilly in Belfast, sixty miles from the terrified children.

My father lived in mortal dread of Mr Eaton, a man with a smouldering and unreasonable resentment against Belfast, the Belfast accent and Belfast schoolchildren. Picked on relentlessly by Eaton, this period was a very miserable one for my father, and I have often thought of him praying his child's heart out in that small Irish village, desperately wishing that the Austin car which drove the dragonish Eaton would crash and kill him. The evacuees' home was comfortless. Talking was forbidden, bed was at eight o'clock and it required the greatest daring to creep out of the bedrooms to hear Alvar Liddell's nine o'clock war bulletin.

Later, there were compensations. My grandmother was able to join them in Rosharkin after a year, bringing the rest of the children and renting at last their own two-roomed accommodation in the village. The family sent fervent but often hopeless prayers that Pop's registered money envelope would arrive from England. If the drink had devoured it that week then Bill was dispatched across the road to the landlord's to explain that the rent would not be paid and to beg for understanding. But they were in the country, which my father loved, and he earned a few extra pennies by collecting eggs for the local farmer who let him keep one from every batch. Indeed, the Branaghs' landlord grew so attached to this enterprising Belfast lad that he approached my grandmother about adopting him. At this point the Belfast authorities relaxed the evacuee regulations and the problem of whether my father should remain in Rosharkin or not was solved by the family's swift return to the city and a new two-up two-down in Nelson Street.

Pop returned from Melton Mowbray and the family were reunited for the last part of the war. Bill and Tommy, when not at the

Mariners' school, would continue to help their Dad with his general 'dealing'. On an old cart pulled by a horse which grew or shrank in size according to the varying success of Pop's ventures, they rode around York Street selling eggs or vegetables or whatever job-lot they'd managed to find. Herrings were a favourite. Pop would pick up a box on the fish quay and sell them round York Street for two bob a dozen. This, with the horse dealing, the saddlery and removal of fireplaces, continued to provide Pop with an erratic income in a Belfast relatively prosperous through the temporary boom provided by the munitions industry.

The street lore of this time was particularly rich and both my parents were beginning to enter fully into the York Street world of Ulster eccentrics. People like Jimmy Foster, who flitted from street to street and house to house as a twinkling handy man who was 'only temporary'. If he mended something, it was 'only temporary'. If he broke an appointment, it was 'only temporary'. Then there was 'Buck Alec', a knotty, sinewy fellow who, it was said, had been a Strong Man in the circus. If the peelers knew they were to deal with 'Buck Alec' on the Saturday night clear-up of the pubs, they laid on extra manpower.

They often had cause to speak to him. 'Buck Alec' kept a lion in a cage in his backyard in York Street. He took this with him round the Fairs in Ulster as a sideshow. Alec would leap fearlessly into the cage, take hold of the decrepit animal's mouth, open it and put his head inside. It was believed that Alec had pulled all its teeth. What everyone was sure of was the incessant roaring of the beast through the York Street night. Alec promised to do something. After a time calm was restored and residents breathed a sigh of relief until another uproar followed as the police station was inundated with people reporting their domestic cats stolen. 'Buck Alec', who could be as 'temporary' as Jimmy Foster, disappeared with the cat-eating cat in tow.

Apart from murmurings in 1935 and the usual Saturday night free-for-all, this period and through to the 1960s was relatively free from sectarian violence or other trouble of that kind. The ratio of Protestants to Catholics in York Street was two thirds to one third, and they worked, ate and played together in peace.

The chief trouble for my mother was her own schooling. Her rebellious streak was much in evidence. On one occasion her sister, Rose, who was in the same class, asked to be allowed to go to the toilet. The teacher refused and after a while, in the scrum of the packed classroom, Rose fainted. Indignant, my mother rose up to tear a strip off the teacher and immediately marched her mortified sister back home and then brought the dreaded Speedy to the school to put the fear of God into the teacher. That kind of Harper spunk made her unpopular with the staff and my mother's response was to refuse to care and to stop listening, a course she has been regretting for the rest of her life, and which she has repeatedly enjoined her own family not to do. She remains lively and intelligent, but haunted by the fact that her education was neglected. This has bred a sense of inferiority, and an inbuilt suspicion of the world and the blows it will inevitably inflict upon her and the family – which is not surprising in the light of troubled family history and of Speedy himself, who seemed dogged by misfortune. Protective coatings have developed to protect this vulnerability, which must be linked to the absence of her own ma, but traces of the rebel child are manifest in my mother's anarchic and irrepressible sense of fun – her giggling fits have punctuated family life for as long as I can remember.

Speedy had moved the family to North Anne Street, where they had four rooms. Like the Branaghs, they lived on barley soups and vegetable broths which lasted for three or four meals. There was shin beef or brisket once a week or once a fortnight. Rationing helped put my father off margarine for life, and egg powder haunts the entire tribe of my aunts and uncles. Speedy was drunk by degrees. The Harper girls preferred him to be paid weekly because then he was only drunk all weekend; if he was paid daily then he was drunk every night.

Late each evening it was the task of the girls to get this dead weight up the stairs, and from time to time they took a secret pleasure in letting him fall, stifling their giggles the next day when he murmured to himself about why the hell he was so black and blue. The temptation for some sort of revenge was great. He would frequently come home plastered and demand that my mother be brought downstairs to sing to him while he became darkly maudlin about his dead wife. Nearly forty years later I appeared in a television play by Graham Reid set in Belfast where just such a scene occurs. All of my mother's family vouched for the authenticity of the scene, one which must have been repeated all over York Street in those days.

The drink and the fags always had the first call on his money. When the girls wanted to decorate he put his foot down about wallpaper, saying it carried bed-bugs and insisted instead that the house should be red-leaded. When he was broke and had no cigarettes he made my mother search the streets for dog-ends. Woe betide her if she returned empty-handed. He insisted despite the shame it caused my mother, who desperately cajoled friends into joining the hunt until they too refused and she felt only the deep indignity of forcibly serving this drunken man's poverty-stricken addiction. She remembers the time and the shame with great force. It remains difficult for her to talk about, and only in recent years has she been able to share these tearful recollections with her own family.

Elsewhere in York Street at this time, papers were being delivered by William Branagh Junior, who was also finishing his education at the ripe old age of fourteen. As with all the York Street kids, the options were few. Mr Burgess, his headmaster at Mariners', wanted him to go on to higher education, but it was out of the question that 'young Willie', as his mother called him, should not start bringing some wage into the house. The obvious place was the textile mill. Burgess was appalled and did everything in his power to save this bright boy from such a fate. Nevertheless a starting wage at the mill for young Willie was £2 10 shillings and not to be ignored. Rescue came in the shape of Billy McMillan, who ran Dad's paper-round and who had a mate with a building business looking for an apprentice. Mr Burgess was delighted, Dad decided on doing his time as a joiner and Lizzie accepted the drop in wage that this inevitably meant. Twenty-three shillings and sixpence was his starting pay, of which one pound was handed into the house. By the Thursday of each week, through his bus fares and the two or three trips to the cinema which was the staple diet of the York Street youngster, Lizzie ended up paying a few bob back so that young Willie could have some sort of social life. But serving your time (if you could manage the immediate financial hardship) was a terrific start, and my father set to it with a will.

For my mother there was the mill, or nothing. She dreamed of getting away, of becoming a professional ballroom dancer. If that wasn't possible, then at least she would try to get to England, the next best thing. No, was the implacable reply from Speedy, not until she was twenty-one. The rest of her adolescence was spent in avoiding his wrath and, whenever she could, dancing. This was more difficult than it sounds. Apart from the cost of going to a dance, maybe borrowing shoes, painting your legs with stain to stand in for stockings, there was also Speedy. If an application to be 'let out' for the evening to go to a dance wasn't lodged at least two weeks before, then you were in trouble. And if there was any domestic work which needed doing, then you were simply required to stay in, regardless of what arrangements had been made.

My mother and father first met properly when they were both sixteen years old at a church youth club – a group of around twenty-four York Street kids, who went on day-trips together; many of them, over the years, married each other. Although the club was attached to the church, my parents both maintained only a nominal interest in formal religion, a reaction perhaps to the religious obsessions which gripped the province.

Dad came out of his time at nineteen and, yet again confounding the apparent rules of working-class opportunity, he was made a gang leader and put in charge of three of the men he'd been serving under for the previous five years. What's more, his boss had special assignments for him. New building systems and materials were developing and young Willie's firm had Irish franchises for important elements of these. He was sent off for a week's course to London and returned starry-eyed and shell-shocked from the first hotel he had ever stayed in, the Strand Palace, which must have seemed like wonderland in 1950 for the twenty-year-old from York Street.

He returned home and then went to the Republic (or the Free State, as it was referred to then) to implement these new skills and at last to earn some real money. He worked all over the south, each job lasting roughly six weeks. The wages arrived on Friday at the local post-office, and a fiver would go back to his mother who at last could be repaid for the sacrifices of his teens. She saved the money and tried to give it back to him when he came home at the weekends.

With plenty of overtime down south, the money was really very good, and meant that on the trips home both 'Pop' and Speedy, the future in-law, were able to benefit. By this time Frances and Bill were writing to each other regularly and seeing each other on his trips back. But their relationship didn't stop my mother sticking to her childhood promise of going to England. At twenty-one she pawned her coat in order to pay her way to Manchester where her elder sister, Jean, was living, and she acted as governess to two young Jewish children in a wealthy northern family. She made a great success of this, and despite pleas from the host family to stay, she was – as she always has been – Belfast to her very bones, and her homesickness drew her back to Nelson Street and into the arms of my father.

They were now officially 'going together', something that must have been a comfort to her when she faced the latest of Speedy's peculiar dispensations. He had had an accident at the shipyard and lost a couple of fingers. He had put in a compensation claim that had taken over a year to be processed, and when it eventually came through no one was quite sure what the amount was, but there was talk of it being a vast amount. In fact, it was around £1500, which was a greater sum than the Harpers had ever seen before. All through the year-long wait, Speedy's slate had been running at the local bar. His credit was good. Everyone knew the claim was in. On the day he got his money he walked into the bar to pay off his slate and buy everyone a drink. His tab ran to nearly £500.

He gave my Aunt Rose £100, and he entrusted the rest to Kathleen, as she'd always managed the household miraculously. From her he received the balance in handouts from which he drank himself slowly to death. To my mother he gave ten pounds, saying that anything more would turn her head. It seems he thought his own was stable enough.

My parents married on 28 August 1954 at St Anne's Cathedral, Belfast. They'd paid for the wedding themselves, and for the reception (six shillings and sixpence a head). Mum wore a borrowed wedding dress and at the last minute, after endless cajoling and a final threat that he would never be spoken to again, Speedy came to give her away. He stayed as long as the photographs and then went off back to the pub. In the wedding pictures he is a haunted, wasted figure. My parents look radiant, handsome and happy.

Married life for the first two years was in one room above Pop and Lizzie's house-cum-shop. They squeezed in a dining-room suite and a bedroom suite and managed to find room for Bill junior, who arrived a year after their marriage. Pop doted on my mother and young Bill, and I'm sure my mother loved Pop far more than her own father. But like Speedy, Pop was often short of the readies. She discovered his own roguish method of acquiring them when he asked her, shortly after they moved in, 'Can I mind ten bob for you?' 'What do you want to do that for?' she asked innocently. Enter my father to catch his own dad red-handed and point out fiscal expedients to his new wife.

After two years of marriage and regular work for them both, Mum in the mill and Dad now working in Belfast as a joiner, they made the huge York Street leap of buying their own house. The semi-detached at £1350 in the Cavehill suburb seemed within their reach, but furnishing the place and bringing up baby was a strain. There were buses to catch everywhere and six pounds a month mortgage plus HP on some of the furnishings. After a while they had to sell their dream home. It was a terrible disappointment and they certainly suffered as a result of this 'fall'. And quite a fall it was. They'd been on the council waiting list for some time but the powers-that-be decided that a probationary period was also needed to see if they were suitable tenants. They were placed at the lowest end of the council's accommodation lists and were eventually housed in the Downview Bungalows estates.

These were pre-fabs, made with asbestos and designed to last for ten years. Some of them remained for forty. My parents had their first shock when they were required to have referees for the baker and the milkman. When trying to buy on HP they were told 'credit was not good in Downview Gardens'. My mother assumed naively that all the men on the estate were doing night work, since she saw them around during the day. In fact my father and one other man on the estate of sixty pre-fabs were the only ones in work. Everyone else was 'on the club'.

My mother finally decided something had to be done when strange male visitors would knock on the door and say that they'd been sent by 'a friend'. She kept sending them off until Dad found out that 55, Downview Bungalows (our address) was being confused with 55, Loughview Bungalows, part of the red light district. It was only this case, specially pleaded by my mother to an (at last) understanding council that persuaded them to rehouse the Branaghs one grade up at 96 Mountcollyer Street, N.15.

Just before that, on Saturday 10 December 1960, in the late afternoon, a second son was born, Kenneth Charles. It was about ten minutes to five and apparently I was just in time for the football results.

My first memories of Belfast begin just after the death of Speedy, who was already becoming a Harper family myth. My aunts had clubbed together to propagate the legend of a man who was hard-done-by, tough but fair, who loved his family to death, despite outward appearances, and whose one fatal flaw was drink. Over the years the family have granted Speedy a Santa Claus-like aura of benevolence. In all of the Harpers there was also a feeling of having been through something of tremendous significance, an impenetrable bond of pride in having survived upbringings of extreme hardship, and a father whose temperament was unpredictable and often cruel.

I never knew Speedy, and although Pop Branagh was not as dramatic (or tragic) a character, for me he was a real grandad – kind, warm, and sweet-natured. I loved him and Granny Branagh to death, and as an infant explorer, running amok in his front room workshop, I was introduced to the Aladdin's Cave that was Pop's factory of commercial ideas. As my father recalls with melancholy, 'He could have been a millionaire, but for the drink. When he did make money, he gave half of it away and drank the other half.'

My mother certainly vouches for his generosity, as she was the first to receive a crisp note after one of Pop's successful schemes. By this time one of his main ventures was removing old tiled fireplaces (then called 'Kitchenettes') and replacing them with wooden 1950s' models. He was still enlisting help from Dad, who provided the mantelpieces for this part of Pop's work.

Both Pop and Granny Branagh took a great interest in me and in Bill, who was five years older than I was. My mother now insists that I was always a difficult child. At the age of three I spoke but could be understood by no one but her. Aunt Kathleen was convinced I was German, and my mother believed I would never be able to speak properly.

The cause of this problem was my tonsils and adenoids, which were promptly removed amid death's-door rises in temperature. I emerged from this brush with death in a considerably calmer state than my family, and with my new vocal dexterity was able to scream the house down about my school dinners. The kitchens of the Grove Primary School were absolutely fine, I'm sure, but a mysterious and morbid dread of puddings and of being forced to eat them – as I was by a dragonish teacher called Mrs Robinson – left me a gibbering wreck.

With Mum and Dad both working, I had no choice. I appeared to comply, but as my weight dropped over the weeks, my parents knew something was up. I was rumbled when a pile of loose change was found in the pans of the boys' toilets. What I'd done was to tell the teachers that I was going home then hid in the loos, where I was so paralysed with guilt that I threw the dinner money down the toilet. I hadn't realised that the coins were not flushing away and I was soon exposed. Whether they felt they had a Freudian textbook case on their hands is unclear, but my folks certainly deemed the problem serious enough to write a note that excused me the horrors of custard, tapioca and bread and butter pudding, and thereby save themselves some money.

Pop and Lizzie came to the rescue and each dinnertime I walked to their house, which was near the Grove, and had their famous broth or 'champ' (mashed potatoes, spring onions and butter) or fish fingers and other treats. Chief among these was a threepenny bit which my Granny produced just before I headed back to school each day and which allowed me a fine selection from the penny tray at the local sweet shop.

As well as my daily visits, the family went to see my grandparents at least twice a week. Belfast seemed to be all about visiting your relatives. As my folks seemed to be related to one half of Belfast and to have been at school with the other half, visiting time was hectic. At my Granny's we were certain to see my Aunt Annie and maybe her kids, Eileen and Joss. On the walk down, or on the bus, we were bound to see Aunt Kathleen and Uncle Jim, Uncle Tommy or maybe his kids (my cousins) Scott and Jackie, or any number of neighbours – Wallace Moore, Peggy Beggs, Mary Page. There was a strong community life which already fascinated me.

I sat listening to these grown-ups as they monitored life in the area – who was marrying who, leaving who, abusing who, moving house, moving country – all of this discussed with continual reference to similar incidents in the past. Everything was linked to their fathers and uncles and aunts, and the daily gossip promoted floods of stories. The past was strongly alive in everyday discourse and was relished by all generations. The built-in Irish preoccupation with history, political and social, was at its most appealing in this context. It is true that the younger working-class generation wanted fridges, TVs, nicer dining-room suites, in short, wanted to better themselves, but never at the cost of rejecting their backgrounds. People like my mother embraced the stories and culture of my grandmother's generation and implicitly encouraged me to do so. It was no hardship. All the Irish, old, young, male and female, are natural storytellers who immortalise the Buck Alecs and Jimmy 'only temporary' Fosters.

The collective yarn session was a colourful occasion, but in the Branagh/Harper clan it did not extend to anyone believing they could 'perform' professionally. There were no actors or singers in the family and none could be remembered by my grandparents. It was hardly necessary. When the sexes got together (for our visits to grannies and aunts were almost always female affairs – the men did their gossip and reminiscing in the pub) it was entertainment of a high order.

These family nights or 'do's' often began informally, growing out of the normal daily visits, or they were arranged to celebrate the arrival of some distant relative from foreign parts. If it had just happened spontaneously then the kids had more chance of viewing the grown-ups and 'the crack' – the Irish word for the pleasure of company, conversation, arguments and songs. On the very rare occasions when I saw my grandmother involved she would sit with a glass of milk or lemonade in her hand and get very merrily weepy. A drink never passed her lips. Like my mother she had an almost pathological distrust of the stuff. There was no such suspicion felt by the rest of my relations, who could even persuade my mother to sip at a Snowball or a vodka and orange. Either drink would last her the entire evening.

While encouraging even greater wallowing in York Street folklore, these do's provided everybody with the chance of a 'turn', which seemed more or less compulsory. My first real impression of my parents comes from these evenings. My father, with a strong compact body, knotty, dark and handsome, had the same twinkling eyes as Pop, and I could already see he was a great 'kidder'. Often in these sessions, when his turn came, he would tell a few jokes or, very occasionally, be persuaded to sing. But singing was really my mother's forte. She always seemed to me to be very fashion-conscious and would sit in her latest pair of glasses – the frames seemed to change every week – and stare at the floor as she tore into her speciality. It was, and is, a funereal ditty called 'Marguerite' which was a great favourite among the rest of the family and for which, over the years, I have tried, but failed, to develop a taste. As the last bars of the song would fade, with more 'ee's' in it than I thought possible, 'I love you Mar-gah-reeeeeeete!', my Uncle Jim would go down on one knee in front of his delighted and embarrassed wife, and croon, 'I'll take you home again Kathleen, to where your heart will feel no pain'.

I watched all this with surprise and delight. I can't recall anyone getting drunk. There was never enough money for a great amount of booze, but there was tremendous merriment, people loving 'the crack', all jammed into somebody's tiny front room, squatting on the floor and perching on the ends of sofas. I wanted more than anything to join in, but entry to that élite came with age, or perhaps with the onset of a talent for performing.

In Mountcollyer Street I was developing my own network of relationships. I knew everyone of my own age in the street, and I'd see many of them in the local corner shop where we'd converge, doing 'messages' for our mothers. The shop was run by Harriet, who had been to school with my mother and was a fund of local knowledge.

The tiny terraced houses were three-up, three-down – an increase with every move. In 1981, on my first return trip to Belfast after eleven years, I went back to Mountcollyer Street and was astonished at how small the houses seemed. It took a while before I remembered that I was smaller then. The streets were tightly packed together and in the evenings, when it was time for our tea, my mum would simply stand on the front step and yell 'Ken!', 'Bill!' – I could hear her streets away. I wish I'd inherited her projection. When all the mothers were doing this at six o'clock in the evening, there was a strange Mountcollyer Street cacophony.

We played in huge groups. 'Raleigh-oh' was a sort of hide-and-seek game on a large scale, involving groups of hiders and seekers and spread across the whole area. We played football in the street too, and the number of broken window incidents improved my sprinting ability no end.

Religion seemed to have as little effect on my early life as it had had on my parents. My only feelings towards it were various forms of resentment. I was made to go to Sunday School, but that didn't seem so bad because at least they gave you prizes at the end of the year for good attendance. If you actually stopped to concentrate on what the teacher was saying, you were in trouble. I remember one dark Sunday when I had been transfixed by the information that when we died we arrived at a fork in the road. One long, straight road led to heaven, the other – narrow and winding – to hell. In my astonishment at this geographical gem, I had paid scant regard to which road was which. I spent a sleepless week certain that I would die early and would not remember which road to take. I cursed the church for not supplying me with some easy-to-read chart, a kind of Tube map for purgatory. The catechism was all very well, but I had enough to think about.

On Sunday evenings we were often sent as family representatives to the big church in town. Whenever I read about actors being fascinated by the ceremony and theatricality of the Catholic church, I remember my own repulsion at the far more sober Presbyterian version. I hated its ornateness, the oppressiveness of the buildings, the clothes the ministers wore, the smell, and to this day I dislike churches, which make me feel physically ill. Coventry Cathedral is the only place I've ever been where the building seems light enough to bear some relation to the joy that organised religion is alleged to provide. My innate aversion was confirmed early on by the bombastic threats of those fire-and-brimstone Belfast ministers, and they were the last push I needed to resist the demon of fear which religion seemed determined to establish in the province.

I'm not sure what set off my interest in the arts, but two events coincided when I was seven or eight that ignited some spark of inquiry. The first was my brother's tortuous rehearsal process for his 'joke' in the Grove School end-of-term concert. He was playing a blacked-up American minstrel (with a strong Belfast accent). There were weeks of agonised practice around the house and I remember thinking that it was a strangely painful activity to volunteer for. I was mad keen to see the results, but on the night I found that I was so transfixed by my brother's black York Street shoe-shine that the delivery of the gag escaped me.

It was around this time that I saw Burt Lancaster in the film *The Birdman of Alcatraz*. It is a gripping story about a convicted murderer who finds peace rearing birds in his prison cell. I was struck by how real it seemed. No one appeared to be 'acting'. Lancaster's own performance was tremendously powerful and affecting, and I was so engrossed that I studied the end-credits list so that I could check the names of the other actors and everyone else responsible for the movie.

It was the beginning of a habit that lasted throughout my youth. I started mentally logging all the unsung character actors – in *The Birdman of Alcatraz*, for instance, Telly Savalas, then relatively unknown, played the side-kick to Burt Lancaster. I began to wonder what 'continuity' was, and imagined it as the person who joined together all the bits of film. And who did 'lighting', which I always misread as 'lightning'? I must have noticed it first on a horror film. Very soon I became a fund of useless information and, if nothing else, I knew that the Westmore family seemed to provide the make-up artists for every Hollywood film and that Michael Ripper was almost guaranteed to play the innkeeper in a Hammer horror film.

I had my first trip to the theatre: a production of 'A Christmas Carol' at the Grove Theatre, which starred Joseph Tomelty, with whose daughter, Frances, I would later work. I was enthralled by the tale itself – which promoted a great love for Dickens – but also by the nature of the performance. They were there, actually in front of me, *being*. There was no other word for it. Magic.

My parents didn't share the same enthusiasm, as the arts did not play a big role in their life. They read voraciously, but only news-papers and magazines, and there were no books in the house: if people needed fiction or poetry it was there in everyday life, in gossip, conversation and storytelling. My folks did enjoy the sheer escapism of movies and there were family trips to the cinema, which I loved, to see *Chitty Chitty Bang Bang*, *The Great Escape* and the deliciously absurd *One Million Years BC*, which seemed ridiculous even to my nine-year-old sensibilities. I've had a soft spot for Raquel Welch ever since.

During the late 1960s the family finances continued to fluctuate. I was never aware of any real hardships, only that some Christmasses the stockings were fuller than others. I was always taught to be aware of 'the value of money', and never to abuse it or to put too much store by it. At dinner I was never allowed to leave an empty plate, because 'somebody in the Third World would be glad of that'.

We took a holiday every year: sixty-seven pounds at Butlin's, which was enough for full board for the four of us for the week. My dad remembers praying that we didn't ask for yet another ice-cream in the middle of the afternoon as he tried to eke out their allowance for the week. I made my own unconscious attempts at household economy. Just before one trip there had been a TV advertising campaign which boasted that everything in Butlin's was free. I put this to the test by leaving a camp-site sweet shop with a basket full of Smarties, only to be nabbed by an irate Redcoat who told my dad that he didn't believe my story.

Money remained scarce, and despite Dad's efforts to go solo in business, he hit a bad patch in which work in Belfast became difficult to find. A slightly better job came up in England, involving ceilings and partitions, and he decided to take it. From 1967 he flew back every third Friday on the Aldergrove standby and brought his youngest a tiny Matchbox car on each trip. By the time we left

Belfast in the Spring of 1970, I had an enormous collection of much-cherished vehicles.

His departure coincided with a resurgence of the Troubles. Tension was high all over the province. Confrontations of gangs and individuals in the local parks and streets were common. You'd be stopped by a bunch of youths, and pushed around, and asked if you were Catholic or Protestant. Sometimes it was impossible to guess what religion they were, so the right answer was a gamble. Often you'd get hit anyway. If you did answer correctly, they'd say you were lying.

Apart from religious trouble, there were the usual adventures of growing up. I went on my one and only inept shoplifting expedition and, although I wasn't caught, I was identified by the manic shopkeeper who, of course, knew my mother. Retribution was the usual clip round the ear, administered by my mother, Dad being away. Punishment was always short, sharp and harmless. It didn't always seem logical, however, and I learned when to keep my mouth shut.

I had my first lesson in this when sitting on the tiny wall in front of the house while my mother chatted with her neighbour, a daily event up and down the street. Most of the time, Dad was away working slavishly, but when he was home he would occasionally slip off to place a wee bet.

'Where is Mr Branagh then, Frances?'

'I'm not sure. I think he's on a message.'

'Sure he's at the bookies', Ma.'

'Oh, that's right, son. Thanks.'

We finished the conversation and went back into the house where the door closed and a fiercesome belt from Mum sent me flying across the hall.

'Don't tell your business to everyone.'

Point taken.

School life was Dickensian in its severity. I was once caned for running across some flower-beds during a chase in a playground game. I had been spotted and secretly reported, and was summoned to see the headmaster. I shall never forget the relish with which he slowly put books away, opened and closed drawers, while he calmly scolded me. Years later, the scene retains a Pinteresque menace. The preamble of quiet, deadly reprimand, delivered in a sepulchral drawl, was far more of a deterrent than the actual blow with the cane.

18

If I later wondered why school discipline seemed much more effective in Ireland, I had only to remember this Donald Pleasance look-alike and imagine him tearing the wings off flies.

My form teacher, Mr Gribben, upheld the tradition of grisly intimidation. He kept two gym shoes on his desk. He called them Dougal and Zebedee after the characters in the then popular children's TV series, *The Magic Roundabout*. If, for an offence, you received a whack on the bottom from Zebedee, you were fortunate. That was his left shoe, which he chose to wield with his weaker left hand. If you had been especially naughty (perhaps talking in class when you weren't supposed to), then you were hauled out to the front of the room and given a whack with Dougal and the full force of his right-handed wrath.

Academic discipline seemed equally harsh. A weekly maths and English composition test was savagely marked and the results tabled so that in the four rows of uncomfortable wooden form-desks people were regrouped on a weekly basis. Those children with the highest marks sat at the desk beside the teacher's table, and everyone else was graded accordingly, with the least successful at the bottom of the fourth row and furthest away from the teacher. A cruel system that did everything to confirm hopelessness and breed conceit.

My maths never allowed me to get to the top desk but I was always near enough to witness Amanda Watson, the object of my unrequited love, elbow to elbow with Edward Brown, the numerical genius. I prayed that when we grew up she might marry us both – although she had eyes for no one but him – and at least I could look at her.

With Mum working and bringing up two boys, and Dad away, it was a worrying time for them both. My mother was in charge while Dad was away but she could do nothing about the rising tide of street violence which, up to then, had not really affected us. Then, one evening, things came to a head. My brother was playing football a couple of hundred yards down the hill. I and a few friends were idling outside my house when we became aware of a strange buzzing, like an enormous swarm of bees in the distance. Then we heard the screams of my brother and his mates tearing up the hill towards us, yelling 'Get inside, get inside!' They were being followed by a dark, clamorous mass which revealed itself to be a crowd of wild-eyed Protestants from the Shankhill Road.

I ran inside to my mother, who stuffed me underneath the

dining-room table and tried to control my terror. The sound of yelling and pounding was horrendous. The mob was the width of the street and a couple of hundred thick. Bill, watching at the window, described how they were lifting the draining grates from the gutters and smashing them. With the broken pieces of wrought iron they smashed a single window in each of the Catholic houses. It was clearly understood that this was a primitive form of marking out the houses of undesirables, like the daubing of doors in times of plague. It meant, we know who you are and where you are, and if you don't move out, then next time we'll set the house on fire.

The great cloud of ugliness passed as quickly as it had come. The reaction of the street was just as swift and just as alarming. I peeked out of the front door to see women on every doorstep talking thirteen to the dozen while every able-bodied man was ripping up paving-stones and carrying them in wheelbarrows and makeshift trolleys to the top of the street, where a fierce-looking barricade was already being erected. The word 'vigilante' was flying around. I was still shaking. The next day there were troops in the street.

On my dad's next visit home it was clear that he was shaken and worried for his family. On a trip to his local pub he was warned as he was leaving to stay away, as the bar staff was Catholic. If he used the place again it could mean trouble. His defiant reaction was to go back in and order another pint.

In the strange intoxication of the time, I joined a local gang who were looting a nearby supermarket that had been bombed. I was so terrified after I'd dared to run into the stricken building that I grabbed whatever was to hand, in this case a family pack of Omo and a jar of Vim. In my innocence I took them back as trophies to my mother, who surpassed herself with the speed at which she knocked me sideways. She made me take them straight back, a nightmarish experience, as the cops were due to arrive at any moment. I made it with minutes to spare, and resolved that my criminal career was finished.

My parents had had enough. The first escape route was Canada, where my Aunt Rose and Uncle Billy had found sunshine and prosperity. But the Canadian authorities were not looking for joiners or mill workers, so the chance of an assisted passage was out. They simply did not have the money to emigrate. Then there was a changeover at work, when Dad's firm was sold lock, stock and barrel to a new company. Fortunately, the new owners wanted Dad to stay on and were prepared to offer him a house at a nominal rent. My thoughts flew immediately to my infant love life. There would be no more dawdling around Amanda Watson's house on the way home from school. The love of my life was not to be. I was in tears as my parents told me about the move, despite their promises of a garden and my own bed. At the end of an evening of sobs, I relented enough to ask:

'So where are we going?'

'Reading, son.'

My dad spoke as if he were talking of Shangri-la.

'Where's Reading?'

TWO

'What country, friends, is this?'
TWELFTH NIGHT

'The best way to see Reading is going through it on a train.'

That was Oscar Wilde's view, but then he had his own reasons for disliking the town of the 3 B's – Bulbs, Biscuits and Beer. Sutton Seeds, Huntley and Palmers' and the Courage Brewery were the three names that distinguished the town in those days. But as the Branaghs arrived, the M4 motorway's new extension was nearing completion, and Reading's second life as a commuter-filled adjunct to London was about to begin.

For me, the most disappointing aspect of Reading was the size of our back garden. Bedtimes in Belfast before the move had been imaginative flights of fancy which turned the new house into a kind of Disneyland castle with croquet lawns and tree-houses, and the chance to do everything I'd seen gangs of adventurous children do on the box. What we had instead was a rather small suburban semi-detached, not much bigger than the house in Mountcollyer Street, but with considerably more pretension. The back garden was the first I'd ever known, but playing football in it would be as dangerous for the windows as it had been in Belfast.

But my new school, Whiteknights County Primary, seemed a real improvement. From my first day at this green and pleasant establishment, I was aware of being a stranger in what seemed – to a Belfast boy used to fierce, grey discipline – like a very strange land. There were nice cheerful buildings, playing fields, even the classes had 'play' corners (I thought I'd read the sign wrong). All was cosily middle-class, quiet and nice. Mr Shanks, the headmaster, was everybody's favourite uncle and always smiling, and introduced me to the gentle lions of Mr Cortiss's class with a generous speech of welcome. The first question whispered to me, a startled white rabbit, by an inquisitive classmate during the maths lesson was, 'Are you any good at football?'

I was competent at it and, more importantly, passionate about the game. This kept me going during the early days when I had to repeat everything I said, in order to give them a chance with my Belfast accent. I was acutely aware of my speech at a school where it seemed to me everyone spoke like BBC newsreaders. The accent problem was already causing friction at home.

For my father, the move had been easy. He had been living in England part-time for three years and apart from a greater natural confidence he had already made the tiny adjustments in speech that allowed for instant understanding in a social context. For my mother, it was not so easy. There were endless arguments between her and my brother about her accent and our non-English status. For Bill, in middle adolescence, the culture shock was profound and the confusion immense. He was in daily fights at his secondary school and chose to deal with the disorientation by changing his accent almost immediately and completely. The suburban sound was like having a new member of the family and my mother's accent became a target for his own divided feelings. There were regular criticisms of what she said and how she said it, which reduced my mother to tears.

It was a traumatic period, for the whole family was undergoing an enforced change of personality. My mother, removed from the support network of sisters and cousins and made to feel almost ashamed of her speech, had a very painful time of it. The outgoing dancer and spunky fighter for family justice was rendered impotent by the isolation of English suburbia. The neighbours were fewer and quieter, community life, as she knew it, almost non-existent. The men were out and about in company most of the day, but my mother suffered from a loneliness and loss of confidence from which it took her years to recover. Her one salvation through this period was the arrival, in her fortieth year, of my sister Joyce.

The early 1970s were not a good time to be Irish in Reading. Many of the children at school had older brothers in the Army. Every death reported on the television news made me try to change even further; I longed just to blend in. After a year or so I'd managed to become English at school and remain Irish at home. It was a dreadfully uneasy compromise about which I suffered inordinate guilt. I instinctively wanted to remain the Belfast boy, but pressure at school was very strong. I was already conscious of being different from people who had 'friends round for the day', who had parties in their large houses, and who ate curries *at home*. I was hardly becoming a cod 'working-class hero', but the differences between me and them were plain.

For as long as I could, I kept up the double life, but my voice gradually took on the twang of suburbia. However I still sounded different, and was very careful when the subject of English casualties in Ulster came up at school. It was another stage in the painful process of learning when to keep my mouth shut.

Soldiers weren't the only people dying in the province. Shortly after our move, Pop Branagh passed away. It was the end of an era for my parents, as Pop had always exerted a strong influence over the family. He had had a long illness, but through it all he urged my parents to leave Belfast and make a new life. The old order and the old good-heartedness were over, he said. The gangsters were moving in and young families should move out before kids did more than looted the shops.

Pop would have approved of Whiteknights. Its taste for theatricals was encouraged by Beryl Levitt, my final form teacher and a great enthusiast for drama. She gave me my first break, boldly choosing me to play Dougal in a hotly-contested casting session for a Christmas production of *The Magic Roundabout*. The show was intended for infant schools and, in a thick brown blanket, with fringes to represent the canine hero, I remember thinking in old pro fashion that I was 'very good with the kids'.

A few weeks later, with a wilful precocity which has been annoying people ever since, I made my debut as an author. It was a five-minute piece for harvest festival. The central character was called Lord Ponsonby-Smythe, a young aristocrat who visits his farm labourers, discovers the extent of their poverty and the difficulty of their labour. Stricken with guilt at this economic and social imbalance, he replaces their tools and ups their wages. A very unlikely parable.

There was always football and music. A local group put on a production of *All the King's Men* by Richard Rodney Bennett in which I thought myself rather thrilling. I played the Royalist soldier with the slightly bigger musket *and* a pennant. Subtle touches, but they made all the difference. Imagine my surprise when Thames Junior Opera failed to renew my contract for the next production.

It was rather a shock for the Infant Phenomenon to hear that another domestic move was being planned. Unknown to us, our landlord had acquired planning permission for a supermarket at the back of our rented house which meant knocking it down to provide access for delivery trucks. Meantime the success of the M4 led to a vast rise in Reading property prices. My parents were in no position to buy, and so we were at the mercy of my dad's boss and landlord, who eventually offered us a dilapidated property to rent on the other side of Reading. The house was much bigger – three bedrooms – but was in a dismal state. Gas mantles, stone floors, leaky roof: a sort of luxury York Street. There was no alternative, and so a couple of months before I finished my primary education, we moved to Berkeley Avenue.

The consequences for me were serious. All Whiteknights' pupils went to Maiden Erleigh School, the cosy secondary complement to the idyllic primary school, where my brother was now happily installed. Moving house meant moving catchment areas and for me a different secondary school. We tried briefly and in vain to get round the council red tape so that I could stay with my new friends, but a place had already been assigned for me at a brand new school, the Meadway Comprehensive, which was opening in September 1972. It had 1200 kids and I would know no one among the 300 children who would make up the first year group. I was terrified.

The omens were not good. At the end of the summer holidays just before I was due to start I asked my dad to drive me past the school buildings. Meadway was to exist on two sites. The first- and second-year intake were housed in what had been the old Wilson secondary school, and my father showed me this imposing Victorian red brick affair. It was a shock after the cosy freshness of Whiteknights. It looked to me like the setting for an Edgar Allan Poe short story. We would remain here for two years before travelling a mile and a half to spend the rest of our schooldays in a spanking new building which the fourteen-year-olds and older students occupied. On the morning of my first day, I was much relieved to find others quite as nervous as myself. The camaraderie of shared terror united us quickly and before we were herded into the great assembly hall, I was breathing a few quiet sighs of relief.

I was assigned to form 1/3. I checked quickly. No seven-foot psychopaths, and the only really mean-looking creature was fat, smaller than me, and a girl. It was looking good. The teacher checking our names off smiled. I was safe. We were going to be OK.

Certainly the faces were rougher. The atmosphere was a little more like *The Blackboard Jungle* than at Whiteknights but certainly less Dotheboys Hall than the Grove Primary, Belfast. I made the fatal mistake of relaxing. Very quickly I was 'good company' in 1/3, and the attention accorded to my schoolboy funnies brought small playground audiences of a pleasing kind, and then its inevitable consequence – the attentions of the school bully.

'You're a divvy.' This was classroom slang for 'prat'. It was morning break. I felt a dig in the ribs from behind.

'You're a divvy, ain't you? What are you?' A small crowd was beginning to gather. They smelled blood. 'I said you're a divvy. What are you?'

Squirming. More breathless fear. Cornered now. Literally against the wall. My lapels were seized.

'What are you?'

Mumble.

'*What?*'

'A divvy.'

Hysterical sneering. Flashman laughter. The bell rang. Escape, thank Christ.

I wasn't bullied for long, but it affected me badly. I was also being terrorised by a boy of my own size who was an honest-to-goodness thug. I lived not in fear of him but of the confrontation. I'm sure I'd have stood a good chance in a fight, but it was the anticipation, the dread of the potential indignity, that ate into me. I began to play truant. Usually I'd skip the last lesson before lunch or the afternoon break in order to escape the horror of playground exposure. I was consumed with guilt and fear and would end up ringing my father at work, pumping misery money into a public phone box. I chose my father for these confessions, as I was terrified of what my mother would say. My father's schoolboy nightmares at Rosharkin bred understanding and sympathy, but my mother had put up with Speedy Harper, and after him school bullies must have seemed trivial.

Eventually the whole family were involved in my daily traumas. They knew the situation was getting out of hand when I tried to throw myself downstairs. I reckoned that one clean break meant a leg dramatically in plaster for a couple of school-free months, and the glamour of those signatures all over it. When I did go back, no one would pick on me if I developed the right kind of residual limp. I had everything worked out. My only problem now was that when I reached the top of the stairs on the appointed morning I could find none of the necessary courage. I finally bumped myself down the last few steps, banging rather noisily on my bottom and attempted to act out the rest of the scenario. My father rushed from the kitchen. I knew he was concerned and upset about the situation. The hall door opened.

'Dad . . . aagh . . . I . . . think . . . aagh . . .'

The groans were quiet but rather effective, I thought. If Marlon Brando could play a con-man cripple in that film with David Niven, why couldn't I?

'Dad . . . I think I've broken something . . . I don't think I can go to school . . . ooh.' (Thump. A final collapse.)

He laughed in my face.

Despite the absurdity of my private melodramas, I was genuinely upset by the situation. My avoidance technique was not working. Despite ridiculously circuitous routes through the school to avoid the bully, I was still regularly disappearing altogether when my nerve failed me. In desperation, my father paid a quiet visit to the headmaster and this made the situation worse. I was a marked man.

My release came in true British fashion when, after a month, the PE sessions developed into organised sports. I was good at rugby and my tormentor, of course, was a physical coward. I was strangely fearless in sport and took a dark pleasure in tackling the fiend as ferociously as possible. It did the trick – a wary respect was accorded me as, once again, sporting ability granted survivor status to the lucky few and condemned the physically weak to even greater misery.

I eventually became captain of the rugby and football teams, more, I suspect, for my innate sense of drama – I loved shouting theatrically butch encouragements to 'my lads' – than for any real sporting skill. I was a plodding workhorse, blessed with physical robustness.

Despite my elevation to Roy of the Rovers, the damage had been done, and it was cheerio to the giggling extrovert who'd been brought out of his Belfast shell. I kept my head down and my mouth shut. Meadway was essentially an excellent school, and, notwithstanding the odd psychopath, there were many genuinely friendly pupils and teachers. I kept my distance from them over the next three years and opted for an isolated adolescence. School holidays were spent alone. Mates did not visit. I was still frightened of the social conventions of my classmates; I simply didn't know what to do in an English house when your friends came round. So after school I simply went home and up to my room. I had £1.22½ per week from a paper-round I did in the mornings and I started to read.

It was a genuine surprise to me that I could buy a paperback for as little as 25p. When I found a children's author that I liked (Malcolm Saville was a great favourite), I would start collections. I loved seeing, for the first time in our house, a shelf with books on it. My father couldn't understand why I had to buy the things – after all you only read them once, and there were libraries for that sort of thing. It seemed a waste of money and certainly very foolish to buy two or three at a time.

But up in my attic bedroom hideaway I was building up a miniature library of my own. The more I read, the more I wanted to write. My imagination grew in proportion to my isolation, and I started to write letters. To everyone. My interest in television and film had never diminished and at that time I was enthralled – as I still am – by Morecambe and Wise. I wrote to them after a fascinating documentary called 'Fools Rush In', and asked for tickets to their show. I remember thinking it wasn't too cheeky, as I was sure I had read that the BBC gave such things away. I sent the letter. It was a small step for anyone else, but a giant leap for the Bard of Berkshire.

I think their reply was the first letter I'd ever had addressed to me as a proper grown-up. The name and address were typed, and in the corner, stamped in red, was the full glamorous seal on the whole event, the letters BBC. My brother was so flabbergasted and curious when he saw it on the mat, that he wouldn't let me open it until I told him who it was from. I protested excitedly, though I was desperate to open it. Quickly sibling tyranny won the day. Morecambe and Wise, I admitted. Curiosity turned to astonishment. My brother tore the envelope open to reveal a photograph of the two, with a message in their own handwriting on the back. 'Sorry. No tickets available. Our series is over. Many thanks for your letter. Morecambe and Wise.'

My brother gave me a quizzical look and then handed it over. He headed off to school while I took the reply back up to the nerve-centre of my literary operation. It was possible, these people *did* write back. I was excited beyond belief. Some sort of door had opened. I made a note to be sure in future to get to the postman first.

I've often thought I should check Equity records to see whether any members had asked for something to be done about me. I was certainly tormenting the actors – Dave Allen, Sally Thomsett, Gillian Blake – and anyone I admired on TV at that time. All sweetly wrote back, and my ambition grew.

My new status as a collector of books and man of letters allowed me to cast a critical eye over the literary world around me. I picked up the *Reading Evening Post* one night and looked at their books page. It was packed with reviews, but only one children's book was mentioned, and that review was written by an adult. I set to immediately, and a letter was dispatched to the editor complaining about the situation. I employed a favourite phrase of the time: we want book reviews '*by* kids, *for* kids'. I'm not sure whether the junior population of Reading would have agreed, but the letter worked its spell on the pape's features editor, June Sparey.

She ran a Saturday half-page section called 'Junior Post'. As it happened, they did receive children's books from time to time, and she took up my suggestion to pass them on to me to review. No money was involved but I could keep the books, and I could tell my father I'd found a way of saving money. She wrote back inviting me to mastermind something called 'Junior Bookshelf'. I had my name just below the title. Fame at last. I was thirteen.

Teenage empire-building extended to the BBC, where I wrote to the Head of Children's Programmes demanding my own junior chat

29

show '*by* kids, *for* kids'. When he wrote back suggesting a meeting I realised that my gargantuan confidence actually went no further than my four bedroom walls. Once it came to implementing these schemes beyond the written word, I was helpless. It was not to be the first time in my adolescence that my imagination would reach beyond my capacities.

My parents had no illusions about my condition. Between the ages of twelve and fifteen I went into an odd form of retreat. I was aware of their concern because, apart from their own enquiries, they cajoled my brother and every visiting relative to try to discover why I stayed up in my room and didn't go out, or even have mates round. So insistent were their worries that even I began to wonder if there was something wrong with me.

I think I really did prefer my own company but had also built some subconscious once-bitten-twice-shy drama about myself and the world. If nothing else, the solitude was providing an obvious career choice: I would be a writer. Although I was having an unpleasant adolescent flirtation with the world of sub-editing and deadlines, journalism seemed the right road.

Ideally I saw myself cutting through all the court-reporting drudgery and heading straight for investigative TV journalism, and eventually to my own chat show. I also thought that I could probably cut the training down, or do without it altogether. I couldn't spell or type or use grammar correctly, but I was sure these were things that you could pick up. I knew that, journalism or not, the last thing I wanted was an ordinary job.

One rainy day in autumn, the drama teacher, Roger Lewis, came to watch the school football team. Something was up. Generally they looked down on all that butchness but Mr Lewis was clearly in trouble. He had planned a school production of *Oh! What a Lovely War* to play in the dinner hall at the end of the Christmas term, and had had a miserable response to his casting appeals. With tickets and advertising booked, he was now stuck. It didn't take much to persuade me to join in, although some of the other lads had to be persuaded that playing soldiers had great girl-pulling potential and could easily be as macho as their activities on the football field.

Roger Lewis was a director of enormous energy and the rehearsals were the most fun I'd ever had at Meadway, partly because I was nabbing parts like flies. The more image-conscious of the soccer team eventually dropped out and Roger himself, who'd had to take on several roles early on, shed some when he saw there was an eager show-off waiting in the wings.

It was still a huge cast. *Oh! What a Lovely War* is an ensemble piece with many scenes. I played the American arms dealer (Burt Lancaster in *Bird Man*), the Young British Soldier (Tom Courtenay in *King Rat*), the Old British Soldier (Robert Newton in *Treasure Island*) and the officer (Michael Caine in *Zulu*). Nothing I did had much to do with acting, but it was a great laugh.

I was astonished by the camaraderie such things could inspire, which was just as much fun as the playing itself. It was an extraordinary new club in which I felt completely at home. I loved the dressing-up. I loved things going wrong. I was completely stage-struck and just waiting for the magic words supplied by Roger: 'Have you ever thought of doing this professionally?'

I was sixteen years old and everything clicked at once. Not only had it taken me out of my old hermit self (I actually started seeing girls – my parents were relieved and delighted) but from that point on there was simply nothing else I could think of doing. Journalism was no longer an option. I was so much better at acting than I was at reviewing books, and the notion of acting for a living made work seem as if it wouldn't be work at all. In short, every dream-filled cliché danced through my head. Others in the cast of that lovely production felt changed, and talked about taking up acting. I knew I meant it.

I felt certain, but also terrified. How was I to go about it? Parents, drama school, money – I decided on a long, slow campaign on all fronts. The obvious thing was to stay on at school from sixteen to eighteen – it was impossible to think of leaving for London any earlier. And I needed the experience: more plays, more reading. I imagined that you had to be very bright to be an actor, and I felt thick. I knew I had to do something about it.

My dad was quietly appalled that I had decided to stay on. English, History and Sociology 'A' levels meant little to him when there was an opening in his own firm. It would mean another two years of his keeping me, but he finally agreed, and I showed willing by getting a weekend job in a supermarket, so that I wasn't forever 'minding ten bob' for him.

In the meantime, I started on my own secret theatrical education. I joined the Berkshire County Drama Library, and visited second-hand bookshops assembling a paperback collection of Shakespeare.

I scoured the bookshelves in Smith's and found that there was a magazine called *Plays and Players*, but that you had to be quick, because only one person in Reading seemed to buy it and I had to get to the shop to read the single copy before it disappeared.

But this covert operation was soon rumbled by the tortuous question-and-answer session of the Meadway 'careers interview'. Parents were invited to this momentous half-hour, and my father dutifully turned up to hear what Mrs Bell, the careers supremo, had to say. She took the initiative, and in the first ten minutes she referred to my academic record, my likely pass levels in future exams, and laid before me the employment riches available in Reading at the time. There were basically three choices: British Rail, the Prudential or the Army. I had to get it over with.

'I'm going to be an actor.'

The air suddenly turned chilly. I didn't look at my father but I felt his little jump of shock and then the deep, weary sigh. He'd obviously seen it coming, and here was the confirmation. His son was a homosexual.

Mrs Bell gave a puzzled smile. 'I'm not sure how much information we actually have on that particular career avenue.' She went to the tiny filing cabinet which housed the school's careers information. 'No, there's nothing. I don't think we've had that one before.' Pause. 'Are you sure about this?'

All the arguments were trotted out, my dad joining in as best he could. High unemployment, fierce competition, my own lack of experience, poor money.

'I want to be an actor.'

'What about something to fall back on?'

'Like what?'

'Banking.'

'I'm afraid I've made up my mind.'

Mrs Bell had done all she could, and I promised that I would go down to the careers department in the Civic Centre where they had more detailed information on the subject. Perhaps that would make me see sense. There had been no hard words in the interview, just an amused indulgence from Mrs Bell. I think she felt rather sorry for me – I'd clearly let school dramatics go straight to my head. My father looked as though he'd been punched, but smiled bravely and shook me by the hand as he left and went back to work.

I stayed in my room all that evening. I had no wish to be part of the conversation that was going on downstairs. My parents' bewilderment must have been immense. My father had only just been given the chance to run his own company, the place was thriving, and his only disappointment was that my brother, Bill, who had originally joined the firm, left it after a year to set up his own company. If I failed to succumb to the lure of this secure opening, it would be the end of Dad's dream of establishing a strong family business. To both my parents' credit, they remained patient over the following months and simply watched to see how I was pursuing entry into this strange, unfamiliar world while desperately hoping that I would grow out of it.

As promised, I went to the Civic Centre for detailed information. The assistant was almost as puzzled as Mrs Bell, and after half an hour one rather sad-looking sheet of A4 paper was placed before me. It was headed 'Advice to those interested in stage careers', the writing was on one side only, and it was dated 1968. I took a deep breath and consulted the oracle, which began 'An empty theatre is a lonely place. Behind the tinsel glitter of the curtain and the greasepaint, the theatre can be a hard, lonely world, especially for the actor.' You can imagine the rest.

Back to the bookshops. I found an old Foyles' Handbook called 'Making The Stage Your Career', which had Tom Courtenay as Faustus on the cover. Inside it mentioned Albert Finney and Peter O'Toole a lot, so I thought it must be all right. It was written by Denys Blakelock, who had been a teacher at RADA in the mid-fifties and had taught both of the above, as well as John Stride, Richard Briers, Sian Phillips, all referred to in the book. Even though it was slightly antiquated, it became my Bible. If his advice was good enough for them, it was good enough for me. He talked a great deal about drama school auditions but, for all my reading, I still knew so little about what plays to use, what speeches to read. I had to act in more plays.

I had read in the local paper about the Progress Theatre group. It was an amateur company and the building was within walking distance of my house. I wanted to join, but once again my confidence failed me. I was all right in private, in books, in dreams of glory, but still desperately reserved in real life. I rang them up, found out when they met, and promised that I would turn up. On the appointed night I walked to the little 100-seater theatre which was on the edge of the Reading University Campus. And then I froze. I stood under a tree and watched as people filed in and simply prayed that some kindly figure would walk across and say 'Hello, you must be the hugely talented youngster we've been expecting. I'll look after you and make sure you don't feel utterly ridiculous and stupid. Come with me.'

It didn't happen, I simply got cold and walked home. It was the second time that this had happened – the same summer, in 1977, I had auditioned (through Roger Lewis's encouragement) for the National Youth Theatre. When I heard that I had been given a place on their summer season, I withdrew immediately. Terror, sheer terror of living in London for the summer, terror of all the new people – I couldn't face it. I was beginning to wonder if I could ever be anything but a suburban Walter Mitty.

I tried Progress Theatre again, and this time God was on my side. Their newsletter had told me they were auditioning for *Who's Afraid of Virginia Woolf?* by Edward Albee, with a part for a young man that I could conceivably have played.

This time I actually attended the audition. I waited nearly an hour to say my first lines as Nick and experienced the sweaty-palmed anticipation of actors at read-throughs. Nearly twenty of us were sitting in a circle, a mixture of potential Marthas and Georges and Honeys, but very few Nicks. The other young auditionees were much older than me, and I thought that my youth might be an asset. Perhaps they needed some new blood.

Groups of four had taken it in turns to read different sections of the play, and I thought my bit was over far too quickly – there hadn't been time for them to be bowled over by my extensively researched and rehearsed American accent (Marlon Brando in *On the Waterfront*).

I revelled in the words 'Some of you will be hearing from us' at the end of the session. This was proper theatre, brutal, tough, Warner Baxter in jodhpurs, the real thing. Then, of course, I recoiled when someone said 'Shall we all go to the pub?' My annoying Irish flush flushed, I mumbled my apologies and made my way back to the bedroom at Berkeley Avenue. This had now become a garret in Greenwich Village where I was hanging out, while making my name in New York. Jimmy Dean was on the next landing, and Marlon often stopped by for coffee and an intense discussion about Stanislavsky. To my utter astonishment, the director of *Virginia Woolf* had decided that she wanted me as Nick. And to my embarrassment, she rang my mother to discuss her one reservation. She had heard that I was not yet seventeen and explained that there were scenes of sophisticated sexual game-playing in the play, indeed a little actual mauling, and she wanted to know if my mother objected, if it would destroy some delicate psychological balance. My mother's surprising response was to say that she thought I'd be fine, and that if I wanted to be a professional, then I'd better get as much practice as possible.

I'd cracked it. Parental acceptance. Three cheers for York Street. My only disappointment was that the director changed her mind anyway and decided that having a son of my age herself, she would be too aware of corrupting me in rehearsals. I didn't care. I was established at Progress Theatre and was on the way to winning over my folks. They still thought most actors were unemployed homosexuals, but one thing at a time.

I did land a part in the next production, *The Drunkard, or Down With Demon Drink*, a Victorian temperance melodrama. I played William Dowton, a simple rustic. Simple was not a word you could use to describe my performance, which resembled Benny Hill crossed with a manic opera diva. The result was an overblown mummerset thicko in the great tradition of 'never knowingly underplayed'.

I also joined the Progress Youth Theatre, and with this and other school play rehearsals, I became a busy actor-about-town, running from one 'job' to another. During the school holidays I made my first trip to Stratford-upon-Avon. I hitched up the A34 with my tent on my back and pitched at a site just outside the town. I was in seventh heaven. After visiting all the Shakespeare landmarks, I had a drink in the actors' pub, 'The Dirty Duck', and went on to the theatre, where I stood entranced by the programme – *The Taming of the Shrew*, *The Tempest*, *Measure for Measure*, Michael Hordern, Jonathan Pryce, Ian Charleson, Juliet Stevenson, Alan Rickman, and more. The weather was lovely, and the whole trip was like a miraculous pilgrimage. Acting it was to be, and Stratford looked as if it was to be my Mecca.

And about this time I was given a wonderful present: hundreds of back copies of *Plays and Players*, *Theatre World* and *Encore*. They dated from the early fifties and were a real treasure trove. Each night in bed, before I went to sleep, I would read a copy from cover to cover with minute attention to every detail.

I was still scouring film and TV titles sequences, and I loved

35

cross-referencing the spear-holders of the sixties to the stars of the seventies. I wanted to know who did everything – music, lights, direction. And I took untold pleasure in building up an encyclopaedic knowledge of post-war theatre, while theatrical biographies were giving me an insight into different eras. At this time – I was nearly 18 – I was reading *Early Stages* by Gielgud, *George* and *Emlyn* by Emlyn Williams, biographies of Irving and Garrick, and the criticism of James Agate. My appetite for theatrical history was voracious and the quest for it was sheer, unadulterated joy.

Part of the great quest was theatre-going itself. I had seen my first Shakespeare at the St George's Theatre, Tufnell Park, when I was fourteen. It was a hysterical schools' matinee of *Romeo and Juliet*, with David Collings as a thrilling Mercutio. Peter McEnery and Sarah Badel gave wonderful performances as the lovers. The whole production was rough and thrilling, completely dispelling the classroom image of Shakespeare as boring.

Now that I'd found my vocation, theatre-going was a wonderful adventure. I banished all social timidity in order to savour all the treats available, such as my first momentous visit to see *Hamlet*. There was a new production playing at the theatre in Oxford; I asked Jayne Thurgood, a girlfriend whom I was trying to impress, and we took the train from Reading. I was completely bowled over and so was my companion, which was a relief – it was not the most obvious evening's entertainment for a young suburban couple. It seemed unbelievably dramatic, dark and rich to look at, full of exciting lighting effects. The production had tremendous pace, and the acting was passionate and electric.

I cheered at the end as he came on. I'd read all about him: Cambridge, Birmingham Rep, understudying at the National Theatre, taking over from Jeremy Brett, Cassio in Olivier's *Othello*, Ivanov for Prospect, and now here he was, live – a completely thrilling Hamlet. I was watching Derek Jacobi.

With all this excitement my school work inevitably suffered. I had patient and understanding teachers who put up with me, mainly because I loved the work in class, however lax I was with homework and background reading. My subjects were all grist to the mill: history is the very stuff of drama, and Miss Sheppard, our history teacher, loved the theatre in it as much as I did. I loved the personalities – Parnell, Lloyd George, MacDonald, Churchill – and wanted to play them all. I enjoyed Mrs Nalpanis's sociology lessons, but it was English that I revelled in and I owe the most thanks for my release into the enjoyment of language to my English teacher, Stan Grue. An actor and director himself, all our lessons were infused with a Celtic relish for words. I fell for the poetry of Dylan Thomas, John Donne, and Shakespeare's sonnets, and for a whole range of modern poetry. We read countless plays: Wesker, Osborne, Shakespeare and Congreve; and our 'A' level course (chosen by Stan) contained far more plays than was prevalent in most syllabuses. Stan could do no wrong for me, and proved it by casting me as Toad in the Christmas school production of *Toad of Toad Hall*. It's one of the most enjoyable parts that I've ever played.

The only problem during this whole golden period was that I was neglecting my homework. The 'A' levels that I promised to provide as a safety net were looking very precarious. No amount of classroom zeal makes up for background reading and notes, and I was really banking on something else.

I'd quietly sent off for prospectuses from all the major drama schools and was putting the next phase of my secret plan into action. I secured auditions at the Central School of Speech and Drama and at the Royal Academy of Dramatic Art. The appointments were within days of each other in early January 1979, and were for admission in September of the same year, just a few months after I was due to leave school. I was required to produce two two-minute speeches, one from a modern play and one from Shakespeare. I knew I wanted the classical piece to be exciting, dramatic and above all, original. With a startling lack of imagination I decided on *Hamlet*. And from an interesting selection of modern pieces I chose the most familiar: a scene from Pinter's *The Caretaker*.

Friends were enlisted to take me through the speeches. Colin Wakefield, a colleague from the Progress Theatre, helped me on making the Shakespeare ('What a piece of work is a man') seem more natural, and Stan Grue tried to curtail the movements of my flailing arms, which always seemed to get stuck in the air at the wrong moment, and accompany dramatic lines with entirely inappropriate gestures. Pauline and Harry Grey, two really fine Progress Theatre actors, took me through the Pinter. Alone, I practised the piece opposite an empty chair, trying to summon up as much menace as possible.

Central was first. The school was housed in a collection of shambling, picturesque buildings just off the Finchley Road, at

Swiss Cottage. Despite preparing some interesting alternatives, I again played safe and presented the judging panel with two very familiar pieces – Edmund's 'bastard' speech from *King Lear* and yet another bit of *Hamlet*, with which I was obsessed. Derek Jacobi had a lot to answer for.

The Central School audition was so casual that I became worried, and took the judging panel's relaxed style for indifference. As I waited my turn in the student common room, nothing seemed to be going on. I don't know what I expected – maybe harlequins and people with leg-warmers doing ballet exercises, and someone rushing into the canteen shouting 'Let's do the show right here'. Instead all was calm and normal, and I did my audition with relative ease. Not a flicker on the faces of the panel, a polite thank you at the end, and no questions asked. Outside a dragonish grey-haired matron shrieked, with operatic grandeur 'You've been recalled' (rather like Edith Evans intoning 'A haaandbaaag?'), which meant that they wanted to see me again. I had got through to the next round, which would take place at some future date.

The experience had been fine, but it was its ordinariness that I resented. Why hadn't Olivier been passing through on his way to rehearsal? He'd gone to Central, hadn't he? I'd seen all those period Hollywood films where the hero walks up the steps to his club and passes a bearded figure on the way down to whom he says, 'Morning, Dickens'. Why couldn't that happen in life?

RADA was a very different affair and appealed strongly to my thwarted sense of glamour. The unprepossessing doors opened up onto a marbled hall full of busts and portraits, names I recognised, and great boards on the wall with lists of people that I'd heard of from the distant past. There was the sense of a real connection with theatrical tradition – the Vanburgh sisters, Maggie Albenesie, Gielgud – it was like breathing in ether. In retrospect the entrance hall was probably a little shabby even then, but it did smell of theatre and of actors and I loved it.

Richard O'Donoghue, the registrar, welcomed a group of about ten of us and promptly learned and remembered all our names. Very impressive. We then filed up to the common room, where I had an inordinately long wait because an eccentric Liverpudlian who was in before me had decided to build a castle. He was doing a piece from *Macbeth*, and wanted to create a setting for it by piling up chairs and tables in the audition room to give a sense of the 'pleasant seat'. By the time I got there the place looked like a furniture warehouse.

I have never been able to tell how auditions go. I simply did it and went back to wait in the common room with the rest of the applicants. We had all been gathered for about ten minutes when the phone rang. No one had explained quite what would happen and so one of the girls nervously picked up the receiver.

'Yes . . . right . . . I will.' Her hand went over the mouthpiece. 'Would the following people please go to see Mr O'Donoghue.' This was it. She started calling the names out. Seven, eight, nine. She'd finished. She hadn't mentioned mine.

They started to troop out and I sat there alone, stunned and not knowing what to do next. I had found what I had been looking for and had bollocksed it at the first hurdle. Total defeat. Then it dawned on me that I was still there. Could Mr Donoghue have made a mistake?

The phone rang again. I forced myself not to panic.

'Hello, Ken?'

'Yes?'

'Come down to the office, will you? Sorry to keep you waiting.'

Eureka. I was through the first round.

Every drama school has its own quirky auditioning system, and at RADA you returned on the afternoon of the same day if you had made a favourable impression with the first three examiners. There were four of these trios at work on auditions day, and the afternoon session was a repeat performance by the applicants so that the other nine judges could see the shortlisted students.

I had two hours to kill and decided on some lunch. I found a working men's café and sandwich bar on the corner of Goodge Street and Tottenham Court Road and sat down to gaze at the limited menu, plumping eventually for a hamburger. As I ate, I turned to the back of my well-thumbed copy of the RADA prospectus. There was a dizzyingly long and impressive list of theatrical luminaries, most of them former students. I knew that this was where I wanted to go.

I also realised with a stab of horror that I'd eaten the wrong lunch. My breath reeked of onion. I ransacked the local sweet shop for some strong mints but, despite risking dental suicide, I re-entered the famous portals sure that I smelled like a portable kebab stall.

If the toxic fumes exhaled by my afternoon Hamlet affected the judging panel, I was unaware of it. I simply couldn't see them. The venue had changed from one of the classrooms to the small George

Bernard Shaw Theatre, a friendly auditorium which, on that occasion, couldn't have been more intimidating. The panel was impressively lit from the back so that the poor, dazzled auditionee looked out at a gestapo-like line of silhouettes.

The figures asked me about my education, about my acting experience. I was in and out in fifteen minutes, and was told that they would be making decisions 'very soon'.

The whole experience had been agreeably formal and well stage-managed, and apart from the grim theatricality of the afternoon's debriefing, quite enjoyable. I got the train back to Reading. I prayed that I would get in.

The phone rang three days later. It was a Saturday evening at 7.30, and I was just about to set out for a party. My sister called me and said,

'I can't make it out, but there's someone called Jo Huttell on the phone for you.'

'What?'

'Hello, Kenneth. Hugh Cruttwell here.'

Jesus – the principal of RADA. His was the chief voice in the darkness. He was going to let me down gently.

'Now look, I'll be quite frank. All the others want to offer you a place here.'

This was too much. I sat down.

'The thing is, I'm not sure. I have to say the kind of acting you came up with the other day is ten-a-penny. I simply wasn't interested.'

'Oh.'

'So look. What I suggest, if you're willing and interested, is that you come back with a different audition speech and you and I will have a work session on it. How's that?'

'Fine.'

If he'd asked me to dance naked in Gower Street I'd have agreed.

'When is your recall for Central?'

'Thursday, sir. Thank you very much, sir.'

The spiritual forelock was being tugged to within an inch of its life.

'Well, why don't you come along here on Wednesday, say 10.30, OK? Good. See you then. Cheerio.'

I was breathless with excitement and terrified to boot. Another speech. What? And what was it he didn't like? Everything, it seemed, and yet he was prepared to give me another chance, *and* he had asked me about Central. I must be in with a shout. I went off to the party elated, had one drink, and was completely plastered.

Pauline and Harry Grey rallied magnificently to take me through the gentleman-caller speech from Tennessee Williams' *The Glass Menagerie*. I thought an American accent should impress him, the slow drawl of Jimmy Stewart in *Harvey*, which at least was a change from *Hamlet*. If it was a total disaster, I could at least use it for the recall at Central, the next day.

I took to Hugh Cruttwell at first sight – a sharpish face with the aspect of a wise old eagle, and a strong, wiry body. He was instantly commanding and completely honest. I started on the speech from *The Glass Menagerie* several times, but he stopped me continually, and made me go back to the beginning. His criticism was very direct – he was saying exactly what he thought, not to wound or play power games, but because it was patently true.

We started again, this time on *The Caretaker*. 'What you're doing is *demonstrating* to me what the character is doing. You're *indicating* what he is feeling. The execution is tremendously accomplished but the overall effect is soulless. I am not asking you to present me with a fully rounded character in a two-minute speech, but I want to see the potential of that character, not your actor's commentary on him. Try again.'

He urged me to abandon my carefully rehearsed moves around the vacant chair in which my invisible victim was sitting, and made me start the speech in a different physical position. He talked about the play and the character.

'Good. Now, you clearly know a great deal about this character, so you must trust me when I say that your actor's instinct is sufficiently developed for you not to have to "present" him. Abandon this point-making and allow, if you can, the character to play you. You'll be surprised at the results.'

I tried everything he suggested and my biggest surprise was drying stone dead after three sentences.

'Excellent. You were surprising yourself then. All that acting had been dropped, and you were discovering things in performance by being true to the character, not your idea of it. Naturally, things come out differently. It's an unfamiliar experience and that's why you dried. Well done, you've dropped all that acting.'

We carried on for another half an hour, and it was exhilarating. I found myself acting in a way I had never done before, and, as Hugh pointed out, I'd had a tiny glimpse of the difference between being a performer showing off and being an actor actually serving a character.

At the end of the session he said, with great precision, 'You've absolutely convinced me of your potential to work in the way I think is important for you. Good luck at Central, and let me know how you get on there.'

I still hadn't cracked it, or at least, I wasn't sure. It was now or never. 'I must say, sir, that even if they offered me a place I would far rather come here. I would really love to.'

He hadn't been fishing for this, but he was clearly pleased that I'd declared my preference. 'Thank you. I'll certainly let you know as soon as I can.'

It had been a wonderful morning, and it was proof, if ever I needed it, that acting was the career I wanted to follow. It had also shown me that there was a place to go where I could really learn, and a person who could really teach me. Acting now meant more than just showing off in school plays – a door had been opened on something far more interesting: the way you could submerge your personality fully into someone else's words, the way you could become an instrument, a vessel through which something else could channel and expand itself, take on colour and meaning. It was frightening to be faced with the truth of the tiny extent of one's knowledge, but hugely exciting at the same time.

On that one magnificent and humbling morning, acting stopped being simply another means of escape for the working-class Belfast boy adrift in English suburbia. It was no longer to do with aspirations to fame and having nice things said about you. An enormous area had suddenly opened up where the attempt to plumb the mystery of real acting offered a lifetime of attractively elusive satisfaction. A profound shift had taken place in my mind, and I was absolutely certain that RADA was the place, and Hugh was the man, to start me on this immense journey.

But he still hadn't offered me a place.

The next day, at the recall for the Central School, I was introduced to the acting profession in competition. We arrived at nine o'clock for a movement session. These sessions usually consist of an hour's worth of ballet-based, aerobic exercises which vary in difficulty. They are designed to improve and enhance an actor's body control, and in this case they were testing whether we had any body control at all. There were around forty of us, a very mixed crowd – and there were several deeply embarrassed males like myself, looking ridiculous in their football kit, and insisting on their heterosexuality with every uneasy pirouette. Then there was a whole selection of dazzling leotards and a few 'pros' who had sweatbands on every available area of exposed skin. We finished half an hour of rudimentary exercises and gathered back in the common room. The silver-haired matron appeared with a flourish. Her name was Miss Grey, and she was there to announce that half of our number were already 'out'.

We were in for quite a day. The next session was audition speeches. Split into groups of five, we were required to perform in front of our fellows as well as the judging panel, a particularly gruelling experience. One was aware of 'favourites' emerging during this process – auditionees whose talent and confidence seemed to shine through. I felt I performed well.

Then there was a ninety-minute wait, and Miss Grey appeared again. Another eight names were read out and people with whom one had quietly been making friends had to pack their bags and hold dignity intact while they made the long exit from the common room.

A nervous lunch was followed by a singing test. I was shown a book with a collection of show songs and asked to choose. There was only one I recognised. Conscious of a certain irony, I launched into 'Dream the Impossible Dream'. It was shaky, but reasonably in tune.

By this time it was late afternoon, and I went back to the common room where the numbers were about to be reduced by another six. One cold sweaty minute later I was through. I was relieved at the decision, but was becoming increasingly resentful of the selection process. This was one aspect of being an actor that I wasn't going to like. There was too much relish in our hostess's ceremony, and there had to be less humiliating ways of doing these things. But who was I to complain? They had a place and I wanted one. Or did I? At around six o'clock, after another nail-biting hour, I said aloud,

'I wish they'd let us go home.'

From my right a girl, who was visibly feeling the strain, turned round and snapped,

'Well, why don't you piss off then, and give us a better chance.'

I was taken aback. I'd hardly spoken to the girl all day and had certainly done nothing to annoy her. What I saw was the naked fear and aggression that tends to be one of the occupational hazards of being an actor. It was a result of succumbing to that helpless feeling of being a pawn in a game that someone else controls. I understood exactly how she felt, but I resolved to avoid that kind of reaction at all costs. It must never matter *that* much. When she was asked to leave at Miss Grey's final pronouncement, the girl's face turned to stone.

There were two of us left. It was 7 pm. We'd been there for ten hours and I was fed up. The principal asked us into his office and offered us both a place there and then. The other successful candidate was a lithe, red-lycred American girl who was shrieking with excitement. I smiled weakly. 'Thank you very much.'

Later, we said goodbye to each other at Swiss Cottage tube station.

'See you in September,' she shouted as the train doors closed. As I waved goodbye, I knew I wouldn't. Whatever the outcome of the session with Hugh, I knew Central, for all its undoubted prestige and excellence, wasn't the place for me. I had a gut feeling about the personality of the place as it then was, and made a simple, personal decision. The day seemed like a microcosm of the least appealing aspects of the theatre and was filled with everything that frightened me. The whole episode was comically capped by my being propositioned by one of the students, a flame-haired Scotsman in pink dungarees who threatened to celebrate my admission by taking me down to Piccadilly for 'a good time on the meat rack'. Suburban sensibilities suitably shocked, I headed for Paddington with relief.

That night I wrote to Central explaining my refusal of their kind offer, and then worked out what to do when Hugh Cruttwell rang to say that, much as he'd like to offer me a place, the course was filled. I got out the rest of the prospectuses. Bristol and Guildhall looked affordable. I prepared myself for the second round.

The next day Reading was covered in snow. There was a hard afternoon at school explaining why the latest history essay was not on time, and when I came home there was an envelope still on the mat, with the words *Royal Academy of Dramatic Art* set out in red letters across the bottom. My heart started pounding, and I stood for ten minutes just holding the letter. I finally opened it. My eyes swam, and I could read nothing while I searched for the magic words, '. . . and so I would like to offer you a place.' They were there.

My mother was asleep upstairs, and I didn't dare wake her. I couldn't stop jumping around, so I celebrated by taking the dog for a three hour walk in the snow. He didn't know what had hit him, and after ninety minutes he was whimpering to come home, but no chance – in my mind I was miles away at Stratford, the National Theatre, Hollywood, playing Macbeth, Hamlet, Hotspur. The dog was so exhausted that I had to carry him for the last half hour.

My parents were thrilled and deeply relieved. RADA was the one drama school they had heard of, and the 'Royal' tag seemed to bestow an acceptably conventional status on it. If I had got in to one of the more avant-garde schools, they would have been terrified. And RADA gave you a diploma – if I didn't make it as an actor I could perhaps teach.

When I re-examined the magic letter, I noted with alarm Hugh's request that I contact the local authority to apply for a grant covering fees and maintenance. The course did not offer a degree, and naturally, because it was an arty course, in a discipline which some felt could hardly be described as work, any award would be discretionary. I did some research. The Conservative-controlled Berkshire County Council had not made an award for a Drama course in four years. Bloody hell. I worked out some figures: they came to roughly £1,000 per term for seven terms, plus maintenance of £500 per term. £10,500 for the whole course, a sum my father could not possibly afford. Despite his pride in the very legitimate status of my RADA acceptance, he was in no position to pay for me. It was a grant or nothing. Hugh had already indicated that there were no scholarships available. I made my application and was informed that the funds available were severely limited.

It was hardly surprising. All available funds had to serve those wanting to study music, dance, sculpture and all fine art foundation courses, and this meant that although candidates had already been accepted at recognised and prestigious colleges, they were lumped together to compete with each other for money which they would have received automatically if they had chosen to go directly to University.

In my case, it meant that despite winning places at both Central and RADA, I would have to audition for Berkshire County Council, and they would decide my fate. It was my first brush with the absurd anomalies in attitudes to arts funding, and I felt real resentment. It wasn't that I didn't appreciate the luxury of individual subsidy, but I bitterly resisted the implicit assumption that the arts were always a borderline case.

I already had strong views about the application of my training.

The Government would not merely be sponsoring a private fantasy: I knew then, for instance, that I wanted to act in or take theatre to Belfast, which was then rapidly on its way to becoming a cultural wasteland. I also watched every piece of drama that came to Reading's Hexagon Theatre, and knew how powerfully good theatre could affect people. I dragged unwilling friends along, and saw their reaction to good work and to rubbish. I looked at the different audiences, and wondered about how they might change, how more people – people like my parents – could at least be offered the choice of becoming theatre-goers. I had firm convictions of the importance of popular art, and of its power to make life seem richer and better. I knew in my bones that drama need not be élitist in the way suggested by the council's attitude.

I was certain, even then, that it was necessary to take a long-term view. It seemed essential that a council, government, or any administrative body had to concede the notion of quality. If you wanted a great theatre, then you needed great writers, directors, designers and actors, and if you didn't encourage them, or allow them to be trained properly, then you reduced the possibilities of widening audience choice. Why should audiences take an expensive chance on any theatrical experience, if what they are usually offered is dreadful? I was – and am – convinced that greater quality can mean greater accessibility.

My half-formed adolescent views were part of an embryonic actor-militancy. I was attracted by the glamour of the theatre, but I was also proud of my parents and my background, and I wanted to do something of which they would be proud in turn. Imbued with the Protestant work ethic, I believed that work was a good thing, that one should make oneself useful and put something back into the world through whatever work one did. I felt that as an actor this was possible and the implication that any aspirant thespian was an effete, money-grabbing waster galled me.

The Council audition was set for May, and as a gesture towards my parents and teachers, who were all worried about me not getting the grant, I applied for University. Lots of actors had come up through University, so I thought I should at least go through the motions. It might give me that old favourite: something to fall back on. The Oxbridge route was suggested at first, and the theatrical alumni it boasted gave it great career kudos. Meadway Comprehensive, with a roll of 1500 and a sixth form of twelve, was obviously keen to boost its academic record, and if I could only be persuaded to stop acting a bit and do some work, I might just scrape in. But I was dead against it.

My one experience of Oxford had been on a visit with a girlfriend who knew people in one of the colleges. We sat in some ancient rooms at midnight, drinking port. Our host put a violin concerto by a little-known composer on the record player. The smooth-talking undergraduate next to me turned and spoke as if the effort might kill him. 'They're taking this at quite a lick, aren't they?'

I smiled and shifted nervously in my seat, moving an enormous working-class chip from one shoulder to the other, and thought that this definitely wasn't the place for me. I felt much the same on a visit to Cambridge, where the weight and complexity of traditional customs made a deep impression on me. If I had experienced a sense of cultural collision in moving from Belfast to Reading, then a potential jump from suburbia to the intricate élitism of Cambridge was even more terrifying. The prospect of London and drama school frightened me enough as it was.

I was given an interview at Manchester University which convinced me finally that academic life was not really the place for a frustrated actor – it was to be RADA or nothing.

At the Council audition I behaved like a sulky child, since I was outraged that they should demand proof of my abilities after I had been accepted by two major schools. But the Council had at least entrusted a recommendation to two drama professors from the borough, both of whom I knew. Alistair Conquer, a great friend of mine who had the ear of the examiners, reported afterwards that I had seemed rather peremptory. I rushed to the dictionary and my heart sank. They wouldn't announce their decision till July.

At that point I had to plunge myself into 'A' level revision, and I tried desperately to cram two years' homework into a month. My renewed efforts had been hastened by the terrible disappointed look in my father's face as he watched me across the dinner table, learning lines for Noah Claypole in *Oliver*. It was a school production and I'd agreed to do it, even though the performances were only eight weeks before my exams. 'Do you think you could pull it together for a couple of months, son? Stop all this theatre gallivanting and do some studying.'

There was a tired, reproachful note in his voice that got to me, and I was stricken with guilt and shame. I knew it was too late. I also knew that Noah Claypole was a delightful little cameo that was irresistible. I'd make it up to him. It happened again, however, when I was cast as Cassio in the Berkshire Shakespeare Players production of *Othello* at Reading's Abbey Ruins. At first my parents were pleased, as it was a successful production, in a magical setting with fine local actors. But the dangers became more real when the production transferred a month later – during exams – to the Cliveden Festival, where it played in the grounds of the famous house. I pleaded successfully to be allowed to do it, and they gave in. I think they knew I was an academic lost cause.

Much good the Cliveden experience did me. Fighting the main flightpath from Heathrow airport, I discovered the peculiar torture that open-air theatre can be. On our final matinee we clashed with the men's singles final at Wimbledon. There were twenty-five in the cast and seventeen in an auditorium which sat 1200. The ticket tearer was very deaf but still intent on watching Wimbledon on the bar-tent TV. The cacophony reached its heights in the fifth act, when the desultory audience of sleepy pensioners were treated to:

'It is the cause . . .'

'Fifteen love.'

'. . . It is the cause my soul . . .'

'Borg to serve –'

'. . . Let me not name it to you, you chaste stars . . .'

'Lovely backhand.'

'. . . It is the cause . . .'

'Extraordinary, he's cracked it!'

Othello carried on gamely as Desdemona was smothered and Borg won the third set. Othello had no choice. The cast had taken a vote, and given the interest evinced by the tiny audience, had decided to listen to the match as they worked.

July came, and with it the joyful news that the County Council would pay my fees and maintenance for the whole course at RADA. My fellow candidates had not fared so well: mine was the only drama award made that year. There had been many applicants, and the snob value of RADA's name had obviously done the trick.

The summer was devoted to earning money to supplement the grant, and I took a job as a hospital porter, working in the supplies depot of Reading's Battle hospital. Orders for equipment would come from the various wards and I would load up the trollies of goodies. I was in charge of shrouds and specimen bottles.

They gave me a day off every week and I used this to travel to London to look for accommodation. I was only just coming to terms with the place, and was still fighting a country boy's awe. It was such a relief to know that you could walk everywhere. In my previous visits to see plays I'd always taken the Tube for fear of getting lost. My terror of living in London had been the main reason for turning down the National Youth Theatre. It was still very intimidating, and seemed a place to be lonely in. But I had things to do. RADA had sent a list of required items for new students. Jazz shoes and dance tights rang alarm bells, but I went at it with a will and strode along dutifully to the leotard emporium in St Martin's Lane with my butchest grin and my lurex under my arm.

Sometimes on these trips I had company. David Longstaff, a long-standing chum from Progress, was hoping to go to University in London and we looked for a place to share. Our daily routine involved calls to ever-shadier accommodation agencies and a dive for the early edition of the *Evening Standard* after lunch. Scouring the paper for flats one day in a Tottenham Court Road pub, David made the fatal mistake of ringing home to see if his 'A' level results had arrived. They had. I followed suit, and both of us were disappointed. My results were bad. I cursed myself for all those plays I'd done, and felt remorse for the intense disappointment I knew would be felt by my teachers and my parents. I'd let them down, and here I was adrift in a pub on the Tottenham Court Road, a thick student actor with no place to live. Life was a bitch.

I left David drowning his sorrows, and walked around the corner to RADA where they sometimes had news of accommodation. The place smelled better than before and Summers, who ran the front door, was charm itself. Apart from having a name like a 1930s' butler, he was understanding of nervous new students. He gave me a telephone number, and I rang a number in Clapham.

'Hello, Angus Mackay?'

'Yeees.' It was the most actor-ish voice I'd ever heard.

'I'm a student from RADA. I believe you have two rooms to let.'

'My deaaar. Of course I do. When would you like to see them?'

'Would this afternoon be possible?'

'Of course. As soon as you like, though I'm not even up yet. There you see, your introduction to what actors really do.' A great hearty laugh. 'See you later.'

I felt as though I'd just spoken to a cross between Noel Coward and Basil Brush. Whether the rooms were right or not, this man had to be worth meeting.

When I arrived, the house – in Manchuria Road, Clapham – turned out to be a roomy terrace. Angus Mackay was tall and distinguished, with thinning silver-grey hair, and an old-fashioned theatrical line in persuasive charm. His conversation seemed enormously flamboyant, and was scattered with references to his late wife, Dorothy Reynolds, the co-author of *Salad Days*.

The house was the sort of theatrical Aladdin's Cave of which I had dreamed. He had even more back copies of *Plays and Players* than I did, and the walls were covered with playbills and prints of famous actors. The place was absolutely crammed with books: a formidable theatrical library and thousands of novels. We took to each other right away. I was his first lodger and the first person to share the house with him since his wife had died, three years before. The back bedroom and the little sitting-room were very comfortable, Angus's company was highly enjoyable, and it was all for twenty pounds a week. I had fallen on my feet.

I returned to Reading that night and gave my mother the good and the bad news. To my mother it all seemed bad. The 'A' level results gave me very little to fall back on, and my academic record was important to my parents, who felt that they had thrown away or had been denied their own educational opportunities. I had let them down and, what was more, now that I had found my own accommodation, another home, the last ties were being broken.

'Well, I hope this place isn't full of nancy boys.'

I left her scowling over the washing up, but I was certain that I was right to move to London. My days as a hospital porter came to an end, and the big day arrived. I left home on a Sunday. Mum had been ironing for days, and I had more pressed shirts than I knew what to do with.

We'd never been a family to demonstrate emotion. We weren't unloving, just reserved. I went for a drink with my father, his custom on a Sunday lunchtime. I came back to find my mother doing the sprouts. I made all the usual protestation about coming back at the weekends, that London was so near, then gave her a hug. I was fine – my emotions were well in control.

I went into the living-room. My dad was sitting there quietly. I noticed an envelope on the mantelpiece, and walked over to it: it was addressed to me. I opened it, and inside was a pink 'good luck' card of absurd sentimentality, a kind that only my mum can choose. After the treacly verse, she had written 'We are both very proud of you son. Here is something to help you on your way.' There was a hundred pounds in cash. I was speechless. Their generosity was extra-ordinary. I turned to my father who had naturally averted his eyes. The words wouldn't come, and I could barely see him. My eyes were brimming with tears.

THREE

It was the Sunday evening before my first day at RADA, and I was nervous and lonely, but somehow ready for anything. I'd occupied myself making the first tentative explorations of Angus Mackay's marvellous house, which looked more and more like a miniature theatre museum. I marched down to Clapham South Tube station to get my three-month season ticket. I had dinner with Angus that night, and a roast leg of lamb made me feel considerably less lonely. I'd already started to torment Angus with questions about the theatre and actors, and the nerve-wracked evening passed quickly and enjoyably.

The next morning all the first day horrors I'd imagined gradually disappeared. I didn't sleep in, there wasn't a delay on the Tube, but yes, horror of horrors, I was the first one there. John Alderman, a huge ex-policeman of Karloffian menace, who shared the reception job with Summers, showed me how to clock in. They were very strict about lateness at RADA.

That done, there was my first appearance in dance tights to accomplish. I entered the men's locker-room trying to look confident about where my locker was, gave a few nonchalant, warm-but-strong smiles to a few of the older students who were already there, and then went down the wrong aisle three times.

The first class was Movement, in room ten, directly opposite the locker-room across a short stretch of landing. I changed as quickly as I could and rushed across into the empty class. I was in room ten and ready to go at 9.45. The class started at 10. I was completely alone and hoping that life would eventually cure me of pathological punctuality. At 9.50, with my paranoia reaching new heights in walked Glen Wyand, tugging at his tights.

'Jesus, how do you walk in these things?'

A tall, tanned West-coast American in his mid-twenties, Glen was kind and generous and about as laid-back as you could be without actually stopping. The sound of that soft, velvety voice, apparently devoid of all worry, relaxed me instantly. We began to share mock macho complaints about what this training would do to us.

The room started to fill up with equally uncomfortable but smiling young men and a smaller number of girls who performed the usual trick of convincing you that they had all been professional dancers. Just before 10, Ruth Eva Ronen entered, a movement teacher of enormous precision and metronomic discipline. Neat, in dark blue leotard and always beautifully groomed, she looked like someone's favourite aunt, but the reality was a sergeant-major of the dance floor. Her technique was a sweet smile as she walked round the room, while she pushed students' legs further up in the air or along the bar or round their necks. After an hour of what I came to think of as gestapo aerobics, I was aching all over and consulting the timetable. Christ. Movement every morning. Still, all part of creating the perfect machine for acting.

We then had our first voice class, with instructions about what was to be prepared, speeches and exercises. And then on to music rudiments, where my grasp of reading the stave could hardly have been more rudimentary.

Lunch at RADA was a very cheery affair, and took place in a heavily subsidised canteen right at the top of the narrow building in Gower Street that was ginghamed, bright and airy. Here was where we first shared Movement miseries and consoled ourselves with some of Mrs P's spotted dick. I'd grown to like desserts by then, and Mrs P, who ran the canteen, could make a mean pud.

The afternoon brought the first spot of real acting, with our introduction to Wedekind's *Spring Awakening*. We'd been split up into two groups and I was rather miffed because the other lot were working on Chekhov's *The Wood Demon*. We did have an excellent director in Jane Howell, but even she was unable to lift the unremitting gloom of this view of troubled adolescence. I was given a long speech by a character called Hans who seemed to spend most of the play in the toilet masturbating (I don't know what impression I'd made at the reading!). Hans gets very carried away during this speech – I took his example, and by the end of the first week I'd have been audible in the back row of the Coliseum.

'Remember, he's in a toilet on his own, not wishing to be heard,' said Jane in hushed tones.

'Ah.'

Having got through the first day, I poured out my impressions to

Angus that night: yes, there were some marvellous actors, it seemed; no, I didn't think I had a second career as a dancer; yes, I loved the building, old-fashioned, wood everywhere, sweaty, a bit frayed at the edges, but a real place for work. Things were going on, the place was full of activity. I was a convert on day one.

As the days and weeks of the first term went by, RADA completely took over my life. The institution was all-embracing. Classes ran from 10 to 6, and in the evenings there were rehearsals, tutorials, singing classes. We often worked on Saturday mornings, and most evenings throughout the term there were productions to watch in one of the Academy's two theatres, performed by the finals students. The place seemed to take up all one's waking hours, which was fine by me, as it not only satisfied my voracious appetite for learning but it made leaving home a relatively painless experience. By the time I got round to noticing the first term was over I was already a Londoner.

I made some good friends, sometimes in unusual circumstances. During our first week we all awaited the arrival of a mysterious student, John Marshall, who was late starting term because of a delay in his flight from Canada. He still hadn't arrived when we began our first 'group project' session. There appeared to be a teacher running it, for the curly-haired, compact lumberjack-type before us was asking plenty of questions. After fifty minutes I rumbled him.

'You're not a teacher.'

'No, I'm John Marshall. I start today.'

There was a general moan from the assembled group who'd spent all that time being well-behaved, and this was my introduction to the mild-mannered Scotsman with the manner of a teacher who was to become John Sessions. This incident provided me with a marvellous stick with which to beat John who had come to RADA at twenty-six with two degrees and a feeling that he was already too old. Activating John's age-neurosis became a RADA sport. He and I formed a student threesome with Mark Hadfield, another actor in our term, and together we went to see practically everything the London theatre had to offer.

RADA's location in central London was an enormous boon. We could walk to every West End theatre, the National Theatre, the RSC in pre-Barbican days, and not only were there student stand-by tickets offered by the theatres themselves, but RADA was often given complimentary seats for struggling shows. Student arrogance knew no bounds when it came to savage criticism of plays and performances.

As the term wore on my faults were catalogued in gruesome detail. I suppose this process might be described as the 'breaking down' process, prior to the 'building up' of a technically competent actor. At the end of the first term I was not so much broken down as broken up. Ruth Eva and her colleagues had convinced me that I couldn't walk, stand or sit. If that really were the case, I sensed limitations in my future work.

The voice teachers were particularly hard on me. At one notable voice class I gave what I thought was a splendidly heroic Hotspur. It was a speech from *Henry IV Part I*, which begins 'My liege I did deny no prisoners'. I'd read about the character's famous 'thickness of speech', which was sometimes interpreted with a Geordie accent, and sometimes (as by Olivier) with a stutter. With my customary originality I went for the latter. A splendid frustrated bark on the line, 'For he made me mmmmMAD.'

It had worked like a treat. You could hear a pin drop. Robert Palmer, a splendid teacher with a voice that was made for sexy chocolate commercials, was effusive. 'Marvellous, absolutely super, tremendous grasp of that. A couple of reservations.'

Here it was. The iron fist in the velvet glove. 'Horrendously stiff jaw there, Ken. That'll lose you all vocal flexibility if you're not careful. You've got to work on that sibilant 's'. Also those dark 'l's are letting you down badly. Don't want to be just a regional actor, do we? The hollow back really is a problem. It's affecting your rib control and contributing to that annoying sailor's roll you've developed. I think also if you can even out those vowel sounds, you'll do yourself a favour. Can't have kings sounding like peasants, can we? OK. Let's have the next speech.'

Exit quivering student.

To be fair to Robert and his fellow voice teacher, Geoffrey Connor, there was never any attempt to 'standardise'. Their points were always specific, and there was no attempt to produce the legendary 'RADA voice'. There was however an insistence on silly-sounding phrases like 'thick, rich, dark, round, brown sound', which you had to say as if you were seducing someone. I can't think of a less likely line for the job.

Weekend trips back to Reading became increasingly infrequent. When I did go home, I was always astonished to see that my parents had grown older. While I was living at home, time had stood still, but now I noticed the deeper lines in my mother's face, and the grey in my dad's hair. My sister, Joyce, was now a young woman and no longer a child, and my brother had married and had children. Mum and Dad asked me about life in London, but I told them little, as all they really wanted to know was whether I was 'all right' – eating well, and getting enough sleep. As far as Mum was concerned, if my bowels had moved, then all was well with the world.

Life in London was becoming frantic, with homework – preparing speeches and reading plays – taking up more and more time. Life at Angus's was also delightfully engrossing, with his actor friends coming round to dinner to be plagued with questions from the gauche lodger. I had also abandoned my Reading girlfriend with a callousness that amazes me even now. I'd known Sandy for a couple of years and had been seeing her regularly for about nine months. She was delightful, both understanding and supportive, but not the right person for the young actor obsessed with independence.

'I'm just too busy . . . it'll never work out . . . it's better this way.'

What was that I was saying about it must never matter that much?

The student Burbage had taken over with a vengeance. *Richard III* was on the menu and I had several scenes to act as the crookback. I'd seen Olivier in the famous film and could do a wicked impersonation. This of course was not quite what was required for the wooing scene with Lady Anne. We'd been rehearsing the scene in different pairs for weeks. On the day we presented our work to Jane Howell, I was inspired. Flying. The first time since I'd arrived that I thought I was *doing* it. It seemed effortless, brilliant acting, and I was also thrilled by the girl playing Lady Anne. We neared the end of this wonderfully constructed scene.

ANNE	Didst thou not kill this king?
GLOUCESTER	I grant ye.
ANNE	Dost grant me, hedgehog? Then, God grant me too
	Thou mayst be damned for that wicked deed!
	O, he was gentle, mild and virtuous!
GLOUCESTER	The better for the King of Heaven, that hath him.

ANNE	He is in heaven, where thou shalt never come.
GLOUCESTER	Let him thank me that holp to send him thither, For he was fitter for that place than earth.
ANNE	And thou unfit for any place but hell.
GLOUCESTER	Yes, one place else, if you will hear me name it.
ANNE	Some dungeon.
GLOUCESTER	Your bed-chamber.

Electric. I could feel people all around completely gripped. The scene ended. I looked at this gorgeous creature who had been part of my triumph. I knew what she must be thinking.

'Well?' I said.

She seemed puzzled. Then she asked, 'Are you always going to play it like a Dalek?'

Well, actors are never the best judges of their own work, but it hardly mattered. I was in love. It felt like the real thing, and was in fact a relationship that would last for several years.

The penny was slowly beginning to drop about 'performing', about the need to create each part or speech, and not simply slot in some carefully remembered voice or mannerism from another actor. Not that I am against nicking things. I do it all the time – from life, or from other actors. It's just that a really good actor will put such borrowings into his own soil and make it his own.

Hugh Cruttwell continued with illuminating definitions of where my faults lay. 'You want to produce great acting. There are three major ingredients: passion, poetry and humour. You often have the humour, though not necessarily of the right sort. You have great access to passion, but you seldom find the heart of the poetry. For this you must surrender yourself much more to the part. Not indulge, but give away your technical awareness to a large extent. Not advice to give to every actor, but certainly to you.'

It was sinking in, but it was also painful. I spent my entire RADA career haunted by the voice of Hugh saying 'not true, don't believe it'. Not that his judgement was infallible, simply that I agreed absolutely with him over the severity of the changes necessary to convert the school show-off into an honest actor. He and I never argued. And as he tactfully pointed out, my acting never seemed vulgar or ungenerous. It was just that for certain roles, i.e. the ones I wanted to play, the performer in me had to be clamped down.

Hugh's great gift was to say out loud what I knew myself. It didn't matter if ninety-nine per cent of your audience, critics and colleagues raved about your performance, if a single voice rumbled it as a cheat, as not true, for all its flashiness and technical accomplishment, then you really had to own up and do something about it. Hamlet was right:

> Now, this overdone, or come tardy off, though it makes the unskilful laugh, cannot but make the judicious grieve; the censure of the which one must in your allowance o'erweigh a whole theatre of others.

These words continue to haunt me. I have always suffered from original guilt. About everything. I don't know whether it's a peculiar part of the Irish inheritance, but it's a powerful and motivating force in me, and my acting has never been free from its grip. The first two terms at RADA let me see that I was gifted in particular ways – good at sight-reading, good at accents, quick in most ways – but that this was not always a help. Being betrayed into superficial performances by these accomplishments was a continual danger.

If I fell into this trap it was never conscious, but the consequent guilt and misery were massive. I knew that it was an acceptance of second best, and an abuse of the advantages I had been given, and I had no choice but to get better and truer by working as hard as I possibly could. This ridiculous extremism has been a major factor in the inner drive that has accompanied my work and career ever since. I find myself unreasonably suspicious of praise; in fact, I am so seldom satisfied with my own work that I become instantly alarmed when other people express their approval. This acts as a kind of puritanical insurance policy against possible failure, and means, of course, that I have rarely enjoyed any true success that I have had.

In the meantime, and before this masochism became too well-established, there was work to do. In any case, things were kept under control by another Irish legacy, that of philosophical acceptance. A drink in the hand and the familiar mantra, 'Ah, fuck it.'

Appropriately, *Fears and Miseries* – Brecht's play set in the Third Reich – was the production that absorbed me during my second term. This picked up on my modest success in *Spring Awakening*, and continued my interesting line of manic Aryans. With thick blond hair and an even thicker German accent I became, for a time, the Anton Diffring of RADA.

Type-casting of this kind did not protect me from improvisation and 'experimental' work. Although RADA subscribed to no specific school of acting, Hugh Cruttwell's policy was to expose the students to as many different techniques and directors as possible. One day I found myself walking blindfold up the Tottenham Court Road, attempting to persuade my 'partner' to cross from the other side. I forget what this was supposed to teach us, but I did learn that artificial sensory deprivation and major thoroughfares do not mix. During the more extreme of these exercises John Sessions, by far the most easily embarrassed student, would hide in the nearest coffee bar until we had all 'found our centres'.

We were also required to visit the Zoo once a week and study an animal, which we would later present in closely observed physical detail to various teachers. This was designed to test students' powers of observation as well as their dexterity. I have to confess to a less than committed attitude to this class, which was run by a soft, pixified lady in beaming middle age who appeared to be visiting Gower Street from Pluto. At the end of each class – in which we might have to be an animal or imagine ourselves a ball of mercury, or a tree, or a Mars Bar – she would stop us and then hold a mystical pause. Slowly she would point her finger at each student in turn. She spoke as if in a trance. 'You had it . . . you had it . . . you didn't have it . . . you had it . . .'

There were often variations.

'You had it for a bit, then you lost it . . . you didn't look like getting it . . .'

Needless to say I never had it or if I did, I certainly didn't know what 'it' was. I sometimes thought that perhaps I'd had it and not known what to do with it. Certainly if I ever did get it, she never saw it.

I don't think she'd ever forgiven me for being a crocodile. I'd chosen this creature because it hardly moved, and afforded me a good view of the rest of the class as I lay on the ground, hooded eyes half-closed, the all-seeing scourge of the jungle. I have never realised my crocodile professionally, although I have of course worked with several.

The world opened up for me at the end of the second term when I stopped playing Germans and was cast as Shakespeare's Pericles. I was remarkable in jeans and white T-shirt. All the cast were dressed alike and my mother said I looked the oldest, at about twelve. She was allowed to see this studio production because the school's policy was to have public audiences invited from the second term onwards.

We all relished the chance to practise in front of real live people from an early stage. I wish I could say that it improved my performance but I remained chronically overparted from beginning to end – the role was simply too much for me to take on at that time and at that age. The reconciliation scene between Pericles and Marina is one of the most moving in all the plays. I fell into a trap here that Gielgud has described eloquently: I did the whole thing awash with tears, genuinely and deeply moved by it, but almost incomprehensible to the audience who strained to hear a barely audible actor emoting to no particular effect.

I was learning rather swiftly about love. My Lady Anne – a girl called Wendy Seagram, who was in the same year – really was the one for me. I left Angus in Clapham with some sadness, but I had no choice, the primrose path was leading me inexorably to Willesden and to the arms of my beloved. We moved in together at the start of the third term. My brother had already broken the taboo about cohabitation, and so my parents accepted me living in sin without a murmur. I think secretly they thought it would ensure that I ate properly.

I certainly entered on full domestic life with a vengeance. There was a regular Saturday visit to Waitrose on the Kilburn High Road, and we bought a 'slo-cooker', which would be left on in the morning when we left for college and would produce something hot and tasty when we arrived back late at night. Favourite and cheapest was liver casserole. (Tray of liver – very cheap – pour over a can of tomatoes and anything else you fancy. Cook forever. Then drink something very strong like Retsina when you're eating it. You won't be able to taste it, but it must be doing you good.)

Our flat had everything we could possibly want but heat. There was a huge window the length of one side of the main room, and a gorgeous tree outside: the room was filled with light and the view was green. In the winter it was different – the tree was bare and the windows iced up on the inside, and there was the horror of making the morning dash from the warm duvet to the tiny kitchen to put the kettle on and then rush back before something got frostbite. However many liver casseroles I consumed, the two-roomed love-nest in

Willesden Green was not good for my circulation. At least it was cheap.

The journey on the number 8 bus each morning, or on the Jubilee and Bakerloo lines to Euston Square, was never enough to warm me up. That happened during movement class, not because of the activity, as I was often a shameless malingerer behind teacher's back, but I did get hot under the collar. Our accompanist was a sweet man, but had a limited repertoire of tunes. I have nothing against Andrew Lloyd Webber, but nearly three years of 'Close Every Door To Me' accompanying what seemed to me impossible movements against a wall was more than I could take. I'm unable to hear the tune now without wanting to put my leg up on the nearest table, bend over, and hope that Ruth Eva doesn't come and double me up even further.

Doubling up was quite another problem. 'Corpsing' – laughing on stage when you're not supposed to – had already become a hazard. I don't know why it happened to me, but I had been doing it since I'd started acting. People say it's a form of hysterics, which I'm sure is true.

At RADA the first of a long series of tickings-off came my way, and similar reprimands have been dogging me ever since, to my eternal shame. They usually begin 'I wouldn't have expected it of you,' or, 'You really have let yourself down'. Sometimes it's an irate fellow actor who thinks that they are the object of your mirth. With me, almost always, there's no particular reason, but it's as if some puff of laughing gas had been sent through my system. It can happen at any time. Later in my career, I once corpsed myself in a one-man show, which must be some sort of record. Nothing had happened, I was just struck by the thought that what I was doing must seem absolutely ridiculous, and so I was off. I then amused myself further by attempting desperately to convert the smiles into 'acting'. Not a chance; once begun, a corpse is a lost cause.

I'm much better these days. The tickings-off and the shame have worked, as has the memory of the excruciating pain when you know that you've let down an audience or a fellow actor. I used to shuffle backstage, head down, aware that the word 'amateur' was written in neon lights across my forehead.

At RADA several people pointed out that in my case I didn't have much to laugh about. They were probably referring to my singing. We had a lesson one evening a week in which the teacher, Daryl

61

Moulton, coached me in classical songs and encouraged a flamboyant, italianate delivery. We worked in the canteen where I was encouraged to stand on the tables and belt it out as if I was at La Scala. I loved it. But only in the canteen.

At the end of each term, on a grim Saturday morning, we had to sing solo in front of the other twenty-two members of the class and all the staff. It was a terrifying experience for nearly everyone, but RADA, quite rightly, insisted on it as absolutely necessary to improve the equipment of a versatile modern actor. Hugh demanded a certain seriousness for these occasions, even though the atmosphere was fraught with the hysterics of frightened student actors. Our group was very supportive, and each time one of us got through it the cheering could be heard in Gower Street.

I managed the first two of these occasions with relative ease. At the end of the fourth term I was given Purcell's 'Music For A While' to sing. Daryl insisted on my progressing from the Cole Porter ballads I loved to this extremely taxing song. I practised hard and felt much the same as I had always done when I entered the packed classroom for the session. When it was my turn I went to the front. The introduction was played, and I sang the first phrase. I faltered, and with that stumble an uncontrollable fear and sickness rose up in me. I was about to cry. So I stopped and walked to the piano, picked up the music from my astonished teacher and turned to the huge group of staff and students. You could hear a pin drop. 'I . . . I'm sorry . . . I can't do this . . .'

I walked to the door and tried to get out. It was stuck. For what seemed like an eternity I waited and prayed for the earth to swallow me up. The door finally opened, and I ran down the stairs and out into Gower Street. The tears were pouring down my face, but I was also furious with myself for having given in to my first horrendous bout of stage-fright. I walked round the block replaying the humiliation. After half an hour I realised that I had no choice but to go back. I was scheduled to sing two other voluntary pieces after the compulsory ones. One was a duet with Mark Hadfield, and I couldn't let him down as well. But voluntary? What had I been thinking of?

There was a break before the next session and during the coffee I arrived back to squirm in the puzzled sympathy of my fellow students. The session started. I got back on the horse, as it were, and stood in front of all those people feeling more stupid than I had done before in my life. The singing was fine – that wasn't the problem. It was confidence, and it had been a shock to find out how fragile mine was. I was determined not to be neurotic about it but it did sabotage my performing for a while. I came out of the depression by resolving one day to be in a professional musical in which I sang the most difficult song imaginable. I'm still working on that one.

A rather more visible fear presented itself on our school's tour of the *Merchant of Venice* – violence. The North London comprehensives we played in made Meadway look like a holiday camp. For the first time I confronted an audience who talked loudly all the way through the play, who heckled and threw things. It probably resembled the crowd's response in Shakespeare's playhouse. When their attention was engaged, at whatever volume, it was exhilarating, but it was also a salutary experience of the barriers that separate Shakespeare and the theatre in general from a truly popular audience.

The barriers are high, but not insurmountable. It depends on how you do it. You have to be good for a start: my Salerio and Prince of Arragon were not creations to win over these urban adolescents. I played Arragon as Don Corleone and threw in dark glasses to complete the effect. I didn't go as far as putting cotton wool in my mouth like Brando, but the accent was impenetrable enough as it was. Another fine addition to my gallery of 'mystics'.

The fourth term brought me the Edmund Grey prize for high comedy. I was Sir Joseph Wittol, a fop, in Congreve's first play, *The Old Bachelor*. Rather than 'high', this performance can best be described as 'orbital'. Orange wig, white face, silly costume. Nothing could stop me. Certainly not good taste, and if the abuse of good taste is the spirit of restoration comedy, then I was marvellous.

'Yes, you certainly get full value from that one, Ken.'

Hugh chose his words carefully. I could think what I liked.

'Maybe we'll move you onto something a little more demanding.'

Demanding or impossible?

Old men. I knew it – a life destined for character parts. This was a classic student fear. If drama school condemned you to wigs and funny walks, then so would the outside world. It was no good if potential employers saw you as a ninety-year-old fop – we were young actors and wanted young parts.

Feelings about casting ran high at RADA, but it must be the same everywhere. Midway through the training I, and everyone else, became extremely rancid about the whole process. Why is *he* playing so-and-so when I'm the right person for the part? She *always* gets the femme fatales . . . he can't even *read* Shakespeare. None of this was particularly malicious, and we were a friendly team, but the claustrophobic, enclosed society had its disadvantages.

The part of Chebutykin, the melancholy, middle-aged doctor in Chekhov's *Three Sisters*, was not without its problems. We rehearsed for seven weeks with a director determined to rehearse as Stanislavsky might have done. In this case, the application of the famous method was a little shaky. To be fair, the director was dealing with a pretty stroppy cast. Things had not started well when she announced on the first day that we would not be using the translation we had been given. Some of the actors had learned the parts and weren't at all pleased to have a new version to learn.

She also insisted that we 'headlined', or described each line that our character spoke. For instance, if Chebutykin said in the text 'Hello, Natasha', the headline would be 'The doctor greets Natasha warmly'. Then a subtext had to be written: 'The Doctor appears to be greeting Natasha warmly, but in fact only slightly covers up his annoyance with her, whilst appearing to be polite for the others.' As this was done for every single sentence of dialogue, rehearsals entailed writing a short novel which was then questioned by the director, who wanted subtextual rewrites every time you discovered something new.

I'm certain that in the right hands this demanding variation on the method can work superbly well. Unfortunately I was twenty trying to play sixty and wanting to learn how to manage this feat, bar half a bag of Homepride over the barnet. I ended up looking like a cross between a demented Brigham Young and an anaemic Abraham Lincoln.

In desperation I did ask for help. I found the address from *Who's Who* in the RADA library and a letter was duly dispatched to Sir Laurence Olivier. Not only had Sir Laurence directed a famous stage version of the play, but he had also made a film version in which he played the Doctor. I wrote asking for information about anything that might have inspired him – books, films, paintings – anything that I could look at or read to help me with the part. The writing of the letter was partly a sort of exorcism of the dilemma, and I posted it with little hope of a reply.

A week later, to my great surprise, the following reply arrived at RADA.

LAURENCE OLIVIER

K. Branagh, Esq.   10th February 1981
R.A.D.A.,
62 Gower Street,
London W.C.1.

Dear Mr. Branagh:

   I think it is really fairly clear the sort of man Chebutykin is in the Three Sisters. Like Hotspur, Mercutio, etc., he is the plain man in all of Chekhov's plays.

   I am afraid I really cannot guide you in a purely literary way in a matter which is entirely at the disposal of your own thoughts and workings out. I don't think you can go very wrong, basically, as the author has it all there for you.

   If I were you, I should have a bash at it and hope for the best – which I certainly wish you.

Yours sincerely,
Etc.

   I don't know that the advice helped me one jot, but the thought that the great man had given it a moment's consideration was enough to send me roaring into the next rehearsal, headlines ablaze – 'Chebutykin goes mad', 'Chebutykin picks his nose', 'Chebutykin walks down front and gets into a much better position than the director has given him' – anything to annoy Miss Moscow Arts. Chebutykin came and went in a whirl of mediocrity.

   Contact with the theatrical gods intensified. It was RADA's seventy-fifth anniversary, and Hugh announced a visit by the Queen and Prince Philip to mark the occasion. They would go on a tour of the Academy, and there would be a small concert in their honour, a miscellany of items that charted the progress of students through the Academy.

   Hugh asked for volunteers who might like to do some Shakespeare or any other solo work. John Sessions and I went to see him, as John had already been developing his one-man shows and wanted to do a three minute solo improvisation.

Hugh laughed. 'Oh no. Oh no, no. no.' (More laughter) 'It's simply not possible, John. Your language is quite unacceptable. I have no objections, but there could be a national incident. I don't know what you'll come out with, and I simply can't take the risk.'

There was room, however, for the extremely boring and conventional student who came up with the least original idea.

'Could I do a bit of Hamlet?'

Although I was by no means Hugh's favourite student, I think he admired my doggedness and enthusiasm, and I was allowed to perform the 'rogue and peasant slave' soliloquy. We rehearsed it in detail with Hugh asking me first to colour particular lines and words and then encouraging me to forget all point-making and let the speech surprise me. It was yielding good results, and at the end of our second session he said, 'Yes, that's really coming alone. Now look, John Gielgud, the President of the Academy, is coming in on Monday to discuss arrangements for the royal visit, as he'll be showing them round. Perhaps we'll get him to listen to your speech. What do you think?'

I heard myself say, 'That would be terrific,' but my feet had left the ground. Gielgud had been one of my heroes since I had first begun to read about the theatre. My next reaction was the worst possible. I went back to the speech on my own in the following days and worked it to death. The margin was full of 'brilliant' ideas, and I stayed late at college to work on breathing and voice. If you were going to do a speech from *Hamlet* for the Hamlet of the century, then you had to be prepared. I ended up over-prepared.

On the day, I waited nervously in RADA's Studio 1. Hugh was due to bring him in at three o'clock. The door opened on the dot. My legs turned to jelly. There he was in the flesh.

'I hear we're going to see a bit of your Hamlet.' That voice. Oh, my God. I began.

And that's about as much as you can say for my performance on that frightened afternoon. My voice had gone up an octave with nerves. I was as tense and tight as a drum. It was terrible, terrible acting.

As I finished I saw Gielgud wipe away a tear. There is absolutely no doubt in my mind that he was moved by seeing a young actor struggling in utter desperation with a part that he had made his own. He must have felt sorry for me. I felt pretty sorry for myself. I knew I'd muffed it. Trying too hard, I was straining and shouting and my delivery was wildly exaggerated. I simply wasn't very good. Gielgud knew it, and Hugh knew it, but I shall never forget the kindness in his tone as he came up to me and put a hand on my shoulder to give the following advice:

'Well done. There are some good things there, but you're really trying too hard. Don't over-colour the early section. You can be much straighter. Give yourself a breather in the middle. Don't stress "I *am* pigeon livered" when "pigeon livered" is much more juicy . . .'

He went on to give me some more specific notes which I failed to take in because I was hypnotised by the humility of the man. He spoke to me not as a teacher but as one professional to another. He was completely beguiling. He left as quickly as he'd arrived and I sat down half depressed at my failure genuinely to impress a god of English theatre, and half exhilarated by his presence and kindness.

The concert was a week later. All the Academy's students and staff were there, along with hundreds of former students and associates, including Ralph Richardson and Peggy Ashcroft. The adrenalin flowed but was under control, and I tried to remember everything Gielgud had said, telling myself that I would never do anything quite like it again and simply to enjoy it.

> Oh what a rogue and peasant slave am I.
> Is it not monstrous, that this player here
> But in a fiction, in a dream of passion,
> Could force his soul so to his whole conceit
> That from her working all his visage wanned?

I did enjoy it, and the speech was a hundred times better. At least I'd satisfied a certain personal pride. Afterwards we lined up on stage while the Queen and Prince Philip went down the cast. The Queen asked me how I managed to remember all those lines. I didn't know. Gielgud followed and said, to my delight, 'Oh, that's much better. Very good. You took all my notes.'

I could have kissed him. I'm sure he forgot the whole episode the moment he left the building, but his remark made all the difference in the world to me.

A few days' insufferable arrogance was soon cured by the latest wrist-slapping events in the RADA timetable. I had made enough of an impression with my student Hamlet to be cast in Peter Weiss's play, *Marat/Sade*, as 'a mad animal'. What impression was I giving?

Further indignity was provided by the Standard English Test. This informal exam tested our command of BBC English, or Received Pronunciation (RP). It took the form of an audition speech which we performed to a panel of staff and then an interview with the same, remaining in RP. Quite a challenge for anyone with a strong regional accent, but necessary.

The point was made early on about the lack of imagination among employers. If you walked into an interview speaking RP, they were prepared to believe you could play a cockney or a Scot. If it was the other way round, they were unlikely to give you the benefit of the doubt.

I expected to sail through. I may not have developed the honeyed tones of a Gielgud, but I thought my suburban twang was neutral enough for the panel. Not so, I was failed.

I'm sure I would have failed in any case, but the test was much more than a speech exam. It came just before our final terms, and it was a chance to be reminded of quite how much work there was left to do. The panel returned to my jaw, my back, my walk, my 'l's, my 's's. I took the test again, was given a weak pass and decided to forget about Gielgud, Olivier and all, and just concentrate on learning to speak properly. A rather humbler young man approached the last two terms.

Finals offered our group of twenty-three twelve productions over two terms, during which each of us should have at least one 'showcase' part. Having been through my run of juveniles, old men, stormtroopers and then, in Edward Bond's *The Sea*, getting a chance to revive my simple rustic, I was clear about what I would like to play. At the beginning of the fifth term Hugh had asked us about what we wanted to play. He promised nothing. He had his own ideas about what was appropriate, but he was ready to listen to anyone who was passionate about a particular play or part.

After this announcement I found myself in Sidoli's, an Italian coffee bar and bacon-roll emporium just around the corner from RADA. The music of lunchtime orders rang round the steaming shop, and I sat down and wrote a letter to Hugh explaining why I wanted to play Hamlet.

There were obvious reasons for the pushy drama student to wish to play the part, but playing it ensured nothing. If I imagined for a moment that it would be guaranteed to impress the casting directors and agents, I had my Gielgud experience to warn me. Getting the part didn't mean you would be good in it.

Nor did I relish the idea of potential envy or critical rejection on the scale which Hamlet induces. What I wanted was to say 'Fuck it' to all that, that the really important thing was having a go at the part, especially at the age of twenty, regardless of the consequences. I'd read everything I could – Gielgud's wonderful description of playing Hamlet in *Stage Directions*; Richard Sterne's account of the same actor directing Richard Burton in the role; Albert Finney's comment that you should play it at twenty or forty, and I was also very impressed by Tyrone Guthrie's *A Life in the Theatre*.

Guthrie's advice to young actors was to do as many of the great roles as you could as early as possible, so there would be more chance of getting them right later on. He cited Benedick, Romeo, Henry V and Hamlet as parts it would be ideal to play before the age of twenty-five. Of course he was writing about a different theatre, but I believed in the principle.

I wanted one day to be a great Hamlet. Not a particularly unusual dream for a young actor. The crassness of my continual mistakes in performance made the advice of Guthrie and others even more potent. A lifetime already seemed a short span to get anywhere near the heart of great acting. I wanted to play Hamlet as many times as possible, so that each time I played it I would get better in the role, and would get closer to the truth of the character.

I had no divine right to a so-called classical career – I could as easily see a fulfilled acting life in situation comedy, or children's theatre, if I was destined to work at all. I also felt that nothing should be ruled out. It was important to be prepared for anything – for washing dishes, selling newspapers, doing Kissograms, being enormously successful, or not working at all.

I said much of this in my letter to Hugh, and put my case as eloquently as I could. The worst he could say was no.

The plays and casting for term six was announced, with no *Hamlet* on offer. There was always the next term, and it was still a great season of plays in which people really did get their own bite of the cherry. *Time and the Conways* by J. B. Priestley, Dusty Hughes's *Commitments*, *The Maid's Tragedy*, a new improvised play – *Dance of Death, No Orchids for Miss Blandish* – adapted from the James Hadley Chase novel, and a great musical, *Lady Be Good*. I hadn't fared badly. One old man, one gangster, one servant, one waiter – a quiet line of parts, perhaps *Hamlet* wasn't out of the question for next term.

The lighter work-load gave me time to attend to my troubled emotional life. Things were going very wrong in Willesden Green and every problem associated with living and working day after day with the same person made itself felt. Wendy moved out, and then I moved out, unable to face the place alone.

I ended up paying double the rent for a deeply poky bedsit in Ealing. One very small room, a broken hot plate, wallpaper that needed a volume control, and it was also freezing. Everything was on a meter and because my Dickensian landlady forgot to empty the bloody things, I lived literally in a twilight world. Most of the time she feigned deafness about these things. She didn't like climbing the stairs, but she was as quick as lightning when the front door opened late at night and she popped her head round the door to check whether you had a 'friend' with you or not.

This was the lowest ebb of my time at RADA. I hated the place in Ealing so much that I went back there at the last possible moment each evening, which meant that I drank and spent more during the evening, and that the journey took longer because the trains were scarcer late at night. My few belongings sat round me in boxes. There was nowhere to put them. I was utterly miserable, and each day Wendy and I faced each other across the class experiencing the horrors of a troubled relationship between two fellow students. On one occasion a director in our improvisation class set up a situation in which two lovers were splitting up and had to decide how to divide up the belongings in their shared flat. He chose Wendy and I to act it out. It was agony, and ended with Wendy bursting into tears and running out of the room.

Moving out of the Willesden flat seemed to help, and once we started to spend less time together we began to miss each other. Gradually the dust settled, and the relationship began to improve. In the meantime, I was able to indulge my moments of despair as Buffo Cole, the character I was playing in *Commitments*. Dusty Hughes's play was an examination of the trendy left-wing fringe in the mid-seventies, a mixture of media people and artists involved in an unsettling flirtation with radical political organisations. Buffo was a sort of refugee from the Blunt/Burgess school of Oxbridge leftists, adrift in disillusioned middle age. My career as a cranky character actor made this the perfect part: dark wig, wild eyebrows, moustache, cherubic expression and a flushed alcoholic complexion. It

70

was an example of the amusing extremes to which a young actor is forced by the absurdities of casting for a drama school finals session. Of course, if I'd left RADA in the early fifties, and was in rep, then I might well have been playing such a role professionally.

Chameleon tendencies continued in *The Maid's Tragedy*. England was in the grip of Adam Ant fever and this look, the director felt, was exactly right for this piece. The result was a parade of costumes and make-up that resembled a gay bordello, and it was also very funny. Sometimes unintentionally. Needless to say, I succumbed to hysterics on one occasion when I was confronted with the latest green-haired, gelled, Red-Indianed student. My ever-growing shame was compounded by a reprimand from a fellow actor whom I very much admired, Douglas Hodge. The poor chap was trying to play a king while facing a lot of shaking students looking upstage towards him in ridiculous costumes, laughing uncontrollably. I was a despicable ring-leader.

'You might have to play a king one day, see how you like it.'

I was learning my lesson painfully.

I brought off a rather convincing Al Pacino impersonation in my next role as Eddie Schultz in *No Orchids for Miss Blandish*. I think I may have been the only one who saw the performance as a tribute to Pacino's role in *The Godfather*, but it created enough interest to draw a letter from an agent asking if I would go and see her. I was wildly excited when the magic envelope sat in the 'B' pigeon hole of RADA's mail rack. It would have been noticed by everyone – these things went round college like wildfire. I savoured the triumph and made an appointment.

The agent was a nice woman but ferociously busy, and the office was full of ringing telephones. I was terrified in advance, and the meeting did nothing to reduce my fear or sense of intimidation. A polite exchange took place, but I had the feeling that she was most definitely doing me a favour in offering to take me on. Of course she was doing me a favour, but I suspected it would have been cleverer of her to have perhaps made me feel more wanted. A delicate relationship at the best of times, I sensed that this particular combination might not be productive.

Still, I was in no position to be choosy. I accepted her vague proposal to 'keep in touch', and assumed that if she saw me being marvellous in something instead of just promising, then we had a deal. A very prestigious agent, but scary all the same.

RADA had provided a talk by a practising agent to give us advice about what to expect when the magic envelope arrived. I recalled that she had said to remember that an agent was your employee, and that finally it was you who had to call the shots. Good advice, I thought, but it was far from what I felt capable of doing with my first option, for whatever one's level of experience, one had to feel comfortable with one's agent. It had to be someone who was almost a family figure, someone who could be charming and tough, and produce the best deal for you without giving offence. Someone who would do more than just answer inquiries about you, but who, especially for unknown drama school graduates, would initiate possibilities for work.

The ideal person was someone, I imagined, a little like our wise counsellor. Her name was Patricia Marmont, but she hadn't seen my work, not unless you counted my Spanish waiter in *Lady Be Good*, and I couldn't be sure whether I'd impressed. I felt very much the secret song-and-dance man. One *could* be spotted in the chorus, I'd seen *42nd Street*. I was third line, second from the left in the hotel number. My heel-kicking could easily have caught someone's eye, and I know my voice stood out in the chorus. Eyes and teeth, love. People must have noticed me.

It was a Saturday morning in July, and the last night of the musical. I went straight for the hall noticeboard, eyes darting down the list. *Hippolytus, A Flea in her Ear, The White Devil, . . . Hamlet*. Eureka! Yours truly as the Prince. Thank Christ for that. I sat down and wrote to Pat Marmont immediately.

It was one of a hundred and fifty letters I wrote that summer. I also had my pictures done so that a 10 × 8 print could hang in the rogues' gallery of the RADA bar to impress visiting directors. I remember the first photographer, trying hard to relax me, a classically nervous student.

'Smile. I'm sure you're going to get lots of work. I think you'll be typecast as a policeman. Lots of parts there.'

Jesus. PC Hamlet. Thank you very much.

I had my pictures redone by a lovely photographer called John Fletcher, who was very encouraging and able to relax me with great ease by pushing a large glass of wine into my hand. Actors are often remarkably ill-at-ease as themselves in front of a camera and need a photographer who can make them feel comfortable.

I chose the right print, which gave me a look that had a balance of qualities – funny but sad, intelligent but wacky, kind but firm. I thought there was an expression in my face which said 'I'm a brilliant, warm, modest actor. Not dull, but no trouble either. Cast me as anything. I'm a chameleon genius.'

Postcards of this unique expression were sent to every repertory theatre in the country with my RADA CV, plus interesting personal touches that could mark my missive out from the rest of the bunch. Phrases like 'I particularly love Plymouth and want to work in the theatre there, having spent a happy childhood holiday in a village really quite near.' Or, 'My Celtic origins have always drawn me to a career in Cardiff.' Or, most desperately, 'I love being near the sea, I bet Southwold is lovely to work in.'

The worst excesses were vetted by John Sessions and the other students in my year who were all doing the same thing. I saved my major personal approaches for the theatres in Reading and Belfast. Not a sausage. Certainly not an audition. My photograph was sent right back to RADA, often with the CV, at best with a photocopied letter saying 'We'll put you on file'. After five months of letter-writing I left RADA without a single audition or interview in prospect, despite some professional good fortune which came my way during that *Hamlet* summer.

I spent the first part of the holiday working as a caretaker in St Martin's School of Art in Charing Cross Road. Apart from the income, it gave me something to do while Wendy was appearing with the National Youth Theatre. We were now very settled and happy and spent as much time together as possible. On one weekend we travelled down to Reading where I had promised to check on my parents' house, as they were away on holiday. Everything was safe and we took a walk around the town while I explained scenes of my former dramatic triumphs in the town whose theatre was rejecting me so cruelly.

Unusually, that week I had not bought a copy of *The Stage*. It had brought me little in the way of luck. Job adverts were nearly always for Equity members, and the rare exceptions yielded little. One week the National Theatre of Brent advertised for a new member, and the same night I wrote and recorded a song with my guitar and cassette recorder. I took the Tube to the address given that evening, CV, picture, and song in hand – such was my enthusiasm and ingenuity. All to no avail. Even though I'd returned to live in Willesden Green, in the borough of Brent, my credentials were not good enough. The song remains a favourite, a sort of cowboy-yodel number that celebrated northwest London, and I sang it in a demented Jim Reeves croon:

Sunriiiise on the Hiiigh Rooooad,
Willesden Haieeeaigh Road,
Kilburn looks good to me today
For you can see so faine
On that Jubilee laiiine
To Willesden Haiiigh Road.

They still didn't want me. I couldn't work it out.

I was nursing these slights on that fateful Saturday when we wandered into Reading's Town Library and looked at *The Stage* in the reading room. I soon wandered off, bored, until a scream from Wendy brought me back to an advert that did not require an Equity member.

BBC Play for Today.
Filming Belfast, Oct/Nov '81.
Requires Actor, 16–24
with authentic working-class
Belfast accent.

There was a number to ring but I resisted, as I knew this ad would draw thousands of bogus Belfast backgrounds, and I'd have no chance. Anyway, *Hamlet* played from 24–28 October, the dates would never work out, RADA would never release me. I really wasn't going to bother, but Wendy was having none of it. I was left in Reading while she returned to the National Youth Theatre threatening a definite parting if I didn't ring the number. On the Monday morning, I tried the number again and again, but it was engaged. I kept going, and eventually got through.

'Hello, Paul Seed.'

'Yes, hello. My name's Kenneth Branagh.'

It just worked. Paul Seed was suspicious of the accent but I reassured him that York Street was inches below the surface. He said he'd consider me if I sent him a CV and picture. No problem, I said, except that I had no CV and no picture – they were in London. I dragged my friend, David Longstaff out of his bed and we drove to

RADA where I took my one 10 × 8 photograph off the wall, hastily typed out a new CV and rushed round to TV Centre where the production office was. It was all done within six hours of the call. We arrived back in Reading breathless at 5. At 5.30 the phone rang, and I was offered an interview the following afternoon.

Paul Seed, the director, was in his early thirties. A former actor, this was his first TV directing job. He explained the plot, which focused on a divided Protestant family, the mother dying of cancer, the father drunk. The son Billy was rebelling against his father while attempting, with his sisters, to hold the family together. It sounded very powerful. Paul asked me to look over a section of the play and then read it. I knew it was fine writing and I knew I was right for the part. I felt it had gone well, but as usual I left the interview knowing nothing.

They rang again the next day. Would I come in on Friday to read with some people who might be playing Billy's best mate? They wanted to put couples together. I was very near. Paul had told me that their searches for actors had been extensive even before they'd placed the ad in *The Stage*. Billy was one of the leading roles and pivotal to the success of the piece. They'd even auditioned in Belfast schools to find the right raw quality, but the part also needed a competent acting technique, and it meant they might have to go with someone like me.

Before the second interview my parents arrived back from holiday. They were dismayed at my news, for, like many people on the mainland, and despite their connections, they saw Belfast as a dangerous war zone. They were praying for me not to get the part. My mother didn't hold out much hope, however. She had had one of her famous 'feelings', which were usually connected with births or deaths but were now directed towards my career. 'You'll get the bloody thing. I know it.'

No mention had been made about dates yet. I'd told the BBC about the RADA *Hamlet*, but it hadn't put them off.

Friday came and in the foyer at TV Centre, I met Column Convey, a pal from RADA with a similar Irish background.

'Are you here for what I think you're here for?'

'Ay, I'm up for the mate.'

'But you are my mate.'

'I know. We're laughing.'

It wasn't that easy, but we were the only people they appeared to be seeing for all their talk of putting couples together. We read the scenes for Paul Seed and Chris Parr, one of the producers. They had obviously discussed what to do if they liked us. The reading had gone well. Chris spoke.

'That's terrific. Look, we'd really like you to play these parts. Although the Equity question is difficult we think we can produce cards for you because of the special circumstances. We really have seen an awful lot of people and you boys are the ones for the job. The real problem is you, Ken.' Oh no. 'Dates. We need to start in Belfast the week you open *Hamlet*. I'm afraid I have to ask the terrible question: will you give up playing in *Hamlet*?'

I let out a sigh. I knew it, you can't have your cake and eat it in this world. I thought long and hard but the answer was clear – I couldn't give *Hamlet* up. I tried to explain. I wasn't sure that I would ever play Hamlet again, but perhaps there would be another TV play, and if I reneged on Hugh, what if an extraordinary film came up while I was doing the TV play? Would I then drop the play? I was genuinely sorry to have wasted their time but it seemed, even at that tense moment, that it was no good starting a career by sacrificing something that meant so much. Hugh had taken a great risk by casting me and I would never have those conditions to enjoy again, that rare freedom from critics and from life-or-death notices.

Chris Parr shook his head. 'I understand what you're saying and I respect it, but we'll have to go away and think again.'

I walked out of TV Centre with Column, who commiserated but clearly thought I was nuts. He had left RADA the term before and knew what it was like to be in the race for a job. I'd thrown away an opportunity that might never occur again.

That evening I sat down with a Chinese take-away in a new Willesden Green flat. I had my trusty copy of *Hamlet* by my side and a volume of *Teach Yourself Conjuring*. If I could work out an act I might be able to get myself an Equity card as a cabaret artist. The Catch 22 of Equity was infuriating: no card without a job, no job without a card, and I'd just thrown away both. I was considering whether to invest in a performing dove when the phone rang. It was Paul Seed.

'All right, you little shit.' He was laughing. 'We'll rehearse the first week in London, then go to Belfast.'

'What?'

'You've got the job. But only on condition that you'll rehearse during the day when you're playing Hamlet, and that Hugh releases you for a month after that to rehearse and record in Belfast. And that you give us one day out of *Hamlet* rehearsals for a bit of filming that we can't move.'

'What about Equity?'

'We'll do our best. So what do you say, you grand bastard?'

I was laughing now. 'OK, love. I'll talk to my advisors.'

I thanked him profusely and returned to my celebration chow mein. It was Friday night in Willesden Green. I had a job (nearly) and on Monday I started rehearsals for my first Hamlet. You really are a jammy so-and-so, I thought. When things go well, I have always tried to stop myself from getting cocky by putting achievements down to good luck rather than to appropriate talents, and if things go badly, then there is a neat excuse lined up to explain it all.

Hugh excused me from *A Flea in her Ear*, but insisted that I return to RADA after *Too Late to Talk to Billy*, the TV play, for the last three weeks of term during which I would be playing a very small part in *The White Devil*.

Although the Equity negotiations would be tricky, I started rehearsals for *Hamlet* in great elation at my good fortune. Graham Reid's script for *Too Late to Talk to Billy* was marvellous and rather than envy, I received nothing but support from the other students. Except for one. For a terrible first week of *Hamlet* rehearsals I imagined that I was back in my first term at Meadway.

To describe what happened as bullying would not be accurate, but my reaction was much the same. The actor in question was a good one with an aggressive, powerfully intimidating presence which had been more or less kept under control during the training. Now, for some reason, an undercurrent of menace made itself felt. From the first day he seemed to undercut my contributions, and, more worryingly, he became violent in his manner throughout rehearsals, or so it seemed to me. I know I was not alone in finding him frightening.

I succeeded, I hope, in betraying none of my fears, but inside I was devastated. I dreaded going to rehearsals with the same intensity that I had dreaded going to school. I even found myself ringing my father with the same babyish complaints. I spoke to Colin Wakefield, who spent a day with me trying to talk me out of this strange psychological intimidation. I was terrified, and I couldn't sleep. One night, after a particularly tense rehearsal, I walked the length of Marylebone Road in the rain crying my eyes out. All I wanted to do was run away.

I felt the performance was suffering terribly, and I was full of self-disgust at the weakness in my character which had allowed this to happen. I watched every minute tick away in rehearsals and prayed for them to end quickly, and I also felt that yer man knew exactly what he was doing and that it was a super-subtle but conscious decision to intimidate. Just because I'm paranoid doesn't mean people *aren't* watching me.

If there were advantages to the situation, I suppose that the combination of fear and my self-loathing at not being able to deal with it were sterling Hamletian qualities. I scarcely worried about the part itself. I worked hard, but for me the whole experience was about getting through rehearsals. There was an excellent director, Malcolm McKay, and it was a fine production – pacy, real and exciting. If it taught me anything, it was that I was unable to work easily in an atmosphere of tension or dangerous animosity. Anything that was good in my performance could have been achieved just as well and even better under conditions where a crazed ego wasn't ruling the roost.

The performance in general received a good response from the RADA audience. All the voice teachers thought that I was the quickest Hamlet ever. (Although Richard Briers claims that prize.) Too quick, they said. Hugh's response was frank and uncompromising: 'Yes, Ken. Lot of work to do. Two fundamental points. First, comedy and humour. There is a difference. You give us comedy in Hamlet. What he has is a deep-seated melancholia producing a black, bleak humour. You give us a sort of gratuitous clowning. Secondly, passion. Hamlet is a haunted man, shaken to his very soul by the deep repulsion about his mother's marriage and horror at the arrival of his father's ghost. You give us a sort of lively irritability.'

I was philosophical: I intended to play it several times. I did learn a great deal and, if nothing else, several bits of personal 'business' from this Hamlet went into my later one. And into everything that followed went a determination never to succumb to fear like that again. What a waste of time.

The first two days' rehearsal for the *Billy* play were spent in a daze. We opened *Hamlet* on a Wednesday evening and the next morning, St Crispin's Day, I started my first professional job. The BBC rehearsal studios in West London introduced me to the aircraft hangars in which the BBC rehearse their dramas. It was a short bus ride away from Willesden Green and seemed like Hollywood to the then temporary member of Equity.

In their infinite wisdom the Union had decided that I deserved a card because I had trained at a recognised Drama school and was one of the few people appropriate for the part. But, on the other hand, they felt this kind of queue-jumping should not be allowed and as soon as the job was over my card should expire, as presumably then – in my three remaining weeks at RADA – I might be taking the bread out of the mouths of needier members. Thank you, gentlemen.

It was tricky balancing two jobs at the same time, especially when the first day's rehearsal for the *Billy* play coincided with my second ever performance as Hamlet. I worked hard through that day, in a smoky atmosphere, high on adrenalin. Paul was kindness itself and there was an excellent cast, mostly young, led by James Ellis, a brilliant and entertaining storyteller.

At 5.30 I had the luxury of a car, courtesy of the BBC, to take me to Gower Street. But no amount of cosseting could change the fact it was difficult to play Hamlet and very difficult to concentrate on two demanding experiences at once. My head was full of the day's events. I talked too much, I didn't rest, and the second performance was a disaster. Such was my wayward concentration that I comically invoked the name of the cigarettes I'd been surrounded by all day:

> My tables. Meet it is I set it down
> That one may smile and smile
> And be a villain. At least I am sure
> It may be so with Dunhill.

It was unmistakable, and there was more to follow. There was a price to pay for telly fame.

Pat Marmont managed to see *Hamlet* on a non-disaster night. I went to see her just before going to Belfast. An elegant and very attractive woman, she charmed me straight away by saying that I must go and see other agents. But there were no other agents to see – she was the only one that had actually written to me. She stressed her love of the theatre and the belief that people should put something back into it, so if I wanted to make an exclusive screen career, she probably wasn't the one for me.

There was nothing pushy in her manner. Her quiet confidence was inspiring and beneath the pussycat that was subtly wooing me, she was clearly made of stern stuff. I was won over. She told me to think about it in Belfast and then talk again. She was pleased but not over-impressed with the TV job and, like Gielgud, she spoke to me as an equal, which I liked. I would think about it in Belfast, but my instinct told me it was a clear choice. I sensed a quick temper. We would clearly have our rows, but we thought the same way about the theatre. A former actress herself and an indisputable pro, she made my mind up. The problem was solved.

I felt apprehensive on my return to Belfast. Of course our relations would persuade us of the 'normality' in the province. Aunt Kathleen and my mother spoke on the phone each week, people could shop and go swimming and take the kids to school and do other everyday things with relative ease, but the news reports were frightening and with short hair and an English accent, I was warned about being taken for an off-duty soldier. I was ready to be very careful indeed. As we approached Aldergrove airport I was struck by the silliest and simplest of thoughts. The place really was the Emerald Isle. The grass was greener than green. Peaceful and calm, an ironic, moving characteristic of that troubled land.

The BBC minibus dropped me on the Shore Road and there on the corner was my Uncle Jim to welcome me home with the firmest handshake an uncle could have. A shipyard man all his life, Jim was a strapping figure of Lawrentian masculinity, all muscle and honesty. He took me round the corner to the small terraced house he shared with my Aunt Kathleen and I sat down to the first of the enormous 'feeds' I was due during those four, calorific Ulster weeks.

Like all families that have done without, good food and its plentiful supply was much enjoyed by all the Branaghs and Harpers in modern Belfast. They all shared the common belief that any member of the family under thirty needed feeding up. As a result, meals were an obstacle course of carbohydrate. Ulster has a terrible record of heart disease, and it is inextricably linked to the horrors of the fat-based diet. Too many 'Ulster frys' must have put many an Irishman into his grave.

Over that month I gained a stone. Lunchtime at rehearsals meant a bowl of stew and a pint; at tea-time, a huge plate of tatties and mince was washed down with a pint of milk and followed by trifle. On a Saturday night it was the works – black pudding, tattie farls, soda bread, fried eggs, steak, tomatoes, bacon and mushrooms. Of course one could always have refused these treats, but I was an

Irishman, and my appetite for the food, the drink and 'the crack' were unquenchable.

A true Irishman in spirit maybe, but in practice the split feelings induced by an adolescence on the mainland made for an uneasy time in Belfast. There were two brilliant child actresses in the *Billy* play. After the read-through on the first day, they heard me speaking in my English accent for the first time.

'What's happened to your accent? What's *wrong* with you, mister?'

As kids do, they had gone right to the heart of this strange situation: an Irishman in Ireland who lives in England and speaks English, but who is making a living as an Irishman. I was working in a world which my Irish relatives didn't understand, and I felt ashamed of opening my English mouth in the street or in the pubs. When you spoke of your background, people sometimes looked suspicious, as if you were merely covering up for some betrayal. I became aware of what Olivia Manning described as the Anglo-Irish sense of 'belonging nowhere'. I felt desperate to belong, but on this first trip back it was not to be. I had very divided feelings. Although the place ignited my Irishness – a love of drinking, of storytelling, of the crack, and although I loved many aspects of Belfast, it was very clear that this was no longer my home. My instinctive need for roots was provided more surely by the acting profession itself. This uneasiness about Ireland would remain for some years to come, and would only be exorcised when I could come to terms with my own guilt over this split in my personality.

My first experience of TV work was made easier by the presence of a committed, excellent team working together and believing in the play. There was a sense of something quite young and original going on. Paul Seed was unjaded, Jimmy Ellis was full of high spirits and BBC Northern Ireland was taking pride in this new drive to establish a first-class drama output. The play was about a family, and a family feeling was created among the team, complete with squabbles and fallings out, but held together by tremendous affection. Watching this convinced Graham Reid of the potential to write the full trilogy that he felt the material deserved.

I learnt about TV acting as I went along, one major omission from RADA's training. Screen acting is sometimes described as 'doing less' – using less voice, cutting out large theatrical gestures, keeping the body and face much more still. In reality, the process is much more subtle and complicated. It needs a supreme technical awareness on the part of the actor, who should know exactly where to place his concentration, how to pace himself for short bursts of intense emotion, when to let go. All of this must be invisible, and if you give anything away, the camera picks it up. I was struck by the immense difficulty of presenting the truth of a character or a scene for the camera. It isn't enough just to feel it, you must know what the truth of the scene and the character is, but you must also know how to convey it.

It is not a question of cold, technical acting, which is often effective in conveying the superficial truth of a character, but of acting where appearance and reality merge into one, where the actor sounds and looks like a real person, and not a performer. At this level, the audience is unaware of any artifice or conscious technique. Acting like this can be seen in a 'personality' performance, where a star gives a portrayal which is essentially an extension of their own screen persona. David Niven, for instance, who was a fine performer, nevertheless remained David Niven the movie star for almost all his film work, and distinctions from character to character seemed less important than his ability to present a truthful naturalism through his very particular screen personality. Character performers can do the same thing with the help of make-up and costume, transforming themselves from film to film. In both cases the magic can work its spell and arrest you in your living room or in the cinema. It is rare, and I love it both on TV and on film.

Billy made me realise that good screen acting depends on collaborative effort. I took in everything. I studied the way the cameras were moving; I questioned Paul about his camera script; I tried to find out all I could about the actual mechanics of TV. I didn't want to fight the technical elements of the medium, but to embrace them so that they wouldn't get in the way of the best acting.

At the end of five days' recording I felt that I'd just begun to warm up. Filming was over and there was nothing to do but pack up and head back for London. I couldn't do any of it again. In any case, the BBC Ulster studio doubles as a cattle shed for half the year and the cows were clamouring for the space.

I came back from Belfast with my instinctive love for my homeland revived. I'd enjoyed meeting the dozens of cousins and aunts and uncles that were on my visiting rounds, and I'd particularly loved talking to my only remaining grandparent, Lizzie, who at eighty years old remained strong and steadfast, humorous and full of stories. I was enjoying the treat of hearing someone who was very much my senior talking to me as if I were a neighbour gossip. It was lovely also to hear her version of my parents' youth, particularly my father's.

Back at RADA I was set to play a villainous servant in *The White Devil*, and decided that this was a part which would rid me of some of my mousy suburban attitudes. I paid great attention to costume and make-up. I'd come across some glossy photo books covering the work of Glasgow Citizens' Theatre – visually very extravagant, flamboyant and camp, the company was an inspiration to me, and I got myself up in long greasy dark wig, painted cheekbones (the first and last I've ever had), earrings and lots of black velvet. On the first night, I walked on stage, with fellow students Craig Crosbie as the other servant and Ian Targett as our master, Lodovico.

There was a great rush of music and we tore down the rake of the black and silver set, Craig and I pulling Ian behind us and flinging him down on to the apron. He starts the play off with an angry cry at his fate.

'Lodovico – Banished?'

Whereon I leaned against a pillar looking sexy, shifted a hip and took an age to say (while fiddling with my nails and looking off into the distance), 'It grieved me much to hear the sentence.'

It came out in a lurid, sensuous whine that was both gross and exciting, exactly right for Webster's universe, or so it seemed to me. The scene finished. We came off stage. Ian and Craig turned to me.

'What were you doing?'

'What do you mean?'

'All that terrible Kenneth Williams meets Liberace stuff.'

Maybe I was going to play policemen after all.

The final performance of *The White Devil*, on my last day at RADA, coincided with my twenty-first birthday. I was bought many a drink that night. I sat clutching a confirmation letter from Equity telling me that I was no longer a member. The *Billy* play already seemed like a dream. No one from our term had obtained work in advance of leaving, although many had agents. Pat had nothing for me at that time.

Where were my ambitions? Did I want to be a classical actor? Not really, I just wanted to work. I was excited about leaving – seven terms had been quite long enough. I had no interviews to go to but I was prepared to work at anything else in the interim to make money.

My dad had some manual work coming up that I was ready to do. There was the caretaking or the selling. Anything was fine till the first chance to work arrived. I would read and write and not be beaten by lack of activity.

As someone keenly self-motivated (there are other words for it, I know) I rather relished the gladiatorial aspect of getting a job as an actor. Not the competition with other actors, but the struggle with myself and with the job. If they wanted a short-sighted, hairy basketball player for a film, I was determined to find the stilts, the glasses and the moustache and then persuade them I was the man for the part.

I'd have done pretty much whatever came along: panto, rep, telly, radio, Shakespeare, comedy, whatever. I'd have cleaned floors, made sandwiches, delivered papers – anything to make a quick buck until professional acting work *did* come along.

I remembered a remarkable conversation I'd had two years earlier. In the flush of my enthusiasm at winning a place at RADA I had written to Derek Jacobi. The Hamlet hero of my youth, he was reviving the role at the Old Vic. I asked if I might speak to him, and to my surprise he agreed. In his dressing-room at the great theatre I asked lots of impertinent questions.

'Do you think of yourself as a classical actor?'

'No,' he said with great emphasis. 'I'm just an actor pure and simple. I have to make a living. I have to be prepared to do anything. Not just Shakespeare. Actors are still just beggars, really.'

I'm sure he believes, as I do, in the positive and creative role of the actor, but he was brutally realistic about the economic and professional restrictions, the almost total dependence on others and on the need for new jobs coming in at frequent intervals. I knew the early stages of everyone's career were different, but I hadn't forgotten what he had said and I attempted to be similarly realistic.

I prepared to leave the famous halls in Gower Street. I hovered at the door of the bar to put my coat on. It was snowing heavily outside. I wondered what sort of an omen that might be. As I knotted my scarf I noticed the bright green poster that had hung on the wall there all through my last term. It was a play that had been on at Greenwich, and there had been good reports of it and some talk of it transferring to the West End.

I looked again.

84

Another Country. Good title. Must try and catch that. I pulled up my collar against the snow, took a last lingering look at the front of the Vanbrugh Theatre and headed off into the London winter.

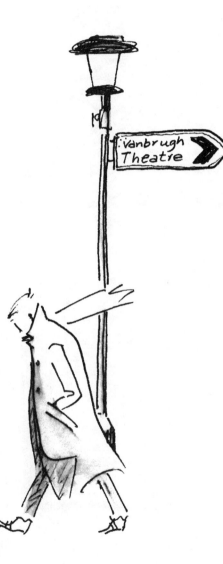

Work

FOUR

'The first suit is hot and hasty'
MUCH ADO ABOUT NOTHING

It was January 1982, I wasn't working on anything else but I'd delayed signing on, and I was now sharing a tiny room in a rather seedy Willesden rooming house. There was one payphone in the hall and an enormous family of Asians upstairs who were clearly involved in the north-west London underworld. Strange boxes were delivered in the middle of the night. I never saw the same faces twice. I had no objections to any of this, except that they ran their business empire from the hall payphone which, of course, was my crucial link to the world of showbiz.

I thought of taking it up with one of the fellows, but chose a moment when the burliest, six-foot, moustached mafioso type I've ever seen was coming down the stairs. Of course he needed free access to the phone. I saw no harm in it, I indicated as much when my voice squeaked out 'Lovely day' and I pressed myself against the wall to let him pass. I could see he was a man who put small children in sandwiches and toasted them. The phone was his. No problem. I could ring Pat myself.

'Hello Pat.'

'Hello darling. What's going on on that bloody number? It's always engaged and when I do get through it's a man grunting "no drop tonight" in a funny accent.'

'I'll explain when I see you.'

'Very well, darling. Now, listen . . .'

She explained about *Another Country*, and I thought immediately of that poster in the RADA bar. Pat had some clients in the play, which was indeed transferring to the West End if they could achieve some key pieces of recasting. They had already auditioned extensively but were prepared to waive the Equity bar at this stage to try and find the right folk. It was the same problem as before. They needed reasonably experienced actors who could look seventeen and who were appropriate for the parts. She'd arranged a meeting for three days hence with the author, Julian Mitchell and the casting director,

Celestia Fox. This was a sort of first round. I was about to put the phone down when I remembered.

'What's it about, Pat?'

It turned out to be a highly funny and dramatic fictional account of Guy Burgess's schooldays and the emotional genesis of his life as a spy. There was no script available, and I was immediately depressed. The upper middle classes I had encountered all had an innate assurance and arrogance that both annoyed and intimidated me. One thing was for sure, I didn't have it. I had confidence on occasion, but that social ease and casual command didn't come naturally to me.

I felt certain that public school changed people profoundly. I found it very difficult to imagine what being a boarder must have been like. I found a book called *The Public School Phenomenon* and set to work. Even if I felt instinctively wrong and phoney, I would certainly give it a go. I fished out an old striped blazer that I had worn to parties when I was sixteen. If I could carry that off, and polish up the accent a bit, I could sneak in.

Julian Mitchell opened the door of his Knightsbridge house. He gave a great laugh. 'Ah, I see you've worn the jacket. Well, you're bound to get the part.'

He seemed enormously warm and funny, but there was my plot in ruins before I'd even begun. How could I have been so crass? Celestia asked me briefly about RADA and then gave me the script. There was a brief scene they wanted me to read, featuring a character called Barclay, the head of house, who is under stress because of a suicide in the school. As I read it over quietly the front door bell rang twice. They were obviously seeing hundreds of people. Oh God. Well, here goes. Remember 1930s' English, Ralph Richardson in *The Q Planes*.

Before I came to the end of the first sentence, Julian stopped me. 'Are you putting on a voice?'

Was I putting on a voice? Is the Pope a Catholic? Yes, yes, yes. I was putting on a stupid, ridiculous voice that was redolent of my Lord Ponsonby-Smythe at Whiteknights. I dropped all Leslie Howardisms and read the scene straight.

'That's better. Thank you.'

Better, but still fucking hopeless. I decided that I'd never get to play upper class parts. It would be coppers, coppers, coppers all the way. I went home furious with myself. Fuck this, I thought. If I do get a second chance, bugger all this residual class chippiness that's confusing me. Just read it as truthfully as possible. I hadn't been to public school. So what? I hadn't studied at Wittenberg, but I'd played Hamlet. What was I going to do if Macbeth came along? Kill some reigning monarch so that I felt I had the experience for the part?

A second round had been arranged which Robert Fox, the producer, would attend with Stuart Burge, the director. It was to be held at the Whitehall Theatre the following Wednesday but on the day before Pat had arranged another audition, which, this time, was with the Royal Shakespeare Company.

Near the beginning of each year the RSC casts for its long Stratford season, and often the small parts are taken by RADA graduates from the previous year. The Company were in a position to give an Equity card with the job and sometimes the debuts happen in marvellous parts – Anton Lesser, for example, made his professional début just after leaving drama school as Gloucester in Terry Hands' production of *Henry VI Part III*.

Several members of our term had been granted auditions for play-as-cast contracts which involved doing just that, as well as understudying. This must often have provided a wonderful chance to watch and occasionally perform. During my years of RSC theatre-going I had followed the fortunes of the small part players, looking out for promotion where it occurred and trying to imagine what the workload must be like.

Joyce Nettles, the RSC's casting director at that time, had seen my student Hamlet. She was in an impossibly busy job and I am astonished that she ever found the time to catch the show. We'd had a brief meeting before Christmas in which she had tested me about my feelings towards the Company – whether I was their type, and whether I would be prepared to go to Stratford for a season. Naturally I answered each question with an eager 'yes', and smiled my face off.

The audition day arrived. I was first on after lunch. I waited in the empty Floral Street rehearsal studio, an enormous, echoing wooden warehouse, with huge, open spaces yawning at me as I sat in the little partitioned corner that served as green room and canteen. Then the first director appeared. Barry Kyle came in clutching a prawn salad sandwich and three bags. A cheerful shambles, he was carrying so many things that he shook hands with his left hand. The others followed. Adrian Noble was courteous and formal, with flyaway brown hair and a wispy goatee beard which convinced me that he should change his brown leather jacket for a tunic in order to complete the look of a dashing Renaissance man. Then came Ron Daniels, crisply dressed in a black leather jacket, with a neat shirt and tie. His hair was very carefully groomed, and he made a strong contrast with the charmingly dishevelled look of Barry and Adrian. I have developed an enormous affection for Ron, but on that day his usual nerves made him behave like an SS General. He looked at me through narrowed eyes, head held slightly back, as if he were highly suspicious.

Then Terry Hands appeared, dressed entirely in black, and received my handshake with an unsmiling nod. He wasn't particularly unfriendly, just eccentric. I half expected Peter O'Toole to walk in, and for everyone to launch into a scene from *Night of the Generals*.

Barry, Adrian and Ron sat behind a long trestle table, and were joined by Joyce. Terry sat to the side, with his back against the wall, very much on his own, and not speaking at all during the interview. Adrian and Barry were really very friendly, and asked about parts at RADA and the audition for *Another Country*. Ron continued with his comic intimidation technique, shifting in his black leather jacket and moving the steel-rimmed spectacles further down his nose. Still the same penetrating, slightly suspicious look.

I went into Hotspur, and then, as the comic piece, I produced Lord Foppington from Vanbrugh's *The Relapse*, a marvellous speech to do at an audition because it needs such attack – you're really forced to produce energy, if nothing else. There were smiles from Adrian and Barry, a laugh from Joyce, a tell-tale movement of the curled upper lip from Ron and in the corner Terry remained impassive, as if he was in the middle of a mantra. I was enjoying this. Ron spoke, feigning disdain and trying to suggest I might have cheated.

'Have you played that part before?'

'Well . . . no . . . I did play a fop at RADA. Sir Joseph Wittol, who I suppose is a sort of second cousin to Foppington . . . but . . .'

'Oh, I see. And you played it like that?'

'Well no . . . I . . .'

'Thank you.' He looked round at the others as if to say, 'What did I tell you? I rest my case.'

Joyce came to the rescue. 'Can we see a bit of your Hamlet?'

The others nodded. Can't be bad, I thought – three speeches. I gave them 'Rogue and Peasant Slave' from my greatest hits album, and as they say, went for it.

As the chorus of 'We'll be in touch' started up I thought that at least I'd given full value. I looked round and said cheerio as I left the room. I'd grown rather fond of this group. Joyce had played my mother to good effect, and even on my exit, Ron was still producing a very charming Goebbels-meets-Clouseau manner. The smiles of Barry and Adrian had reached Noel Edmonds proportions and there, in the corner, was Terry the black Buddha, still staring into the middle distance and waiting for the latest casting advice from Olympus.

My first RSC audition. What larks, Pip.

Next morning was the second round for *Another Country*. Just before I went in I was asked to look at the scenes featuring Barclay, the character I'd read at the first audition. I obliged, and when I entered the auditorium was taken aback to be asked to read Judd, a part that I hadn't even looked at. I shook hands with Rupert Everett, who would be playing the part of Bennett, the Burgess character, and climbed onto the set. I relied on sight-reading and discovered the scene as I went along. Rupert judged his reading beautifully. He could easily have bulldozed me, having played the part of Bennett already to huge success; alternatively, he could simply not have bothered. Instead, he played the scene with me so that I could start to understand it as we went along.

It was marvellous writing. I hadn't seen the rest of the play but if Judd had only this scene it was still a terrific part. He was a natural rebel of tremendous intelligence, with a colourful temperament and a lacerating wit. Judd was the school outsider, and an example of the heroic, committed English Communist of the 1930s, extravagantly indignant at the hypocrisy of the English public school and of English politics. Inspiring, hugely funny, warm and passionate, Judd was a brilliant creation.

I somehow assumed that because it was being put on in the West End, the leading roles must be for grown-ups, for adult actors. Surely a part this good couldn't be entrusted to an unknown, and yet Judd was only a schoolboy. I didn't know what was going on. We finished the scene, everyone was very kind, and I went back to Willesden to recover from the excitement of the last two days.

Miraculously that afternoon the drug-dealers of NW6 appeared to be having a tea break, and Pat Marmont got straight through to my number. The RSC were offering play-as-cast and, wait for it, Robert Fox wanted me for *Another Country*. The catch was Equity. Rehearsals for *Another Country* began in three weeks' time which was not long enough to allow me to secure my card, but it would be too long to keep the RSC waiting.

So began a couple of nightmarish weeks where the question of my membership remained uncertain. The whole job might fall through, and I would have then lost the chance of a job and a definite card at Stratford. My first obligation was to Robert – I'd seen him first, and if the reading was anything to go by then the part was a great deal more stretching than anything the RSC would offer at such an early stage.

Pat appraised both parties of the situation, and they were understanding. The RSC suggested that in the meantime I should meet Howard Davies, who was directing the first play of the season and who had not been present at the original audition. I admired Howard's work enormously and found the man a delight, polite but still informal. More to the point, he also felt he might have something specific to offer me.

True to his word he rang Pat and offered me an excellent juvenile role, but he did stress that the RSC couldn't hold on forever. Meanwhile the wheels at Equity were turning very slowly. Eventually the dispute went to arbitration and Robert Fox reiterated the point that they'd seen literally hundreds of people, and if he couldn't at least have his first choice then there was no point in taking such a huge commercial risk on a new play with no stars. This must have clinched it.

At the eleventh hour they relented. Yes, I could do it. Pat let the RSC know. They had very patiently kept their offer open but were very understanding of the situation. That done, Pat filled me in on the terms of my first engagement: £150 per week for six months.

The longest I'd ever been in anything was two weeks. I had no idea how I'd deal with a much longer run, but guessed it would depend on the character I was playing. I was still in the dark to a certain extent – I had a job and a salary but still hadn't been given the play to read. It arrived on the Saturday before Monday's first rehearsal, 1 February 1982. I read it with growing amazement: not only was the play riveting but the part of Judd was demanding and very long. I finished the play and sat in a state of shock. I simply couldn't believe my luck. Although I'd read very well at the audition and had sensed that I might get the part, I had completely underestimated the scale of the opportunity. As a first professional role in the theatre, it was an unbelievable break. Christ.

I started to learn it that afternoon. Eight of the strong cast of twelve had been in the play before, and with only three weeks to rehearse I would have to work quickly to catch up. To help break the ice for the new boys, Julian Mitchell had arranged a drinks party early on the Sunday evening for us to get to know each other. Riddled with nerves, I arrived at South Kensington station an hour early and wandered around in the freezing cold for an hour and a quarter and mused whether I could ring in sick. But there was no turning back, it was all part of the job.

I was one of the first to arrive and took a large slurp of white wine to calm me down. Then, with an uncharacteristic punctuality, in bounced David Parfitt. Bounced rather than walked, for one of the trademarks of the most optimistic person I have ever known is to travel with a marked spring in his step.

This Peter Pan figure with the toothsome grin was already part of my youth. In the course of cataloguing British Equity members through my days of adolescent TV watching, I had grown up with David. The familiar trampolining movement had been one of the chief pleasures of *And Mother Makes Three*, a situation comedy in which the young Roscius had played Wendy Craig's son. The beaming smile which lit up when his name appeared in the jaunty end-titles sequence was a memorable pleasure, and series after series brought David into my living-room.

Although a veteran of stage and screen he still looked (and looks) very young. He claimed to be twenty-four but though he looked about eight, I suspected his real age to be nearer forty-seven. He played Menzies in *Another Country*, and we struck up an instant rapport, the start of a friendship which would be an important one for me.

It was a very lively group. Rehearsals began in a draughty warehouse building in Old Street. A quick reading of the first scene took place round a table, then we went into the blocking or setting of the physical moves. I tried my first line, binoculars in hand, staring out of the 'study window'.

'What's this? What's this? Three o'clock from bushy-topped tree.'

The director, Stuart Burge, stopped me. His style was amiably offbeat.

'Er . . . (scratch, scratch) . . . I think we need . . . (scratch) . . . I think we need more suspense on that line.'

Suspense. Right, will do. I tried again.

'No, still not quite right. Never mind, let's move on.'

The rest of the day and the week were spent blocking and learning the lines. The only drama was the predictable one of being ticked off for corpsing. Rupert was quite as bad as me when it came to giggling and the tea-party scene which took place between Rupert, David Parfitt, Piers Flint-Shipman and I, was too much. David William, the one senior member of the cast, and an inveterate giggler himself, feigned rage and turned on us all.

'Just STOP. This really is boring. Balls-achingly boring.' Silence and stifled whimpers followed.

In the second week we rehearsed on the stage of the Royal Court Theatre, where more detailed work began. Stuart Burge kept up his stance of distracted eccentricity, but he was in fact as sharp as a knife and very stubborn. He let nothing go and wasn't afraid of using abstract directions to get what he wanted.

'Rupert, there's marvellous detail in all that. But I do think overall in that scene you must convey ecstasy about your new love, and certainly about your own secure future. You must be more golden.'

'Golden?'

I was relieved that Rupert was given the tough ones, too.

'Oh, and Ken.'

'Yes?'

'More suspense.'

Rupert and I seldom talked about the parts we were playing, and our acting relationship was almost entirely instinctive. Rupert, like myself, seemed to prefer to get on and do it, and to put an idea into practice instead of describing it. We had a quiet and wary respect for each other which acknowledged our different backgrounds and characters, but I shall never forget his kindness during those rehearsals. It would have been very easy to be resentful of a newcomer arriving to throw the rhythm of his role. He had already had a huge success as Bennett and nearly all his scenes were with Judd, but he positively welcomed the chance to change and rework the scenes to allow for my slightly different interpretation of Judd.

The whole experience of these rehearsals was a very gentle

introduction to the harsh world of commercial theatre. Robert Fox kept a low profile but offered words of encouragement at the right moments. He was clearly excellent at his job, and he introduced me to my first press interviews, he was present at all significant run-throughs of the play and acted as an occasional go-between between the director and cast.

'I think Stuart feels that on that first line there could be a little more . . .'

'Suspense?'

'That's it.'

If the first line remained dodgy, the rest of the character was shaping up well. Judd was a deliciously meaty role – intellectual, yet capable of real feeling and humour, a great soul in embryo. He was a man who really might have gone onto become something extraordinary. Julian Mitchell had the character of Judd based on two men, both dead. The first was Esmond Romilly, who married Jessica Mitford and who provided the anarchic streak in Judd and the second, John Cornford, the poet, who died on his twenty-first birthday while fighting in the Spanish Civil War.

Cornford provided the intensely lonely and romantic side to the character. Judd is a visionary capable of a knowing sadness far beyond his years, a quality which the play suggests he shared with the young Bennett. Both are outsiders, and both have an uncomfortably prophetic awareness of their probable futures; both, in the course of the play, rebel against their prospective fates, Bennett selfishly, and Judd, by trying to change the system. Through Judd's anger and irony Julian Mitchell presents a memorable picture of genuine goodness, an altruism and hope of a kind that was uniquely possible in the 1930s. The total effect was most moving.

I seemed to spend most of my real life moving house, and the most recent move was a mile or two from Willesden to Harlesden, an even less salubrious part of north-west London. Wendy had joined the Royal Shakespeare Company and was moving to Stratford. I swapped one underworld for another. Evan Carruthers, my landlord, was a car dealer. He looked like an ex-RAF fighter pilot, with a twirly moustache, distinguished, greying hair and a kind, military manner. He had a professional shiftiness which offered much to enjoy. He stayed up very late each night and never rose before lunchtime. The curtains of his room were permanently drawn and he chain-smoked Gauloises.

Evan advertised weekly in *Exchange and Mart*, sometimes under different names. Part of his work was quick escapes, and he'd sold plenty of 'dogs' in his time. Each week I was an unwilling party to his attempts to pull more wool over more eyes. He used a secret mixture in dodgy engines which kept them sounding sweet until the punter got home.

I would know when he'd been up to his tricks when he mysteriously disappeared and I had to deal with irate customers at the front door. Some of this was dangerous, as invariably the 'big bruvver' would have been called in, but Evan kept cheerful about all this. He'd been involved on the edges of petty crime for thirty years, and belonged spiritually to the Soho of the fifties, shifting a motor for someone. The real appetite had gone, but he kept his hand in.

I'm sure he wasn't short of a bob or two, but I suspect it must have been kept under a floorboard in that funny old flat. I certainly had to be on my toes in this house: apart from complaining punters, there was Roger, Evan's business partner, and a visit from him and his boys was like the arrival of the Kray brothers. I often thought I'd arrive home to find Evan in a wooden box.

Still, it did take my mind off West End nerves, but these had pretty much disappeared as the part began to take over. It was one of those rare experiences where the more you put in through research and reading, the more you got out, and I was already an expert on fellow travellers, the Spanish Civil War, the English public school system of the thirties, Romilly and Cornford, and it all helped towards drawing the emotional graph for Judd. By the time I got to the first preview I thought I had built up a convincing tragic hero, an earnest, misunderstood romantic. There was a light side to him, but I knew it was important to present his seriousness and weight.

The audience laughed themselves stupid. I was outraged. I was playing Hamlet, not Lancelot Gobbo. By the end of the first half I calmed down and realised that this was what Julian had intended. The more seriously I took it the more they laughed, until the play started to twist and the truth of Judd's earnest rebellion became clear. It also began to dawn on me that Judd knew he seemed funny and, up to a point and with certain people, enjoyed it. I took this and a million other bits of information into the second preview and hoped I wouldn't be so surprised if they giggled. It was much better.

Better still was the shock as the dressing-room door opened afterwards and Albert Finney walked in. His company, Memorial

Films, had money in the production and he was taking a very personal interest. He's a big man in every sense and he was so warm and encouraging that when he'd gone I ran all the way to Green Park tube station and rang my mother in a breathless shriek.

'Albert Finney! Albert Finney, Mum! He was in tonight and he came round to say well done.'

'Very nice, son. What would I have seen him in?'

The preview days went by with friends from RADA visiting and Stuart calling us in each afternoon for comments and advice on the show. By now I was taking the initiative.

'I think I should go for more suspense on that first line, Stuart.'

'Good idea, Ken. I'll leave it with you.'

The day before we opened I rolled up for the afternoon session to be greeted, to my great surprise, by a hug from Mr Finney.

'Congratulations, you've won the Bancroft Gold Medal.' I was absolutely thrilled. It was the top RADA prize for the outstanding student of the year, and my joy was intensified because I knew the folks would be thrilled, and the whole thing would help the management for *Another Country* to flog their unknown actor playing Judd.

It was a week of giddy pride for Mum. The week before, *Too Late to Talk to Billy* had been shown on BBC. The response had been tremendous, especially in Belfast. This was a huge relief to my father who had read the script before I'd done it and had dismissed it grumpily. Despite having left Northern Ireland, he didn't care for anything that showed the old country in a bad light. And the truth of the matter was that the script touched too many raw nerves in both my parents' experiences. Indeed when my Uncle Charlie witnessed James Ellis's bravura performance as the drunken father, he said, 'That was Speedy Harper, that was my father.'

On reading the play I think my father expected a gloomy re-enactment of all that was bad about the Belfast he was brought up in, but what he found was a story in which the Troubles were for once in the background, and in which the humour and warmth and passion in working-class family life was made accessible to everyone, and not just to people living in Ulster. The province became fiercely proud of the *Billy* plays because they appealed to families everywhere. The RADA award coming on top of this five-minute fame caused my father to write to me, the first time he had ever done so, to express his pride.

He was largely on my thoughts the next day when I prepared for the first night of *Another Country*, 2 March 1982. He had always told me to face nerves on a full stomach. We were called late that afternoon and before we went to the theatre I lunched alone on a large steak in a tacky Berni Inn in the Strand. I was remarkably calm.

The fact was that I was enjoying myself, I'd had four weeks of being a professional actor and I loved it. In a way, the importance of the evening's events affected me little, and in fact I had so little sense of the 'occasion' that it was only late in the afternoon that I thought about buying first night presents.

Panic set in and I ended up rushing round Soho buying the most inappropriate and stupid cuddly toys. So un-West-Endy was I that it was only at 6.30 that it struck me that I should need some drink to offer round afterwards. Wine, where was I to get wine? What was I thinking of? Champagne. That's what it should be. Shouldn't it? I was rescued by one of the two dressers who worked on the show, and once the curtain had gone up, he whizzed round Soho for bubbly and plastic cups.

The performance was that of a typical Press night, and the atmosphere was tense with friends willing us on, but it was a good tight show and Rupert, driving the piece, was in marvellous form. I didn't know what to expect after the show. I went to my dressing-room, changed as quickly as I could and waited for a knock at the door. Robert Fox and Celestia were there first with large hugs and well dones, but after they left, the place flooded. Two schoolfriends appeared whom I hadn't seen for years, Hugh Cruttwell was there, and so were my parents. My mum and brother were in tears, and I knew my father had enjoyed it because he employed an adjective he reserved for moments of greatness, 'Tremendous, son.'

He clutched my hand firmly, but then, like the rest of the family, took a step back when anyone entered the room. It had taken a great deal of persuasion to get my mother to come at all, as she was terrified of 'letting me down', but I plied them with champagne and told them to stop tugging their forelocks whenever people came in.

It was a great pleasure that evening to see my mother get tiddly. The champagne and excitement had gone straight to her head, and by the time Joan Plowright and Albert Finney had been and gone the intoxication was complete. Finney had been marvellously entertaining. The family had stood agog as he put his arm round my giggling mother, champagne and cigar in hand.

'Your young lad,' he said, sending up some northern actor laddie, 'has just got off the bus, as we say in the business. But . . .' – Dad's jaw was on the floor at this point with anticipation – 'he's not half bad.'

Later, as we walked to my parents' car in Berwick Street, there was general agreement that Mr Finney was a good sort, that Julian Mitchell was very nice, that Robert Fox looked just like his brother, and all kinds of giddy instant recollections. They all piled in, Bill, Sally, Joyce, Mum and Dad. My father spoke.

'We'll never forget tonight, son. Thanks very much.'

Wendy had arrived as the last visitors left my dressing-room. An RSC rehearsal had meant that she had missed the whole thing. This was not her fault at all, but she was very upset, and it seemed inauspicious that we should not be together on such a momentous occasion. With a long, enforced separation ahead of us, I felt that there were problems to come. We stood forlornly in a wet Soho watching my dad's car drive off. No official party had been arranged and I wasn't sure where the other actors had gone. It was midnight, and I had no idea how you were supposed to celebrate a West End first night – my chief worry had been whether my parents would enjoy it or not, and my chief pleasure had been watching their delighted faces afterwards. I wouldn't have known where to celebrate even if I'd known how, but we opted for a Chinese meal and took a minicab back to Harlesden. I was in bed by one o'clock. I wondered if Noel Coward ate take-away on his first nights.

The show was a great success with the critics. The play and company were both praised, with Rupert and I singled out for special mentions. There had been worry about whether the show could run without stars, but it looked as if these fears would be proved groundless.

Six months seemed like a very long time, and I had decided to take the long run business very seriously. As I'd read in all the best biographies, I rose late and had a good healthy breakfast of cereal, toast, bacon and eggs. I then took a walk, and had a sleep in the afternoon – very important this. A light meal at around four to allow plenty of time for digestion before the evening performance, and I would arrive at the theatre at 6.30, read my mail, say a few hellos, then lie on my back to do some breathing exercises. All very virtuous, all very boring and all destined to last three weeks.

A number of factors came together to rock the paragon of virtue. I arrived home one night to find that Roger, Evan's crooked landlord, had decided to redecorate the flat. One of his 'boys' was already on the job, and this highly unprepossessing type claimed to have his own decorating system which would take 'as long as it takes – OK, Mister?' Neanderthal man could have shown this one a few tips in DIY. He had started in my room, had moved nothing and had stripped one wall of paper, leaving the scraps all over my bed and covering my books. He had then got bored and moved on to another room. It was chaos.

I got out as quickly as I could, and as a stopgap, Julian Mitchell said I could use his house in Knightsbridge. This was not without its complications. I was feeling guilty because the corpsing in *Another Country* was getting a little out of hand, and I was doing very little to stop things. Although Julian lived in the country, I was terrified that he might come up and catch us, and then I was convinced I would be marched out of the house and out of the play.

There had been various sticky moments – girly pictures in the copy of *Das Kapital* that my character read throughout the play, spiders in the sandwiches during the tea scene, and apple-pie beds in the dorm scene. On a particularly wild matinee, halfway into the run, with about seventeen people out front, a decision was made to try the antique gramophone that sat on the set. Not only did it work but it completely drowned the dialogue. The first half ended with one of the staider characters in the piece coming on in a kilt.

It was all very amusing to us, and we flattered ourselves that these little private jokes could not possibly offend anyone in the audience, who would assume that they were part of the play. Unless, of course, the author was in the audience, as he was that Wednesday afternoon.

I have never seen fury as white and as hot as Julian's on that afternoon. It seemed highly appropriate that we should be in a play about schoolboys, and Julian's fiery lecture invoked the familiar adjectives: 'pathetic', 'arrogant', 'stupid', 'amateur'.

This hysterical corpsing was partly induced by the unusual demands of a long run on inexperienced actors. After three months I began to go a little stir crazy. Much as I loved the play, I began to pray for the safety curtain to stick so that the second half would be cancelled and we could all go home.

At the same time, after a marvellous start, I felt my own performance to be set on automatic pilot. It grew wooden and heavy and my concentration wavered in performance until I dried desperately in the middle of one show and had to walk off while Rupert saved the day with an ad lib – 'I think Judd must have a headache or something'. This produced a terrible stage-fright for the next two weeks where all acting stopped as remembering took over. I would stare glassy-eyed at my fellow actors, thinking of my next speech, and waiting for their lips to stop moving so I would know when to speak. I think we all went through such a phase, but particular visits would perk us up. Gielgud came to a matinée and saw me afterwards. 'Very good. Didn't I see you at RADA?' A gent.

Sitting in bed one day, I pulled out the script and started to read it again. I felt compelled to do this, not just because of my reaction to the long run but because my lack of freshness was letting the side down. In the last few performances Rupert Everett had been producing astonishing acting, and in the last scene between Judd and Bennett I really had a sense of him soaring away on a flight of great acting. It was a high voltage scene and demanded that I try to keep up with him.

I looked at the lines and started making new notes in the margin about what I thought Judd meant. It worked: it not only cured my stage-fright by giving me something new to think about but it really did rejuvenate the performance. Towards the end of the six months Rupert and I sometimes really did catch light together and it was exhilarating to play the scenes with him. He can be an electrifying actor.

Most of my colleagues shared my resistance to the supposedly conventional daytime life of a West End actor and towards the end of the run we decided to mount a lunchtime production. Gogol's *Gamblers* really marks the beginning of my involvement with independent production, and it was significant because it produced all the usual problems – the performances were for charity, we had no venue, no money and no organisation. We were simply a small company of actors learning this as we went along, naive but wildly enthusiastic.

Julian Mitchell provided a new translation for the piece, on condition that he could direct it. The Upstream Theatre Club became the venue and we tried to cast it in order to give the understudies and people with smaller parts in *Another Country* a decent opportunity. We found props and furniture ourselves, designed the set between the ten of us and let David Parfitt (who else?) work out a 'deal' with the venue. It was hard, often shambolic, amateur work but it was great, adventurous fun. There was great co-operation from everyone, except on the issue of my performance where I was allowed to get away with a third-rate Charles Laughton. I was playing Captain Cropper, a gambling shark, and my ever understated make-up talents were devoted to creating an impression of that particular beast. You can imagine the results.

The performances of *Gamblers* took place at the end of the run. Robert Fox now wanted to extend the run by at least another six months. We were asked to stay on, and there was great loyalty to Robert, Stuart and Julian but, in the end, the rigours of eight shows a week outweighed any considerations of security or finance. Julian and Robert were gracious, but obviously very miffed, and I was certain I would never work again, as I was leaving the show with nothing in view.

The day after my departure was confirmed with Robert, Pat rang to say that a book was on its way to me, *The Boy in the Bush* by D. H. Lawrence and Mollie Skinner. I was a great Lawrence buff, as I'd started reading his letters in a moment of emotional crisis and had been hooked on the man and his work ever since. I had heard of this novel which Lawrence had recast for Mollie Skinner during his journey through Australia in the early 1920s. Channel Four were planning to make a four-part serial of the book and was I interested in the central part of Jack Grant, the book's central figure?

It was a wonderful read. Jack Grant is in disgrace after being sent down from public school, and is packed off to Australia to stay with relatives. The new country starts to make a man of him, and he learns to love and to fight. Lawrence had infused this conventional adventure story with great psychological detail, particularly in the character of Jack, and the book had tremendous atmosphere. The sounds and smells of Australia were powerfully evoked, and there was a great deal of very provocative Lawrentian discourse on the subject of marriage.

It would make a very arresting and offbeat film that combined action with some rather interesting philosophy, Jack Grant would be in every scene, and the series would be shot in Australia over a period of three months. It sounded like an ideal opportunity. But this was August, and it wasn't scheduled to start until April. They weren't absolutely sure that they had the money and the project was put on ice. This still left me without work.

Another novel came to the rescue: *To the Lighthouse*, which was to be made into a two-hour television film. I had read no Virginia Woolf, and with an actor's typical lack of shame I decided, after a quick glance, that the whole thing would be too much to read before the interview, so I scoured the text instead for the name Charles Tansley, the character I was up for. I filled in the rest of my knowledge by buying the appropriate 'O' Level 'Study Notes' for the novel – these small volumes provide helpful short précis of character and plot for the poorly read actor.

Colin Gregg, director, and Simone Reynolds, the casting director, both kept straight faces as I bullshitted my way through the audition.

'Of course, I've always loved Woolf. She's a marvellous writer, and Tansley is absolutely my favourite in all the books, really.'

No shame. They let me take a script away and asked that I come back to do a reading. It had been quite beautifully adapted by Hugh Stoddard – it read like a Chekhov play, and Tansley was a wonderful, cravenly ambitious, snotty little loser. A small man, depressive, vulnerable, and with an enormous chip about his background. I began to wonder what sort of vibes I gave off at interviews.

By the time it came to the second interview I knew that half the cast of *Another Country* were up for parts in the film and that the rest of Equity weren't far behind. I read well and, more than that, I got on very well with the director. Colin Gregg, a resolutely independent film maker, is fascinated by actors and by the process of acting, and really quizzed me about why I'd made particular decisions about the character. It was a very enjoyable meeting but as I left the room I walked past a line of potential Tansleys. I knew it was a part that a dozen young actors could play, in different ways but equally well.

The RSC rang again. They were halfway through their Stratford season and someone had fallen ill. Would I be interested in another juvenile role? I would, but before I had to consider being swallowed up by the RSC machine, Colin Gregg called to say that he would like me to play Tansley. It began shooting on the Monday after the final Saturday performance of *Another Country*. The gods were obviously stringing me along – all this good luck, he whom the gods would destroy, they first make cocky.

Another Country ended its first run with a manic matinée and a spectacularly good Saturday evening performance. There was a quick meal at Kettner's in Soho for the entire cast, and then I was off.

103

I left early as I'd already begun to loathe goodbyes of this kind. It stemmed from cowardice, as it was painful to bid farewell to people who, as in this case, had become like brothers. I knew we would all meet again in this small business, but it never felt like it at the time.

The next morning I was on my way to Penzance, where *To the Lighthouse* was being filmed. It made a change from the drive to Stratford which I'd made every Saturday night for six months to see Wendy. The pressure on our precious Sundays was immense, as there was great tension involved in making this one day as perfect as possible. Apart from being in the same business, we had ceased to have any shared life together, and it was very hard spending our limited time simply catching up with each other. I was now off to Penzance for five weeks, and would be unable to get to Stratford at all. The perils of long-distance relationships in the acting profession were already upon me.

I was lonely at this time but thrilled by the work. I was on my way to meet several heroes: Rosemary Harris, who had been a definitive Yelena to Redgrave in Olivier's famous production of *Uncle Vanya*; Michael Gough, whom I'd first noticed as the First Murderer in Olivier's film of *Richard III*; T. P. McKenna, Suzanne Bertish, Pippa Guard, Lynsey Baxter, all really good actors.

It never follows that this will automatically produce a happy experience, but in this case it did, as it was a blissfully happy five weeks where cast and crew mixed with abandon. There seemed to be a different huge restaurant booked every night, there were parties and Sunday trips to the sea, and in the middle of it some very good work was being done.

I continued my crash course in film technique. On my first day I introduced the character's walk in long shot. Tansley is out on a cliff stroll with Mrs Ramsay, played by Rosemary Harris. I'd read what Alec Guinness had said about finding a character's walk and how important this was; I knew Tansley was tense, repressed and splenetic, and that the walk had to reflect this. After the first take, Colin Gregg asked, 'Why are you playing it like Charlie Chaplin?' He wasn't trying to raise a laugh. Colin's great gift was for seeing what actors offered up in quite literal terms. If it wasn't truthful, he would say so, and his method was as simple and honest as that. I soon stopped acting and calmed down.

Michael Gough was a delight, and like Rosemary, he'd worked with everyone. I would torment him at the dinner table for stories, and asked him about his career and ambitions. I couldn't resist asking him about the Olivier *Richard III*.

'Yes, talking of ambition, I nearly didn't get that.'

'How did it happen?'

'Well, I'd been out of work for a while and was pretty rancid about it. There was all this talk about *Richard III* and gossip about the casting. It seemed as though it would be full of stars and when I heard that Richard Attenborough and John Mills were lined up to play the two murderers I was enraged. I started moaning about it at parties and complaining to my agent and generally making a stink. Anyway, late one night the phone rings. I was in bed, and it was midnight. I say "Hello". Then this sinister voice says,

"Well, you've been stirring it, haven't you?"

"What?" says I, not knowing who the hell it is.

"A right little shit."

"Who is this?"

"It's Larry."

"Oh Christ. Oh Larry, I'm so . . . I mean . . . I'm . . ."

"Which one?"

"What?"

"Which one of the bloody murderers do you want to play?"

I wasn't sure how I should take this. I jumped in. "Whichever one's got the most lines."

"Fair enough. You start Monday week." Then he laughed. "And I hope that's the last bloody trouble we get from you." ' Olivier kept to his word and even broke up the filming of the scene over several days so that Michael, who was really very hard up, could earn some more cash.

Green I was, but I had been introduced to the notion of 'waiting'. In July, a month or so before the filming of *To the Lighthouse*, I had met briefly with Miloš Forman, the director, and his producer, Saul Zaentz. They were making the movie version of Peter Schaffer's play *Amadeus*. I, along with the rest of the acting world, was up for the part of Mozart. Maggie Cartier, the casting director, had alerted Pat Marmont to the opportunity.

The brief for the role was Mozart as small, bright, childlike and charming. Bright and charming I could manage, childlike I would busk, but small was tricky. They reckoned Mozart at around five foot four. At five foot nine and a half I'd always been too short for the tall parts and too big for the small ones, so I bought a pair of flat-soled plimsolls and tried to walk with my knees permanently bent.

I was so childlike at the first interview that I could barely put a sentence together, and I even attempted a version of the cackling laugh that Schaffer gives Mozart in the play. It was a complete performance.

A week later I heard that I was now through to the next round of readings, to be held at the Connaught Hotel when Mr Forman was in London. A date was set for a fortnight ahead and I went to work, with a thick biography of Mozart, a Sony Walkman playing the music, and another read of Schaffer's play. I'd been told that the film script was considerably different but in that helpful way of film companies paranoid about secrecy they sent only selected pages so that I could prepare for the reading.

These sessions took place over five days and I was Tuesday's Mozart. I arrived at 10 and was shown up to Mr Forman's suite. He was standing at the window eating a sandwich from a tray which would come and go all through the day for the nervous auditionees. He had dark hair swept back, wore glasses, appeared permanently preoccupied and had the charming accented English which is the prerequisite of the International Film Genius.

During the course of that day we got on very well. Actors and actresses would appear for Mozart's wife or teachers or neighbours, and after their read-through would depart. There was often a gap while we waited for the next one and we would talk about the play, acting, his home in Czechoslovakia – everything. I was reading well. The part is a marvellous one for any young actor and I attacked it with relish. Forman made comments on each reading – too funny, too sad, too mad, whatever. I was enjoying it, as he seemed to be considering me seriously, and I was also enjoying acting with the idols of my *Plays and Players* youth, all of whom seemed to be turning up for the audition. Such is the lure of the big American movie for the English acting profession, that I was reading scenes with really marvellous actors.

Next morning they rang to ask me to come back for the Friday readings. Either I was being used as a Mozart dogsbody or they were very interested. They also wanted to be clear about my availability for the filming in early 1983, and Pat told them of the possibility of the Australian job, but they thought it could fit. 'Only checking' they said, covering themselves. The second day was even better, as I was beginning to see what Forman wanted from the character. I tried desperately to relax but I was getting so excited now that in our interim chats I could barely restrain myself from crying out, 'Tell me, tell me I've got the part, please.'

On the following Monday the news came back that they were very interested indeed, and there would be a screen-test as soon as Forman was back in London.

Three weeks later I was at a small studio in Cricklewood, dressed up in a wig and period jacket, once again playing Mozart for the day. I had gathered that a shortlist of four had been established, and I was told that I was favourite. I don't know what they told the others. Once more a British acting roll-of-honour arrived, and superb actors strutted their stuff for Mr Forman's video. He seemed far more distant now, and I tried to seem less friendly, as if I wasn't desperately hoping for the job. He was clearly concentrating more now that he was actually at work.

I was still on form. There was only one funny moment when a mad English actress who was screen-testing for Mozart's wife succumbed to the fear of losing the role. Forman had shouted 'Cut' and then thanked the actress for having completed the scene.

'No, no, no, no. I want to do it again. *Please*, Mr Forman. I can emote more. *I can emote more.*' A great deal of emoting went into this plea, which was accompanied by arms thrown around the neck of the besieged director. We tried again and I played the scene with someone who appeared to be in the grip of a nervous breakdown and was having an epileptic fit. There was little I could do but throw my lines in whenever I could. Her arms were flailing around in demented fashion and I'm sure the sobs could have been heard in the street. It may have been emoting, but it certainly wasn't acting.

Pat rang that night. She could barely contain her own excitement. 'Darling, you are *so* near. It's accent now. They've never been sure whether to cast Americans throughout or English throughout or do a mix. They wondered if you were capable of a sort of mid-Atlantic accent, take the Englishness off it, maybe taking James Mason's voice as a model.'

I was outraged. I'd been to see them endlessly, I'd acted it every conceivable way except on my head, and now they thought that because it was a great part in a huge American movie I would compromise my voice, my very personality.

'And when do they want this new accent prepared for?' I said as sniffily as I knew how.

'Tomorrow.'

'Done.'

That night 'cahn't' became 'cehnt', 'class' became 'cless', and the James Mason of Harlesden was born. Pat had neglected to tell me that these thoughts about accent were provisional and that Maggie Cartier was simply marking my card for the next day. I tested the water with the even more distracted Miloš Forman.

'I wondered if you'd had any thoughts about accents?'

Oh no. He'd smelled a rat. He didn't like actors doing anything but act. No suggestions.

'No, no, no. Don't you worry about accents. We'll sort that out some other time. Please don't worry.'

Oh God, I'd made him irritable. It was clearer and clearer that he wanted puppet actors, folk who seemed so natural for the parts that he could pull all the strings. He didn't want troublesome input or actor cleverness. Either my accent was right and natural or it wasn't. I went on with the screen-test, and Pat rang later the same day.

'The phone call came, darling. The part is ninety per cent yours.'

'Wonderful.'

'Hold on, darling. Look, they're going back to New York tomorrow and next week they have to go through the same process there in order to satisfy Equity, but they are so keen on you it's not true. They simply have to go through the motions with the others.'

I now entered the never-never land of 'you'll know very soon'. A fortnight passed. 'They've found no one in New York. They've got to do the last stage in LA before they get back to us. It's still very hot.'

A month passed. 'Now they've got that time-consuming thing of going through all the tapes of actors' tests. I'm sure it'll work out.'

Two months passed. 'Pat, don't you think we should check on this?'

'OK, darling.' She rang Maggie Cartier. The last time she had spoken to them I had remained their number one choice. By now *To the Lighthouse* had come and gone and I had completed a second *Billy* play. It was December, and nearly six months after the first meeting. I'd had enough practising my Oscar-acceptance speech, and asked Pat to send a telex to America demanding that they declare their degree of interest. The reply came back the same day.

'Acknowledging your cable STOP Plan has changed STOP Now casting American actors STOP'.

Pat prevented me from sending my proffered reply: 'Thanks for the wait STOP Good luck with the film STOP Why don't you stick it up your ass and don't STOP'.

I took Pat's advice and decided that it would be nice to work again. Another part came up almost immediately in Julian Mitchell's new play, *Francis*, a dramatic reconstruction of the life of Francis of Assisi. We staged a reading of the piece at the Queen's Theatre with myself reading Francis and the rest of the cast made up from the second cast of *Another Country*.

The politics of the piece seemed particularly meaty and relevant. Robert Fox and Albert Finney were there and afterwards Julian rang me to say that he felt the play would be given a production, but that it might take a year to organise. When it was ready would I play it? I had been forgiven for leaving *Another Country* early, and I answered with a firm yes.

We were both in a good mood. We both had nominations for the SWET awards, Julian for 'Best Play', and myself for 'Best Newcomer' along with Rupert, whom I was sure would win. On this occasion, I won, and Rupert picked up two awards elsewhere for his performance. I was both pleased and very shocked – my instinctive fear of being carried away by any success that might later blow up in my face told me to play the whole thing down. It was also meaningless and unpleasant to have a television camera shoved up your nose to record your reaction, although I was able to enjoy celebrating with my parents, who were genuinely thrilled, and did not share my complicated response to winning awards.

The following day the producers of *Boy in the Bush* shook themselves out of their lethargy and decided in the wake of my award that now was the time to sign up the award-winning newcomer while he was hot. And so my name went on the dotted line and I knew that on 7 April I would be flying 12,000 miles away at the tender age of twenty-two.

The rest of the profession seemed not to be taking the lead from these far-sighted folk, and the expected avalanche of offers did not appear. I spent a whole afternoon reading for every character in Terence Rattigan's *While the Sun Shines*, for a season at the Royal Exchange Manchester. 'We don't think it's quite his thing,' was the reply that came back. Too common, love – that was my trouble. If there'd been a policeman in the play I'd have been laughing.

Short of carrying the award with me to interviews, I could see no way of actually organising work that might fall neatly before the trip to

Australia. I had plenty to occupy me, but it was the money I was after. I had to learn to ride before I left London, as Jack Grant spent much of the story on horseback. At the interview when I had been asked about riding experience I came out with the usual actor waffle: 'Oh yes, born in the saddle . . . I mean my grandad made them . . . I haven't actually . . . I'm sure that with sufficient . . . I love horses . . .'

Lies, lies, lies. I was terrified of the bloody things, but I was determined to crack it. Alas, English riding schools aren't necessarily the best place to learn, and I think they saw me coming. It's hard to gain confidence or improve as a rider if you don't have a decent horse, and I was sure that when my car appeared in the driveway, most schools rang the knacker's yard and brought some poor beast back from death's door. My horses always combined the following remarkable attributes: aggression, disobedience and extreme old age, so it was impossible to expect them to do anything that might tally with the image I had of myself galloping one-handed through the bush.

All I needed was to look as though I could ride, but I was up against impossible odds. If I pretended to be a normal learner than I was reprimanded for wanting to get on too quickly and told to abide by the 6,000,000 Pony Club rules of training which would take several lifetimes to complete. If I revealed myself as an actor desperate to learn quickly for a part then out came a great squeak of embarrassment followed by silence, and then, 'Are you famous?'

'No.' I tried to be as firm as I could and would start asking more questions about instant galloping. It was no use.

'What would I have seen you in?'

'Hardly anything.' Time was ticking by. I needed to be a brilliant horseman, but it was no use. I could hear them thinking.

'Ah . . . were you in that Hovis commercial?'

'No.'

'The one with the paper-boy who . . .'

'No.'

'He visits his grandad and . . .'

'No.'

'Yes, you were. I bet it was you, you're just shy.'

'Really, I've never done a Hovis commercial. I'm just an unknown actor. I've hardly done any telly at all.'

'That's what they all say. Well, I bet it was you in that one where there's a human cabbage in the saucepan and . . .'

In the midst of my equine depression the RSC rang again. They were obviously fed up with being turned down. Pat said that they were now asking, with no particular end in mind, what part Dame Branagh would deign to consider if she were to come to the RSC at all? I asked Pat to point out that I had never actually turned them down, that other jobs I had been committed to had come off. Still, I knew the part I'd like to try, as I'd been working on it since drama school. It was a young man's role, and the play was littered with references to his youth. They hadn't done it for a bit. Why shouldn't I ask. I was only twenty-three and I hadn't done any professional Shakespeare, but surely that made it all the more exciting? Have a go, love. They could only laugh in my face.

'Pat, tell them I'd like to play Henry V.'

She informed me later that day that the laughter had been deafening. Ah well.

At last, after three interviews, I got another job. It was a couple of episodes in a series called *Maybury*, about a psychiatrist played by Patrick Stewart. The format was described to me. 'Pat's there every week being the problem-solver, and every episode we have a guest nutter – your character is so bananas that he has to have two shows.' A complicated creature indeed – Robert Clyde Moffat was the fictional ego of the author, Douglas Watkinson, and this was the story of Douglas's highly dramatic attempts to come to terms with epilepsy. His adolescence had been plagued with 'the falling sickness', and marked out as 'odd', his life interrupted by a series of embarrassing fits, he had developed something called the epileptic personality, which took the form of a pathological unwillingness to accept his condition. There was great heart in the writing, and it read as if Douglas was exorcising some demon. In the process he had produced a wonderfully showy part.

The phenomenon of what one might coldly describe as 'disability acting' is a strange one. For this role I had to research and produce epileptic fits and various other clinically detailed symptoms and manifestations of his condition. Once an actor does a very physical role like this, accurately portrayed, I've noticed a disproportionately favourable response – people seem extraordinarily impressed. The fact is that when there is a very specific thing to reproduce like an epileptic fit, then the tangible details are available in text-books. A degree of physical dexterity is required to bring them off in performance, but the details are often surprisingly easy to reproduce.

111

I could feel this strange, enhanced status being accorded me in the rehearsals. This virtuoso part was fascinating to play but I knew that I had been just as good in parts that weren't as showy and hardly been noticed. When I watch acting, it's the latter I prefer. I love theatricality, I love detail about real physical conditions, but for me a great naturalistic performance in a quiet part can be just as exciting as seeing someone in heavy make-up with a physical contortion very clearly 'acting'.

The risks are different. With virtuoso histrionics you can be accused of going over the top, but at least you'll be noticed. I think it's much braver to eschew spurious theatricality and be as truthful as possible, not worry about the notices and hope that the multitudes will see that even though you're simply walking, talking and sitting (which of course anyone can do), a great deal of work and thought and research has gone into it. These are crude distinctions, but when this reality *and* theatrically can combine, the results are riveting.

All the great actors have done it, but two favourite examples of mine are by Michael Bryant and Anthony Hopkins. I came upon Bryant's performance quite unexpectedly, in an episode of the TV wartime escape drama, *Colditz*. Bryant played a prisoner who was attempting to escape by feigning madness in order to be repatriated. The Germans smell a rat when they see him behaving oddly and a particular soldier is asked to keep an eye on him. The German has a brother who had gone mad and he is considered an expert, and the episode develops the relationship between Bryant's character and the German. Throughout the series Bryant shows quite brilliantly the descent from feigned 'acting' madness into the real thing, with great theatricality, but utter conviction, and it is heart-breaking to see the character, with his last glimmer of sanity, wave goodbye to the real world. It's a performance which has always haunted me and I've noticed that whenever I've mentioned this performance to actors, almost without fail, they've mentioned it as being in their own 'top tens'.

In *Pravda* Tony Hopkins produced a physical eccentricity which seemed to be the perfect manifestation of a convincing inner drive and tortured ugliness that was caught magnificently in his portrayal of a ruthless newspaper magnate. An absolutely riveting combination.

My attempts to scale such heights were looking a little bleak. I'd finished my very raw performance in *Maybury* and the weeks were rushing by towards my departure for Australia. A third *Billy* play was now planned for August of '83, and it suddenly struck me that since leaving *Another Country* a year before, I had done nothing but screen work. If I wanted to work in the theatre (for which I had been trained), then I had better do a bit of conscious planning. The classics were what I fancied doing but I had no faith in parts just presenting themselves out of the blue. Leicester were doing the two parts of *Henry IV*, I auditioned for Hal and didn't get past the first round. I decided that I would have to do something myself.

In a state of desperation about my riding skills, I'd taken a riding holiday, which meant that you could be on terrible horses all day instead of just three times a week. At the end of two days I was no better as a rider but I did have a bottom that shone. I'd also found a classical piece to do.

I had taken with me Tennyson's *Maud* which he referred to as a 'monodrama'. Its subtitle was 'The Madness'. The word 'monodrama' had appealed immediately to my actor's instinct for one-man show or audition material, but I didn't read it until the riding holiday. There were 1400 lines of often very complex verse, the most famous lines of which began 'Come into the garden, Maud', a refrain I'd heard in the languid Edwardian musical arrangement. This treatment seemed rather incongruous in the context of the whole piece, for *The Madness*, as I preferred to call it, was a full-blooded, passionate, poetic tour de force. I also felt that it was meant to be acted, and not just read aloud. It would be a hell of a job to learn and a very tricky piece to present, but there was a great narrative hook which I was sure would keep people interested for an hour and twenty minutes.

I knew I had money coming in through the Australian job and the third *Billy* play, but I needed to find somewhere to do the piece. I would finance it myself. But before I found a venue, I decided to find the director, and Colin Wakefield was the obvious choice. He had made a late decision to become an actor and had left Reading at the same time as me to train at the Webber-Douglas Academy. He had worked steadily as an actor, we still kept in touch and I knew he was very keen to direct. He'd known my work since I was sixteen, and he was scrupulously honest – no flannels, no 'Darling, you were marvellous'. I decided to charm the pants off him and entertain in style.

We ended up in a rather dowdy trattoria in Southampton Row. He didn't know the piece but after the prawn cocktail he would certainly consider it. By the time we'd finished the spaghetti alle vongole it was a 'very exciting idea', and in the middle of the zabaglione we shook hands. This was the Wednesday night before the Saturday I was due to leave for Australia. Although I was very keen about the project, my old timidity held me back when it came to dealing with the world about it. I knew I wanted a venue but I was terrified of picking up the phone. What would I say? What sort of deal would it be? Who looked after the money business?

Time was running out, and I had no choice. On the Thursday I rang the Upstream Theatre Club, who knew me through *Gamblers*, and on the Friday at four I was sitting in the crypt talking to the vicar, David Wickert, and his assistant, Anne Hopkinson discussing rents. I was terrified but determined to go on with it. They had only two spare weeks available for their theatre: I could have it from 6 September (my mother's birthday, a good omen) for a fortnight. I would have to pay for everything – the printing of tickets, programmes, lights, the whole production costs, set, and so on. In return I had a 150-seat theatre rent-free and we split the income (after overheads had been deducted) fifty-fifty.

I didn't know if it was a good deal, but then I wouldn't have known a good deal if it had stood up and punched me in the face. I didn't care. I had nervously got through my first professional negotiation as a manager and I had a deal – a theatre and a run for *The Madness*. I was ecstatic. I rang Colin. He knew the theatre, had acted there and was delighted. We would communicate by cassette when I was in Australia to discuss the production, and I would spend any spare time I had learning the text.

Pat Marmont was out when I rang, so I left the details with Rose, her brilliant assistant. I was rather relieved that I didn't have to explain why I was mounting this independent venture – there would be none of the usual ten per cent commission and I was rather afraid that she might ditch me for going it alone. Anyway, cross that one later. After a year away, I would be back in the theatre with a huge, frightening classical challenge that would teach me more in a fortnight than months of hanging round for the next telly. If Australia turned out to be a disaster I had this delicious agony to look forward to. One step ahead. That's the way.

The next evening I shared a tearful goodbye with Wendy. After prolonged separation, another three months at the other side of the world was particularly painful. But there was nothing to say – it was part of the job.

My brother drove me, a tear-stained wreck, to the airport on a gloomy Saturday evening. He shook my hand as he left me at Passport Control, and gave me – with typical Irish sentimentality – a horseshoe that he and his wife, Sally, had brought me as a goodbye present. I was as butch and brusque over the farewell as I could manage to be, and, as I strode off purposefully towards the departure lounge, I started to dramatise the whole situation to myself. This was an important turning-point in my life, I told myself, there was no going back, chin-chin, old man – any old rubbish to help me deal with the intense loneliness. Turning up the dramatic volume, I marched down the long airport corridor and on, like some great hero, towards the brave new world that lay ahead.

FIVE

'Upon the rack of this tough world'
KING LEAR

It was the first time I had flown Club Class, and I celebrated the new luxury by eating and drinking anything that came my way. By the time we left Bahrain I was sozzled and had developed an allergy to dry roasted peanuts. I was desperately trying to remember something I'd read about how to avoid jet lag, and sensed I hadn't made the right start. I perked up on the last stage of the leg between Singapore and Sydney, and as we flew over Sydney harbour the sun was shining and I caught my breath at the first sight of the majestic Harbour Bridge. As I looked down I saw the Opera House to the left of the bridge, and the two structures made an eerie, beautiful combination in the early morning light. There was something strong, comforting and honest about the Bridge, and the Opera House was flamboyant, stylish and fun. It all looked wonderful.

I had momentary doubts just before we disembarked. A hairy man wearing a mask sprayed the entire cabin with fly spray, and I wondered what this ritual was supposed to represent. I was convinced it was a charade. The Australians basically believed everyone else had bad breath and this was a large can of Gold Spot.

The producer and director met me from the plane and I was driven through Sydney, which seemed a curious mixture of English bungalowed suburbia and American-looking shop fronts and malls. We drove over the Bridge and had an even better view of the Opera House. I found the combination awe-inspiring, if nothing else because they seemed to be screaming out, 'Yes, you really are here.'

We roared over the crest of a hill and the Pacific was stretched out before us, roaring a great, happy-go-lucky 'Hi!' We drove right down to the front and arrived at my hotel, the Manly Pacific International, right on the beach and facing the magnificent azure-blue ocean. Dickie Bamber, the associate producer, suggested that I go to bed and ring him whenever I woke. I'd slept only fitfully during the twenty-three-hour flight. The hotel was new and fancy and had everything the seasoned international traveller might want, except home. It was all too much for me, so I rang Wendy. Monday morning in Australia, it was Sunday evening in London, and the disorientation turned me into a snivelling wreck. Three months, I'd never last.

On the first day I was introduced to a bewilderingly large crew at the ABC's French's Forest Studios. Channel Four and an Independent British company were making the series with the Australian Broadcasting Company, and all the production people were ABC staff. On that first morning I met the make-up and hair artists, and had the first of an endless series of costume fittings. In the process of Jack Grant's transition from callow English youth to butch Australian bushy I would need a large number of costumes and varying degrees of tan. I had tried to help out in England by having sun-bed treatments in order to warm up my milky Irish complexion. The normal happened. I either remained deadly pale or I switched the control up and I emerged like a small strawberry. Mad dogs and Irishmen weren't meant to go in the sun. For *The Boy in the Bush*, it could all come out of a tin. The excellent wardrobe department had already produced a marvellous pair of leather riding boots which seemed to me half the battle in convincing myself that I could ride like John Wayne.

The producers had insisted on a two-week acclimatisation period, which was intended to allow me to deal with jet lag but also to give me time to familiarise myself with my horse. As I had yet to become familiar with any horse, I was glad of the time, and lessons started straight away. I was to be taught by a wrangler, Graham Ware, whose farm was an hour's drive from Sydney. We pulled up at the quiet house and were greeted by the man himself. Small, knotty and apparently made of leather, Graham shook my hand with the bone-crunching firmness that I'd come to expect from the real boys in the bush and said, 'Hez yah roidun?'

Graham's accent wasn't impenetrable, it just took a little getting used to, and I think I was so beguiled by his appearance that at first I didn't concentrate. Stocky, with a gap-toothed grin, he walked at an angle, leaning forward with a pronounced roll of his slightly bandy legs. We walked to the corral.

'Oim pootn yoo on Dollah, Kin. 'E's a rockin' horse ter roid.'

I mounted, and to my great surprise Graham clicked his fingers and set the horse off on a cantering circle. No warm-ups, no walks, and no preparation. I was delighted, and I bounced around like a

bag of beans. Graham watched me through narrowed eyes. He looked like a character John Carradine would have played in a gangster film. We got on like a house on fire. He saw immediately that I had lots of work to do if I was to fulfil my riding commitments in the series, and he introduced me to the much simpler and more relaxed 'cowboy' riding style that the Australians use. It had none of the British Pony Club stiffness, although it was a little harder on the horse. But it was Graham's horse, Dollar, that made all the difference to my confidence: after weary riding-school nags I was on a highly trained, responsive, good-natured beast that was used to dealing with incompetence. Within a week I was transformed and very, very cocky.

The evenings would still catch me unawares with stabs of home-sickness and, of course, there was Sunday. The Irish Protestant in me had always hated Sundays, and this first Sunday in Sydney was particularly miserable, and it was pouring with rain. However it also provided a farce. Jon Blake, the actor who played my bosom buddy in the film, was concerned about our riding, and we decided to visit a friend of his who lived just outside Sydney and who had horses we could ride for the morning. We pressed ahead, in spite of the rain, and got to a farmhouse that was littered with people who were asleep, drunk or stoned. There had been a wild party the night before, and if the human inhabitants were anything to go by, the horses would be on the ceiling.

In the middle of our visit the police raided the place and I found myself running across the backyard in the rain, hoping I wouldn't celebrate my first week in Sydney by getting arrested. Jon was mortified, but I could have forgiven him anything, for like the rest of the crew and cast he had a professional welcoming instinct which is common to Australians and to the Irish. The number of kind invitations to welcoming dinners that I received in those first two difficult weeks was rather moving. And deeply un-English.

That night Alfie Bell, a Pommie actor who lives in Australia, who was to play the mysterious Dr Rackett in the series, insisted that I come to Sunday dinner with some friends of his, including our director, Ken Hannam. I whimpered something about wanting to be on my own.

'Rubbish. I'm coming to get you now.'

I've never been so warmly looked after. Ten days in and I wasn't sure that I would ever want to go back home.

Filming started. Jack's story was shot out of sequence, which was very tricky. The callow youth who arrives at the outback farm of his distant relations develops considerably over the four episodes, and his clothes and appearance change as he becomes used to farm life, wins the respect of the natives, and falls for the local girl, played by the great Australian star, Sigrid Thornton. As the story progresses, Jack becomes a miner, and later a gold prospector with two wives. We would sometimes shoot scenes with the weathered, rough Jack in the morning, and then return to the younger Jack in the afternoon, which would mean a change of stubble, hair, make-up and costume. This was particularly difficult as I was in practically every shot and my film-acting education really began here. There is really no substitute for practice, and being in front of the lens all day every day for three months was a great crash course. Ken Hannam's direction was patient and thorough. He was determined to capture the special atmosphere of this piece, and not just allow it to become a cowboy romp. He used faces as landscapes, and there were many close-ups to reveal Jack's internal isolation, and indeed to explore the complexity of the other characters.

Each day after shooting, at around six or seven in the evening, the entire crew would watch rushes of the previous day's work. This was a very brave thing to do, especially for the actors, and directors often banish actors from these sessions as dreadful damage can be done to a performance if an actor's hysterical subjectivity is brought to bear. The Australian actors took these sessions in their stride and were very grateful for the opportunity to monitor the filming, particularly as the story was spread over several years, and it was always a very jolly occasion with people cracking open a tube (a can of beer – I was becoming steeped in the culture). This daily process cured me forever of obsessive worry about my own appearance – gosh, do I really look that awful? This feeling is a waste of time, and after a couple of days of seeing myself on film, I was so used to the uninspiring features which, short of plastic surgery, were with me for the rest of my days, that I stopped worrying. I found myself able to look at the character objectively and use the sessions as a useful tool for looking at the character and seeing how the different aspects of the part fitted together. If some quality or other was missing then a discussion with the director would mean that you could be sure to include it at some other point.

It was still early days and the material looked good. We were shooting three and a half minutes of film every day and the spirit among the crew was good. Roger Lanser, the brilliant camera operator, who became a close friend, shared the crew's relief. They'd been working on a series with a particularly demanding director who seemed to share little of Ken Hannam's concern for detail in the acting or for the atmosphere of the piece. He was glad at last to be working on something of real quality. I asked him who the director had been.

'His name is Rob "Rocket" Stewart.'

'Rocket?'

'Yeh. Because he works so fast.'

'Christ, save us from that.'

It was clear after a week that something was wrong. The atmosphere on set remained very positive but there were rumblings in the administrative corridor. Each night after rushes I would have a shower and then make my way to the car, and as I passed the producers' office I would hear noisy arguments about the rushes. Poor Ken Hannam.

The problem was more serious than I thought, and at the end of the second week's shooting gossip was rife. On the Friday night Dickie Bamber picked me up at location and drove me back to the studios.

'Don't worry, Ken. There's a bit of confusion over what we're all after. Mr Warren' – this was the series producer – 'is coming over at the weekend and we're all going to have a chat to sort it out. Nothing to worry about.'

It sounded ominous, but I decided to give Dickie the benefit of the doubt. I knew there had been talk of there being a lack of 'production value', in other words, there had not been enough footage of landscapes or our marvellous sets, anything that showed where the money had been spent. The first two weeks had been spent in concentrating on character work, but I felt sure that production value would come later in the schedule.

I decided not to worry. I had enough to do, with lines to learn and a new flat to move to. It had been suggested that I might be better off financially if I moved – I would be given the money it would have cost to keep me at the hotel (a contractual arrangement) and if I found a flat that was cheaper I could keep the difference. I found an extraordinary place overlooking the ocean. It was perched on a rocky outcrop of Queenscliff and the main room had miles of window and 180-degree views of the Pacific.

I'd begun to change into costume at 6.30 on the following Monday morning when one of the wardrobe girls came in.

'Haven't you heard? No shooting today. Ken's been sacked.'

Moments later the gang of four producers descended on me with all sorts of explanations for their action. I was panicked and wanted to know what was going to happen to him, to me, and to the production.

I protested weakly on Ken's behalf. It was completely hopeless. I had no idea what to do. 'I'll need to ring my agent,' I said, and it threw them.

'Oh, I don't think there's any need for that . . .'

It was no use, I was on a very high horse. 'I'm afraid there is. I signed to be in a show that Ken was directing. The situation has changed, and I need to review my position.'

I didn't know what I was talking about but it was clearly alarming them. I was growing up quickly.

'Now come on, Ken, just calm down . . .' Calm down? I hadn't realised that I'd heated up. I decided to listen. 'No look, we're going to have to stop shooting for a week while we get this thing sorted out. Obviously we have some thoughts about a new director. If you have any ideas we'd be glad to hear them.'

Cobblers. They already knew who they wanted. I had a very uncomfortable feeling.

'Perhaps over the next few days if you fancy spending a little time at the Barrier Reef, we'd be very happy to send you up there.'

'No. Absolutely not. I don't need to salve my conscience.' I had no idea where my bottle had come from.

'Well, of course we don't mean it like that. Just think about it and please don't do anything rash. You've got an international career to think about.'

This was the stuff of which Hollywood legends are made – hirings and firings and tough-talking executives. I loved reading about it but I didn't like being in the middle of it. The cast got together later the same day, and the Australians put forward suggestions for alternative directors. We all knew what was coming and we all knew we would have no choice but to accept it or be out of a job. Pat Marmont was sympathetic and advised caution but felt there was no choice but to stay, however frightened I felt about being in a vulnerable position, and however much I feared the return of old dreads from the days of *Hamlet* at RADA.

The next day the expected news was announced. We were all called together and told that our new director was to be a marvellous and sensitive director called Robert Stewart. Perhaps some of us had worked with him before? There was an audible groan.

I suddenly felt as I had done in the first term at Meadway, and through those awful *Hamlet* rehearsals – terrified, intimidated, and small. Well, bugger it. This time I would not be bullied. I started to fume and marched into the producers' office. Only one was there.

'I'd like to see you all. Now, please.'

'Well Ken . . .'

'*Now.*' My God. I was starting to frighten myself. They filed in.
'Two things. Firstly, don't give me any sweet talk about this fellow's
reputation. I know exactly what it is, and if I get any trouble from
him, and if there is any attempt to interfere with my work, then I'm
on the next plane home. Understand?'

'Now, come on.'

'Don't think I'm joking.'

I tried to control my body, which was shaking all over. They were
not going to treat me like a child. Until then I had been all sweetness
and light. Mr Pro. Now they would see what I was made of.

'Second, I want a car.'

'A car?'

'A car. Good morning, gentlemen.'

God knows why I had asked for a car. They sent cabs for me every
morning, but as they drove on the left in Sydney it felt like home, and
I fancied the independence outside work. The car arrived by lunchtime of the same day. I had taken no pleasure in blowing my top.
Afterwards, I was wracked with guilt, certain that I had done the
wrong thing and finally (actor to the very core) I was worried they
wouldn't like me any more. The toughening-up process had only just
begun.

Three days later a new read-through was called so that our second
leader could tell us his view of the piece. 'Rocket' was about six foot
two, blond and well-built, and looked like the original Medallion
Man. His shirt, when it was on, was undone to the navel, his legs
were permanently spread while he performed ad hoc exercises, and
his handshake was so strong I thought I would faint. His opening
remarks laid out the kind of relationship that was ahead:

'G'day, Ken. Now look here, mate. Old D. H. Lawrence was a
funny bastard, wasn't he? Well look, I'm not interested in all this
motivation shit. I think we wanna just shoot some film, have a few
tubes, fuck a few women and fuck off home. What do you say?'

I couldn't believe my ears. He knew how provocative he was being
and this was clearly meant to test what an arty Pom I really was, but
I suppressed the queeny outrage in me and decided to credit him
with being nervous. I would give him the benefit of the doubt.

The first week proved quite how wrong I'd been. Rocket's hero
was Sam Peckinpah. If Rocket had been making *A Room with a View*,
Maggie Smith and Judi Dench would have been blown up in the first
ten minutes. Alas, Lawrence's delicate tale had far too much cowboy

in it for Rocket to resist the 'rip, shit and bust' adventure style. This was fine up to a point, but there was much more in the story and I took it upon myself to defend atmosphere and character. It was difficult.

Week one. 'Ken, what do you look like with your shirt off?'

'What?'

'The girls, Ken, the girls. All this fucking chat's boring the ass off me. We've got to get the girls interested. Whip your shirt off, get a bit of tan and oil on there, we'll be laughing.'

That was what I feared.

Week two. Shooting had gone up to eleven minutes of film a day. 'And . . . Cut! OK, moving on, next set up.'

'Hold on, hold on, we've only done it once. I'd like another go.'

'Fuck me, Ken. It's dialogue. We need to get on to the fucking action.'

Too much for me. I could butch it up with the best of them but I hadn't come to make *The Dirty Dozen*. He was walking away. I exploded.

'*The dialogue is interesting, you Philistine git.*'

Pause.

'OK, the fucking Queen of the May gets another take.'

I was so angry by this time that acting went out of the window. Next day I tried a new tack: humour. In all truth, Rocket, who to my annoyance I was growing increasingly fond of, was highly risible. His macho-ness was so exaggerated that you expected him to open cans of beer with his teeth. I'm sure he'd tried it. Bully though he appeared to be, he was very conscious of his image among the crew. He didn't mind being thought a bastard, as long as he was a big butch bastard. The mickey-taking did the trick, and I was the only one with sufficient professional status and power enough to challenge him.

It was a rather dangerous game. After all, he really was a big bloke. In the end I took to him because he cured me of whatever weakness had made me susceptible to intimidation in the past. At last I had begun to stand up for myself. Twelve thousand miles from home, in a situation from which I couldn't run away, I had developed new muscles that I feared I didn't have. I hoped it wasn't producing a stroppiness that would plague producers and directors ever more, but it certainly meant that I would not be walked over in the future.

Except possibly by marsupials. Rocket pitched me into the ring with a one-eyed, one-armed, arthritic kangaroo called Smokey.

We filmed Jack Grant's kangaroo fight at an antipodean extravaganza called Nature Wonderland. If Smokey was an example of Australian wildlife, then the wonder was that any wildlife survived at all. I wrestled with this decrepit beast, but Rocket still wasn't satisfied. He found an animal sanctuary nearby which housed a crazed 'roo'. This was obviously going to be more dramatic. We went into the compound and exited one minute later minus a camera and with Roger Lanser in shock, having been attacked by the meanest marsupial I've ever seen.

Because of the original stoppage over Ken Hannam's sacking, the filming had been delayed by several weeks. The limited rehearsal time for *The Madness* had been further reduced and Colin tried to guard against it with trans-continental tapes in which he described how the set would work in the Waterloo Road. I sat listening to the tapes in Bulahdelah, a one-horse town almost in the middle of nowhere, trying desperately to learn the lines between takes of sheep-shearing and logging.

The job ended in a flurry of intense social life. I really had made some good friendships, and at the party on my last day, Graham Ware pulled a cart full of presents onto the lawn at French's Forest and finished me off. I was still awash with tears the next day as I left Sydney, where I had been made so welcome. I would even miss Rocket. Maybe he could come and help Colin with *The Madness*. Exploding Tennyson. That would be new.

As I weepily settled down into the long flight, I felt that I had – rather like Jack Grant – matured a little in Australia. I'd dealt with being away, being bullied, working on a film and had experienced a care and concern from friends that allowed me to see once again that professional problems should be seen in a wider perspective. Frightened though I was by the prospect of *The Madness*, I felt certain that it was the right thing to be doing while I was in this more realistic frame of mind.

I returned to emotional madness. The inevitable effects of a four-month separation wreaked havoc on Wendy and me. After three and a half years of a more or less steady involvement, we decided to go our separate ways. It happened in the first week after my return from Australia – Wendy instigated the break, and I played the wounded martyr, but we both knew it was for the best.

Much more therapeutic was the feeling that I was a real actor once more. I returned on a Saturday from Australia and on the following Monday morning I was walking along the Waterloo Road at 9.30 with a take-away tea and a bacon roll in my hand. This is what I always did when going to rehearsal at RADA, and it felt proper, it was what you did. One never got the same sensation arriving for a television production.

Rehearsals for *The Madness* were tough. A one-man show is a delicate affair. One performer plus one director can equal boredom, and puts great pressure on both of them to provide enough energy to keep rehearsals flowing. *The Madness* had particular demands: it's a high-voltage piece, which combines an atmosphere of Edgar Allan Poe gloom with something of the romantic intensity of *Romeo and Juliet*. It was difficult to rehearse for long hours in any piece of this kind under such conditions, but the delays on *The Boy in the Bush* had left only one week before I was due to fly to Belfast for *Billy III*. We did our best in the seven days, and the rest of the rehearsals were held on Saturdays and Sundays over the following month. I would fly back from Belfast on a Friday night learning the rest of the text in the aeroplane, and the next day we would try to cram a week's work into one day.

The combination of an unusually tough work-load and my own depressed emotional condition made it a rather bleak time for me. The recurring Hamlet in me was much comforted by Alec McCowen's *Personal Mark*, which gives an account of his work on the one-man show *St Mark's Gospel*. The comfort it offered to someone engaged in the same lonely process where self doubt was the name of the game was immense.

Colin Wakefield's patience was extraordinary. In the latter stages of rehearsal when we were attempting a run-through I would often stop speaking and just give up in utter despair. Very quietly, without bullying, he would make me pick it up and carry on, ignoring the fact that I was on the verge of tears with exhaustion and a sense of my own impending failure.

I did wonder seriously about who would come and see it. Colin and I were learning fast about independent production. When rehearsal fatigue overtook us, we would be on the phone pumping in coins and trying to persuade *Time Out* and *Ms London* to give us a mention. We had no press agent, and had no real idea of how to secure publicity.

Back in Belfast during the week being the Ulster James Dean, the cast of *Billy III* were plagued with requests to hear my lines. This was the latest drama: would I be able to remember it? Any spare time was spent filling envelopes with leaflets for the show and sending them off to journalists, friends, anyone. We were twisting arms all over the place. I had already had the artwork for the poster done by the design department of *The Boy in the Bush*. Incidental music for the show had been cajoled from Kate Edgar, an excellent musician who was a friend of Colin Wakefield, and Colin had also managed to obtain the services of Kate Burnett, a highly talented designer who produced a set that could allow a dramatic, poetic monologue to come to interesting stage life. The piece changed locations from the Narrator's house, to the moor, to the manor where Maud lived, to the woods where the father had died, to France, to the sea. The overall effect was achieved by the simplest of means – a naked wooden stage dripping with blood-red paint and a selection of dramatic scaffolding poles, cut and placed to form a miniature wood at the back of the set. When it was properly lit, it ignited the imagination in a powerful way that managed not to conflict with the text.

When *Billy III* was finished I had confirmation that Julian Mitchell's play, *Francis* would go ahead that Autumn at the Greenwich Theatre, and that I would be playing the lead. Rehearsals were due to start a week after *The Madness* closed. I was back to the theatre with a vengeance.

I had yet to complete a run-through of *The Madness* without drying or being overcome by the panic and fear, and wanting to run away. The single preview was on the Tuesday night, and we opened on the Wednesday. All sorts of chums and associates were dragged in to the dress rehearsal on the Monday. Several of them fell fast asleep, which was a disaster for me as I could see every single person in the tiny auditorium. I didn't dry, but I did do a little Tennysonian paraphrasing.

Pat Marmont came to the preview. 'Brilliant, darling, but too quick. It's so dense you must give us a chance.'

It was what Colin had been saying all along, but fear prevented me from taking his advice. The quicker I went the less chance I had to be scared and also the less chance the audience had to be bored rigid. But I decided I would try.

With unswerving loyalty Pat also came to the first night, and I was undoubtedly slower and better. It was nice to have a fuller house than before, although disconcerting to see the three or four critics who had turned up, scribbling noisily in my many significant pauses. Colin was very pleased with the performance. A great party of his friends were in and we trooped off afterwards for supper in Covent Garden. People had enjoyed it, and if nothing else, they felt as if they had been at an event. Wherever else would they see eighty obscure minutes of a Tennyson poem performed on stage by an actor?

There were no notices the next day, and the bookings for the remaining performances were dismal. Colin and I continued a rallying-round of persuasion, David Parfitt helped us, and even lent a hand by selling programmes. These few days really were tough. Colin had seen the show so many times that he really deserved a break. I told him not to bother coming in on the Friday and Saturday nights. It left me even more lonely. Before the show there was only the stage manager to talk to, an unemployed actor who was doing it for the prospect of a profit share which I'd promised to him and to Colin and Kate. Not much chance of that.

On the Saturday night, things reached rock bottom. The show started with twelve paying customers in the 150-seat auditorium, of which six were my family. I might as well have been doing it in the front room. I spent eighty minutes acting my face off and being permanently on the edge of breaking out of it and saying, 'This is ridiculous, let's all go home.' That Sunday, with no girlfriend, no audience and a new room in Brentford to get depressed in, I was a sorry sight.

On the Monday morning a notice appeared in *The Times*: 'The most exciting young actor in years.' And at lunchtime the *Evening Standard* also ran a review – 'Dazzling, virtuoso performance.'

I rang the theatre. The phone hadn't stopped ringing, we were sold out from Wednesday onwards, and Monday and Tuesday had really perked up. Several actors who were in shows had rung to ask would I do a midnight matinée, so that they could see it? In a moment of real madness I agreed. There would be two shows on the last Saturday, one at 8 pm and one at 11 pm. My God, what a difference a day makes.

My confidence was transformed and the performance began to grow. Many people I admired came: Ronald Eyre, Jimmy Ellis, Edward Petherbridge and his wife, Emily Richard, lots of young actors and, to my delight, Alec McCowen, whom I was able to thank in person for the comfort his book had provided. Even Mary Wilson, the former Prime Minister's wife, and a Tennyson devotee, made an appearance. She endeared herself to me for ever by bringing round to the dressing-room a volume of her poetry which she had signed.

'I hoped you might like it.'

I thanked her profusely and when she had gone looked at the inscription. 'To John Branagh, Congratulations on your performance.' I'd clearly made a great impression.

That week of packed performances also brought Joyce Nettles and Genista McIntosh, another high-powered RSC colleague. They'd been threatened by Pat Marmont who sat through the show a remarkable four times, and I was told that the RSC might 'be in touch'.

The last performance on Saturday produced a wonderful standing ovation from a lot of fellow actors, mostly friends, who were amazed that I was still on my feet and who were mostly high as kites on having finished their own two shows that day. It made a great celebratory end to my first fully independent venture. Many lessons were learned, and over the last day or two David Parfitt and I chewed the cud over how to make the administrative side work efficiently, and how to work independent ventures of this kind so that they actually paid people like Colin Wakefield and Kate Burnett who had both heavily subsidised it with their talents. It was the first of many such discussions.

A brief holiday followed – three fascinating days in Rome, and then a research trip to Assisi where I was able to examine the way of life of modern Franciscan monks. I also spent a day with David William, an actor from *Another Country* who was to direct *Francis*. He had seen *The Madness* and wanted to pass on a few comments that might be useful to take on into *Francis*. Like Hugh Cruttwell, David's precision with words and desire to present the truth on stage was inspiring. We discussed how an actor presenting the visionary quality of a man such as Francis must be able to show the character's remoteness from real life at certain moments. It was a form of spiritual isolation, the ability to see 'some other where', a quality that any actor playing Hamlet must give to these lines:

> There is a special providence in the fall of a sparrow
> If it be now, tis not to come. If it be not to come
> It will be now. If it be not now, yet it will come.
> The readiness is all.

David William believed I *could* present this sense of vision and spiritual gravitas but that at present I was much happier in the emotions of the here and now. At the same time it was important to present Francis's spiritual qualities without the performance seeming ponderous or dull. Francis was neither of these things, and his faith was a practical one. He was an exciting charismatic leader but he was still set apart. The part was a tall order but very exciting, and the play contained all these possibilities, but with David there to describe all the different aspects in such an illuminating way, I felt confident of learning a huge amount in the four-week rehearsal period.

I came back from Italy inspired and also convinced that holidays abroad alone when you were recovering from a broken heart were not a good idea. It was better to call a mate, get pissed and have a good moan. I did plenty of that when I got back.

Rehearsals started, and by the end of the first week we had 'blocked' the whole play. By the beginning of the second week I had learned the part. (*The Madness* had done no harm to my retentive memory.) David encouraged me to develop a 'spiritual vocabulary', an extreme receptivity to the man and the ideas in the play. It was very un-modern and very unfamiliar to me. The play dealt with profound themes, and I felt if I could get to grips with the imaginative demands of the part, I could draw new qualities from my acting.

There was a brilliant team effort over those four weeks. Frederick Treves was producing a superb performance as Cardinal Ugolino, Francis's chief adversary, a part he conveyed with real compassion and intelligence. At the final run-through, in the British Legion Hall at Putney, his acting was as fine as any I have seen. From an audience that included wardrobe and stage management personnel, and the artistic director, Alan Strachan, there was a unanimous response. Tears poured down their faces and the response from everyone there gave the impression that they felt they had witnessed something very special.

Introduction to the theatre part 74: new plays need time. Julian's piece was in good shape when we began rehearsal, and it was fine when we moved it to the stage. After only one performance in front of an audience it was seen by the critics, who savaged it. The play would have benefited enormously from a week of previews, which gave the actors a chance to work on the text and also to adapt the set and costumes to fit the needs of the play. There was no time to learn from a single preview. The rough edges threw into sharp relief elements of medievalism which a modern audience can find boring and difficult. I believe this obscured an excellent production of a fine play.

At the time I was certain that I had produced the best work of my career and that the high sights we had set ourselves had been met. I was in a tiny minority, but, for the first and only time, I was completely unaffected and unworried by the reviews. I knew the work was honest and real and powerful, and the difficulty lay in conveying this, but there was still no denying that it wasn't going to catch on. The first night faces told the story. All the ecstatic fan mail in the world – and there was a great deal – could not salvage the show, which played to rapidly dwindling audiences and finished its Greenwich run a week earlier than planned.

I have two glorious memories of the first night. One was the sight of my grandmother in tears in the foyer. She had been persuaded to brave the terrors of aeroplanes at the age of eighty so that she could see her grandson on stage for the first time. She had been deeply moved by the play and only came out of her post-show reverie to giggle wildly at the mention of my nakedness. At one point, when Francis rejects his father's wealth, he takes all his clothes off in the village square in order to make his point. My granny found this scene hysterical, as did my fellow actors, who were playing villagers and peasants, and, facing upstage, couldn't be heard hissing, 'Christ, I've seen more meat on a dirty fork.'

Nor shall I forget the marvellous diplomacy of Robert Fox, who had been keeping an eye on the play with a view to transferring it if it worked. He came into the dressing-room and gave me a great hug accompanied by an awe-struck, 'Extraordinary . . . absolutely extraordinary.'

We looked at each other and his face forbade further comment. He looked as though either his life had been changed or that he was so appalled that he couldn't bring himself to speak. He said one more 'Extraordinary', and then left. I loved him for it. He was in an impossible position, and going round after the show is a ghastly business at the best of times. Now I could choose to believe that the whole thing was 'extraordinary . . . crap' or 'extraordinary . . . brilliance'. I went for the latter and have never troubled Robert for his real choice. The sadness produced by the notices in the subsequent weeks was alleviated by the company spirit, which was high to the point of danger, and corpsing had to be kept under strict control.

Something was definitely afoot at the RSC. Ron Daniels came to see *Francis*, and a trip to see other work was a rare event for a busy RSC director. He stayed behind afterwards and was kind about the play, but he still acted as though he were in a World War II film. This time, I thought, he thinks he's in the French Resistance – he spoke almost in a whisper and kept looking over his shoulder, and I was sure his parting line would be a wink and then 'Ze blue moon eatz ze lazee dog in zee evening,' or some other code phrase. He wanted to meet to chat about . . . something, he wouldn't say what. We would have to go somewhere very quiet – I half expected that he'd want me to wear a trench-coat and stand under a clock with a carnation. The next day his secretary rang to say that there was a table booked at Joe Allen's. Short of putting an ad in *The Stage*, I couldn't think of a more effective way of alerting the entire acting profession to our plans. Still, I was sure there would be method in his madness.

We were on the pudding when I thought it was time to prize Ron out of his Peter Lorre impersonation.

'So what actually was it that you wanted to talk about, Ron?'

'*Henry V.*' Yippee. Ron went on. 'I passionately believe that this play must be done. I passionately want to do it, and I passionately believe that you should play Henry.'

His intensity was convincing. All that passion. 'Well, that's great, Ron.'

'Ah. It's not quite that easy.'

Here we go.

Ron explained the complexities of the RSC's planning system. There were more considerations than individual ambitions for particular plays.

'But you do passionately want to do this, Ron?'

'Passionately.'

Well, that must be a help. 'What do you see in the play?'

'Mud.'

I checked the wine. No, it was OK, we were still on the first bottle. 'Mud?'

Ron explained about the earthy, filthy approach he wanted. Sounded fine to me. 'When will you know?'

The eyes narrowed again. The chances of pinning Ron down like this were small. We finished the meal and agreed to keep in touch, but quite how I was going to keep in touch with him, short of sending a weekly telegram declaring my interest in the part, I wasn't sure. I asked Pat if she knew what was going on in the RSC planning department. 'God knows, darling.'

A fortnight later she rang to say that Barry and Adrian would like to see me. Yes, they were confident of offering me a line of parts, but they needed to chat. I was filming Edward Bond's play, *Derek* for Thames TV during the day, but they gave me the afternoon off to make my first visit to the great airport lounge that is the Barbican Centre. I waited in the RSC's casting office where Siobhan, the casting assistant, tiptoed over to me and spoke in hushed tones that suggested she thought I might hit her. 'Ron has asked me to say that he's sorry he won't be directing *Henry V*, but there is another play he passionately wants to direct and the two couldn't work out.'

Gosh, I thought, all that passion in one man. He'll explode.

Barry Kyle and Adrian Noble, the two senior RSC directors, were equally passionate, so they said, about my joining the Company. They were as pleasant as they had been before and I had no reason to disbelieve them. Ron, it turned out, was directing *Hamlet* and passionately wanted me to play Laertes. Before I became worn out with passionate pleas, Barry explained that he was directing *Love's Labour's Lost*, and thought that I might be very good as the King of Navarre. I was encouraged by the fact that he was interested but didn't feel it passionately.

The real crux of the talk and the offer was Adrian's production of *Henry V*. It was definitely going to be done at Stratford in the following year and Adrian – rather than Ron – was going to direct it. He was interested in me but had not – bar my original audition – seen me in the classics. Perhaps I could go away and prepare a piece of *Henry V* to come back and work on. I offered to do it there and then.

They took me at my word, Adrian suggested 'Once more unto the breach', and we walked down onto the vast Barbican stage. I put down the book and started. I knew the speech by heart and was so excited that I decided to go for it, regardless. Empty theatres have always thrilled me – the fantastic response with which you can imbue your imaginary audiences can sometimes be more rewarding than the real thing.

Barry and Adrian made helpful comments and I did the speech half a dozen different ways.

'Terrific. We'll be in touch with your agent.'

I suppose that that meant I was through, but I wasn't sure. I didn't dare hope. As I was leaving the stage door, a friend who was in the company rushed up to me. 'Well done, that was great.'

'What was?'

'Your audition.'

'How do you know?'

'The tannoy and the video monitor were both on. We were all in the green room having a bite between shows and cheering you on.'

'Bloody 'ell.'

'I'm sure you've got it.'

He was right. Two days later the offer was confirmed: the three

Shakespearian plays, and a part in a new play which Barry was directing which was still at an early stage. The contract was for the sixty weeks of the Stratford and Newcastle season, with an implicit understanding that if, as was usual, the shows transferred to London, then I would stay with them for another nine months. Two years' employment. I hoped I'd made the right choice. *Henry V* opened the Stratford season, and if it was a disaster, I'd either be kicked out or have to suffer it for two years. At twenty-three, I was the youngest Henry ever to play at Stratford. What chance did I stand? It was exactly what I wanted and it was frightening, but there was no turning back.

SIX

Ever since that first camping trip to Stratford in 1978, I had felt
destined to join the RSC. *The Wars of the Roses* in the early sixties, the
work of Peter Brook, and the Trevor Nunn seasons in the mid-
seventies all seemed to indicate an extraordinarily versatile and
skilful company, and it became my ideal. The variety and quality of
the work were consistent, and it was full of immensely talented
people – Trevor Nunn, Terry Hands, Adrian Noble, Barry Kyle –
with whom I was longing to work. I felt very privileged to enter the
RSC at such a level, and I was determined to be a model member of
the Company. I bought my copies of the Arden Shakespeare and set
to work, hoping that a successful first season would lead to a long
relationship with the company that I felt was my natural home. In
the meantime, *Henry V* demanded attention.

Adrian Noble and I sat on either side of a rusty gas-heater in a
freezing dance studio near the Barbican; at the other end of the desk
were the Assistant Director, A. J. Quinn, and the Assistant Stage
Manager, Ian Barber. This was how the luxurious ten-week rehearsal period for *Henry V* began and in the first ten days it was really
just the four of us. The lengthy preparation period was in part
because *The Merchant of Venice* would open directly after *Henry V* and
several key actors were in both productions. *Henry V* was to be the
prestigious opening show of the 1984 season.

The wonderful advantage of that first week or so was to be able
to establish my fundamental instincts about the character.
Shakespeare's Henry V has been described as a jingoistic warlord, a
brigand, and a thug. Despite the huge success of Laurence Olivier's
film, made in the forties, the character continues to create great
uneasiness in the minds of modern actors, directors, critics and
academics, and we had a particular media spotlight focused on this
production. It had already been labelled a 'post-Falklands' version
of the play, and there was suspicion from both sides of the political
spectrum that the production would set out to condemn the war in a

crude way or, conversely, to celebrate it with all the jingoism that the piece can offer.

Adrian and I discussed this problem in great detail, as much would depend on the portrayal of the central character. Studying the part at RADA I had been struck by the sense of Hamletian doubt that runs through the part. Henry was haunted, I felt, not just by his father and their troubled relationship, but also by the ghost of Richard II, whom he invokes at the end of the famous 'Upon the King' soliloquy. This seemed to me to reveal a massively guilty man who was quite terrified, and the speech was not a perfunctory plea from a pious zealot certain of his own victory, but expressed the anguished fear of a young man whose mistake would cost thousands of lives.

HENRY   Oh God of battles, steel my soldiers' hearts;
Possess them not with fear; take from them now
The sense of reckoning if the opposed numbers
Pluck their hearts from them.
Not today O Lord!
O not today, think not upon the fault
My father made in compassing the crown!
I Richard's body have interred new
And on it have bestowed more contrite tears
Than from it issued forced drops of blood.
Five hundred poor I have in yearly pay,
Who twice a day their withered hands hold up
Toward heaven, to pardon blood; and I have built
Two chantries, where the sad and solemn priests
Sing still for Richard's soul. More will I do;
Though all that I can do is nothing worth,

                    Since that my penitence comes after all,
                    Imploring pardon.
GLOUCESTER   My liege!
HENRY   My brother Gloucester's voice! Ay!
                    I know thy errand, I will go with thee:
                    The day, my friends, and all things stay
                          for me.

It was clear from these early discussions that Henry's genuine
humility in relation to God would be a cornerstone of my interpretation. I wanted to infuse 'and all things' with the dark dread of a man
who would expect to go to hell and for whom the place was an
absolutely real concept. Right from the start he attempts to make
everyone genuinely aware of the same thing, of his vision of 'how to
war'. Despite political and war-mongering intrigue, despite irresistible pressure from the Church and from the nobles, he insists on
fighting an honourable campaign. I wanted the first speech to
Canterbury to put this man of God very explicitly on the spot with an
injunction directed at the wily archbishops.

                    And pray take heed how you impawn our person,
                    How you awake our sleeping sword of war:
                    We charge you in the name of God take heed;
                    For never two such kingdoms did contend
                    Without much fall of blood; whose guiltless drops
                    Are every one a woe, a sore complaint
                    'Gainst him whose wrongs gives edge unto the swords
                    That make such waste in brief mortality.
                    Under this conjuration speak, my lord
                    For we will hear, note, and believe in heart
                    That what you speak is in your conscience washed
                    As pure as sin with baptism.

I wanted to produce a moral gravitas that would arrest the clerics
and the court with its weight. When my Henry used words like 'sin'
and 'baptism' and 'conscience', I wanted the audience to feel that
these were real and practical concepts which were deeply felt. It
seemed the only way to make the audience care, and thus to make
them genuinely question this man's actions. It also created dramatic
conflict: the archbishops are faced not with a warlord who simply
wishes a plan for invasion to be given the Church's approval, but

with someone who is asking real questions and underlining their own sense of responsibility. Such a Henry could put everyone on edge, and start to make the story more than just a *Boys' Own* adventure tale, but leave the audience thinking 'What happens next?', 'Will they go to France?'

We felt that the play had to be shaken out of its superficial militaristic pageantry, and given new force. The large numbers involved make it an expensive play to put on, but I was sure there were other reasons for *Henry V* being performed so seldom – even the RSC only does it every ten or so years. Poor productions of the play which portray Henry and the English as thugs have failed to win audiences over, and critics have condemned the play's political standpoint.

All this was healthily challenged by Adrian. He didn't want Henry to be a saint throughout the play, and neither did I, but I was determined to examine and expand what David William had described during rehearsals for *Francis* as 'a spiritual vocabulary'. It is an area of Henry's personality which is viewed with suspicion by critics, but the richness of the text told me to believe in Henry's concept of honour. He is a man with a close understanding of what war involves, and an intense, visionary appreciation of its consequences. He is a killer, a brilliant politician, but much of this is in embryo and is subject to change during the course of the play. Above all, he is a complicated, doubting, dangerous young professional – neither straightforwardly good nor consciously evil.

Adrian and I both agreed that we should not try to explain this man but rather explore all these paradoxes and contradictions, with an awareness of his historical and social context. We wanted to be faithful to the complex inner debate that Shakespeare conducts on the subject of war, and as we discussed the play it seemed less like a historical pageant and more like a highly complicated and ambiguous discourse on the nature of leadership.

After a fortnight the new Company started to assemble. Brian Blessed, who was to play Henry's warlord uncle, Exeter, was a very striking figure, and his capacity for enthusiasm and encouragement seemed boundless. Ian McDiarmid was playing both the Chorus in *Henry V* and Shylock in *The Merchant of Venice*, and seemed a shy and reserved man, but was really leading the company from the front. He would turn out to be one of the most significant influences on my Stratford season. By the seventh week we had run each half of the play several times and I had finally learned the part. I had deliberately set out to delay this process for as long as possible in order to take advantage of the rehearsal period, and to remain responsive and adaptable.

Although Adrian worked very methodically and was moving towards a very particular conception of the play, ideas and approaches changed daily, and it was important not to become locked into certain ways of saying the lines too early on.

There was also a great deal of technical work to accomplish, and it was a great pleasure to work with the legendary Cis Berry, the RSC's voice supremo. With her assistant, David Carey, one could work specifically on difficult speeches and passages that required the special attention of voice and speech experts. Cis did not come from the 'red leather, yellow leather' school of speech training, but she did have her own idiosyncratic methods, which sometimes involved running round the auditorium singing 'Once more unto the breach', or standing on my head bicycling while reciting the St Crispin's Day speech. There was rather more dry technical advice, but the idea was always to keep the words fresh, however silly you might feel. Words and thoughts and actions must always be linked to provide the correct clarity and tone of sound. I could have spent ten weeks just doing this. The Stratford auditorium sat 1500 people. I remember from my own experience of watching shows from the balcony that projection could be a problem, and I had to be on top of it.

And I had to be on top of the part. I had already been through the usual selection of actor tools – I'd read every biography of Henry V I could get my hands on, and had been wooed in and out of a number of absurd ideas. I discovered in one book that Henry, who had been fighting from the age of twelve, had received a facial wound which had left an enormous scar running from the corner of his mouth to one ear. The effect, the historian wrote, was to make Henry seem as though he was smiling all the time. A very sinister disguise for this most mysterious monarch. Ha, ha. The idea fired me immediately: a marvellous make-up job would ensure that the audience were aware of the king's savage past and would allow the critics to hail my extraordinary new interpretation. A few home experiments allowed me to see that my aspirations to be the Lon Chaney of the classical stage were doomed. I looked as though someone had driven a Reliant Robin across my cheek and appeared about as sinister as Shirley Temple.

140

If the visuals were to remain straight then the internals would have to provide the character's fascination. Work on this was proceeding slowly. I was remarkably diligent. Each evening I would record details of that day's rehearsal on a small tape recorder and, in the act of speaking it, I would attempt to make clearer sense of the part. Henry was a young man, and so was I. He was faced with an enormous responsibility. I didn't have to run the country and invade France, but I did have to control Brian Blessed and open the Stratford season. I was sure I could convey a certain sense of responsibility. With Adrian's expert guidance, I could analyse the text in great detail, and although it was difficult to convey everything he revealed to me straight away, I was getting there.

The major problems by the eighth week, with all this experience swilling away in my acting tank, were two elusive areas of Henry's experience. The first was war, and I tried to do something about this by reading Clausewitz, Sassoon, historical documents about the combat detail at Agincourt. I was very slowly beginning to picture the horrors of a hand-to-hand medieval combat. It was quite easy to get a graphic impression of what fighting could be like from people in the company. Sebastian Shaw, for instance, had been in the RAF during the Second World War, and his account of the terror of a 'night raid' was a chilling highlight of one of several fascinating rehearsal discussions.

But it was much more difficult to get my imagination around Henry's royal status, the isolation of his role as spiritual and military leader. Quite simply, what was it *like* being a king? As with war there was plenty of written material, but there was no one to talk to, no one with whom I could exchange ideas. In a welter of indulgent frustration I would bore my friends at the numerous suppers that accompanied my last weeks in London before the move to Stratford. Very early one morning, after a spectacularly verbose evening, my dinner party host rang me to say that he felt something might be done about my problem.

A week later I was motoring up the long gravel drive to Kensington Palace. After a week of meetings, I had been vetted and through several contacts had been given an introduction to the Prince of Wales. Getting the afternoon off rehearsal had been rather tricky, but I decided to abandon the notion of toothache and come clean with Adrian. A director of the *Royal* Shakespeare Company could hardly refuse such a request, and I swore him to secrecy. The heir to the throne did not wish to be plagued by the membership of Equity, all requesting advice on regal roles. I felt several bonds of allegiance: firstly to the chum who had helped organise it, to his friend, and, of course, to the Prince himself, who I felt must be fed up with continual minor betrayals.

My grubby green car came to a halt by the security hut, and the policeman waved me through. My God, they really did expect me. I walked to the front door without being ambushed by three hundred security guards and when the door opened the footman greeted me with, 'Mr Branagh?'

I waited downstairs in a room filled with Royal Wedding memorabilia. The footman who brought me a cup of tea explained that the trays, pictures and mugs were all gifts sent by members of the public, and that this was one way of using them. I wondered with alarm what exactly I was going to ask the heir to the throne, but the time for panicking was over, and I was shown upstairs and into the Prince's drawing-room where he shook my hand warmly, smiled and said, 'I really have no idea how I can help you, but please sit down, and let's have a chat.'

I felt an instant rapport. I had never encountered such an extraordinary and genuine humility. It would be all right.

'Well, sir, I know it seems rather strange. I'm not intending my Henry V to be an impersonation of you, but I simply wanted to explain some of my feelings about the character, particularly his role as king. They're not necessarily highly academic or intellectual observations, but as you're in a unique position to comment, I'd love to run them past you, and if you have anything to say about them I'd be most grateful. You don't *have* to say anything.'

I began Henry's spiritual checklist. It seemed to me that royalty involved the suppression of many facets of one's character. In Henry this meant (as has been proven by many productions) that the sense of humour which I felt belonged to the man was often missing, as was his latent violence, in fact, all the normal extremes of human behaviour which in ordinary mortals find their own balance but which in a pressurised monarch could emerge with even greater force. I wanted my Henry to display these unexpected qualities with tremendous intensity, and I felt that Shakespeare's text encouraged this view. Prince Charles concurred: yes, there was a tremendous pressure and temptation to be at times either very silly or very violent. As with most people, these impulses were resisted but the

142

underlying pressure was greater than most people would ever experience.

Henry's isolation was another fascinating area. Through the course of the play a number of betrayals take place: his 'bed-fellow', Lord Scroop, is discovered leading an assassination attempt; his former mentor, Falstaff, dies; and later still he is required to order the execution of another former drinking companion, Bardolph. His loneliness is intense and his hurt at the various betrayals and losses is very acute. I asked Prince Charles whether the various newspaper betrayals of events, dramatic and mundane, had changed him. Yes, it had, profoundly. And it had, as I suspected was true of Henry, produced an extraordinary melancholy. It was a sadness that could either produce bitterness or a more useful but painful wisdom, and Prince Charles had clearly developed the latter. He bore the inevitable bruises of his position with great courage, and although, sitting opposite him, I could detect the haunted look of responsibility, the very fact that he was speaking to me was an indication of his continuing desire to give people the benefit of the doubt.

Loneliness, however, was unavoidable. Henry makes one desperate attempt in the play to be like other men. During the famous night-time sequence, he walks among his men in disguise. The experience is extremely unsatisfactory: he wants to be one of them, but he can't be; he wants them to understand his position but they resist it. Had Prince Charles ever felt like doing the same? Yes, while he was at Cambridge he'd attempted to do the same thing, but the results were disastrous. By the end of the night-time sequence in *Henry V*, the young king's only comfort is the very certainty of his lifelong isolation. The young Hal had at least the taste of the Boar's Head life, but when he became king there could be no such contact with an ordinary existence.

There is little solace to be found in such remoteness. I believed that Henry's only real comfort could be his faith, and Prince Charles was in total agreement. Some kind of belief in God was the only practical way of living from day to day, it was the only way to deal with his position. This confirmed what I felt I should try to convey in Henry. I didn't wish to present Henry as a tortured martyr, but I did feel strongly that a complex psychological portrait had been set up by Shakespeare which included guilt, doubt and self-questioning. Prince Charles's comments were immensely helpful and I had the impression that he shared with Shakespeare's Henry a desire to strike a delicate balance between responsibility and compassion.

I left Kensington Palace on that grey March afternoon in considerably more awe than when I'd entered. My blind actor's ambition had emboldened me to undertake the meeting, but by the time I left I was aware of having met a quite remarkable man. He did not possess the same political power as Henry but his influence was considerable, his humility genuine and his desire to lead an honourable life was most striking. The taint of politics made Henry a much darker figure than Charles, but my abiding impression was that leadership could incorporate the finer spiritual attributes that, I felt, lay at the root of Henry's character. I had no desire to beg an audience's forgiveness for a man who had invaded another country on dubious pretexts and with enormous loss of life. They had to make up their own minds about the fascinating, enraging conflict between the ruthless killer and the Christian king. I continued to read about war and politics, but Prince Charles had enormously increased my understanding of many aspects of the role.

I had decided that I would live outside Stratford, for when I had visited the town during the 1982 season I had felt that the heavy workload of the actors and the presence of a whole army of tourists had created a kind of midsummer madness. I couldn't work *and* live in the same claustrophobic atmosphere. Alcester was about eight miles outside Stratford, and I found an idyllic country cottage with lots of room for visitors to come and restore my sanity. There was a large garden running down to a river and almost everything about the cottage and my life seemed lovely.

The first bleak Sunday evening brought its share of fear and loneliness, as I imagined myself ruining my career with a terrible performance as Henry, and living a lonely, loveless life. It was the first morning in Australia all over again. The seventh cavalry arrived that night in the form of a phone call from the actor Richard Easton, who was building a strong performance as the Constable of France in *Henry V*. He was giving a small dinner party at his flat in Stratford for a limited number of the new boys, and Boeuf Bourguignon-ed hospitality has never been so welcome. I drank too much red wine, told too many stupid stories, but went to bed in a pleasant oblivion. When I woke the cottage was already warmer and the first day's rehearsal in Stratford seemed slightly less intimidating.

This was our last week before technical rehearsals and at first my chief worry was about Adrian Noble. I have never seen anyone consume so many indigestion tablets – if digestive disorders are any guide to artistic ability then Adrian was a genius. When he wasn't correcting his stomach he was rubbing his eyes. He wore contact lenses and when he was wrestling with an idea his fingers would be pressed so violently into his eyes that I was terrified that the lenses would slip round the other side of the sockets.

The week was full of exciting new experiences. We were rehearsing in the 'Conference Hall', a huge room which had housed the original Stratford theatre that had burned down earlier in the century, and it was here, sixty years before, that Sebastian Shaw, our King of France, had played Romeo. The atmosphere was thick with ghosts and living memories of its illustrious past. Here for the first time, full of the excitement of Stratford and the adrenalin of the forthcoming opening, I tasted what the great speeches in the play could produce. Slowly the production was beginning to take off. I had been so engrossed in my own role that all the other elements of production had escaped my notice. I was aware, through costume fittings and drawings, that Bob Crowley was producing a brilliantly simple set, but not until the end of that first Stratford week did the whole thing start to come together.

The next big excitement was the arrival of the band. We rehearsed the musical cues out of sequence, and I remember with a thrill the sensation of hearing the end of one of my speeches accompanied by a great brass section:

> Cheerly to sea,
> Tarah, crash, boom, da dah.
> The signs of war advance.
> Badah, badum, beWAAAAH. (I nearly fainted)
> No King of England if not King of France.
> WAAAAAAAAAAHH WAAAAAAAAHH!!

Blimey, I thought, I wish I was watching this.

On the following Monday we began the technical rehearsal. We were falling behind schedule, as the rehearsal of lighting, sound and costume changes was a time-consuming affair. By the morning of the first preview on Thursday we had still not finished, and there was a grave danger of not having a dress rehearsal at all. This terrified me, as it was so long since we had 'teched' the first scenes that we were all in danger of forgetting everything. Adrian seemed to accept this as part of the process but my mounting terror made me throw a mini-wobbly. In a slightly shrill, hysterical falsetto I demanded the chance to run the part before facing an audience. Adrian breathed a heavy sigh. I wasn't the first queeny actor he'd run across. At three o'clock that afternoon we started our first dress rehearsal of the play. At 7.30 we did it again for the paying public. I went through the first performance in a daze. The first time you play a large classical role your energies are completely absorbed in how to get on and off the stage, where your costumes are, and how you can manage to drink a cup of tea during the first half. Remembering and acting the lines seem to come a poor second. Rehearsal room revelations, psychological detail, conversations with prospective monarchs are all out of the window while the old pro inside you is screaming, 'How do I get *off*, love?'

All was fine until we'd won the Battle of Agincourt. I was wandering o'er the battlefield looking suitably moved and about to go into the scene with Fluellen and Williams where Henry sets up a complicated plot involving the exchange of gloves and lasting several pages. This works very well if you are in possession of the gloves. Mine were supposed to be tucked into my belt, but weren't there. My crash course in Shakespearian paraphrase began there and then.

> Fluellen, . . . as I do remember me,
> I bethinkst myself that I did have some gloves
> For which it was my full intent
> That thou should'st with them work.
> But see alas they are not here,
> Nor know I when'st they be.

By this stage every actor at the Battle of Agincourt was regarding their monarch with new amazement. From off-stage the noise of scurrying stage management drifted onto the battlefield. There was no stopping me now – I'd have to get us out of this.

> Good Fluellen, although the gloves I do desire
> Be not here i' the field.
> My mind does't tell me of another pair
> That thou shoulds't find
> Were'st thou to look elsewhere.
> Be busy about this errand
> And return again I absolutely prithee.

146

Siòn Probert, who was playing Fluellen, had turned green. What was I talking about? This wasn't what he'd rehearsed. He ran off-stage and as I continued through the thick, interminable pause, marching around the battlefield, being (if it were possible) even more moved, I saw his arms waving up and down in the wings, and the Stage Manager whispering frantically, 'I haven't got any more fucking gloves.'

The moments passed and by this stage I had mourned individually over each of the Agincourt dead, and the shuddering shoulders of the English army told me that concentration was at an end. The air of perplexity coming off the audience was palpable. At last Sion ran back on carrying what looked like two motor-cycle gauntlets, and yelled,

> I have found thine gloves, my liege.

A moment before I had spotted the original pair lying amongst the dead bodies. I had just snatched them up ready to carry on with the scene when the mad Welshman rushed on. Now the audience really were confused.

> Well done, good fellow.
> Thou does't thy office fairly.
> But I have found another pair
> Which suiteth me more goodly.

Before I could wrench myself back onto the text I heard an audible 'Fuck me' from under Sion's breath. He clearly thought I'd done this on purpose. The rest of the show was performed on sheer adrenalin. The age that the gloves incident had seemed to take was clearly exaggerated by actually being part of it, but by the time I walked out of the theatre and to my car I was sure that the audience had not noticed.

I'd got through it, which was a huge relief, and Adrian was pleased. There was lots of work to do next day, but the reaction had been good and we'd got away with the one major embarrassment. As I opened the car door another vehicle drove past and the window was wound down. 'Superb, absolutely superb.'

That was nice. There, I knew we'd got away with it. They called again.

'Loved the gloves!'

As the previews continued I began to put my rehearsal ideas into practice and stopped worrying about whether the crown was on straight. On the Saturday afternoon before the preview matinée performance Adrian came into my dressing-room for his daily progress assessment. By this stage his eyes had been rubbed so hard the contact lenses must have been in his nostrils. God knows what his stomach was like – I kept a packet of Rennies on the dressing-room table just in case. We had our first real argument.

'Look, Ken . . . I think that er . . . I mean, the er . . . performance is certainly developing enormously er . . . but I do think that you must try less hard to er . . .'

'What?'

'. . . be liked.'

I was enraged. 'What do you mean?'

'Well, I think that um . . . specifically . . .'

'What? What is it?'

'I think you should cut your hair.'

'*What?*'

It turned out that my blond mop, on top of a glorious red and blue costume, was fighting the 'Dirty Harry' that we were trying to present. I was apparently looking too glamorous, although I found it very hard to believe that a short-assed, fat-faced Irishman could possibly give this impression. Still, I decided to be flattered and compromised my matinée idol look by applying my trusty Max Factor black pancake and that wonder of the world of modern coiffure, hair gel. The first application made me look like Al Jolson crossed with Jack the Ripper. Adrian intervened. 'I think you've taken me rather too literally, Ken.' A Henry that looked like the Boston Strangler wasn't going to work either. We did crack this look, but it took several performances. I have never really been any good at stage make-up. Before the photo-call for *Henry V* I made the fatal mistake of listening to a fellow actor who had watched part of the dress rehearsal from the gods. 'You're so fair, lovey. We can't see your eyes. You've got to fill in your eyebrows and use more mascara.' Never listen to advice like that. Always take a look from out front at other people first. As a result of all this I am now haunted by pictures of that production where I look like Joan Collins *and* Groucho Marx.

The audience reaction to the previews was mixed. Some people wanted their warrior king in red, white and blue with no inner doubts, while others wanted the play to come firmly down on the anti-war ticket. Very few could ignore the emotional impact of our production which, if nothing else, was distinguished by the sight of Branagh looking all of twelve in the title role.

The days during the last previews had been occupied with the usual process of persuading my mother to attend the opening. Both she and my father were very intimidated by the 'Royal Shakespearian Company' (as my father called it), but the major problem for Mother was the meal afterwards. As it was a special occasion I suggested we eat in the very grown-up Box Tree restaurant next to the theatre: there would be Mum and Dad and the rest of the family, David Parfitt and his girlfriend, Sue, Alistair Conquer and his wife.

'I can't have anything with sauces, son. I'd better not come, I'd let you down.'

I went into my familiar routine. 'You don't have to *have* anything with sauces.'

'I'll never be able to read the menu.'

'*I'll* read the menu.' I couldn't remember if it was in French, but I spoke even less than my mother, so we both had a problem. 'I'm sure they'll do you something plain.'

'Sure, that'd be embarrassing.'

'Do you want to bloody eat or not?'

'Don't shout at me, I'm not coming now.'

'I'm not shouting and yes, you are coming.'

Christ knows how many conversations it took before we established that my mother would come, but only if she wasn't forced to speak to anyone, and only if I sat next to her at dinner. The annoying thing was that I knew she would talk to *everyone*, enjoy herself hugely and be the star of the evening. At least it took my mind off the merry monarch.

It wasn't until months later that I realised, because people told me, quite how much tension had been flying round the Memorial Theatre on the night of the opening. Everyone was terrified that I would cock it up. There were over a hundred members of the press in the audience, and adrenalin was high. The RSC had taken a great risk, and were extremely tense, but fortunately I was insulated by my obsession with the part and with domestic catering arrangements. I was nervous, but it was a first night that I rather enjoyed. I don't think I was especially good, but somehow I didn't expect to be, the important thing was to get through it. I felt sure the production was rooted in the right soil and having planted myself, I assumed that it would take the full two years for the performance to fully grow. There were so many things to develop: my voice and speech, all the different aspects of the role, and I hoped that the critics would give me the benefit of the doubt.

The response from the packed Stratford auditorium was very enthusiastic, and backstage there was the usual hysteria. Adrian walked backwards into my dressing-room partly because he was drunk, but mostly, I'm sure, because his contact lenses had disappeared into his bloodstream. His internal organs were confused, but he was delighted, and within seconds it was a re-run of *Another Country*. The dressing-room was full of family and friends who were visibly relieved because, although it was Shakespeare, they had actually understood it. My dad offered the usual qualification. 'Mind you, son, we wouldn't know.'

In the restaurant my mother was presented with a plaice in some mysterious sauce which I managed to scrape off before she left the table. Although I enjoyed the meal, I probably expended more energy on the post-show domestics than on the actual performance. 'Twas ever thus. The next day I did not rise at 6 am to buy the newspapers but allowed Pat Marmont to choose the nicest remarks and read them to me. The reviews were obviously mixed but the general consensus seemed to be that this was a rich production, sometimes controversial, which would only get better as time went on. Some critics thought I was over-parted, and some thought I over-acted, but several thought I was good, and I convinced myself that we had got away with it so that I could relax and start enjoying the season.

I had built in a rather clever tactic to relieve me of possible post-opening depression. I had twelve days off (the one holiday I would have that year) while *The Merchant of Venice* opened and before *Golden Girls* started rehearsal, and very generously, the RSC gave me permission to fulfil a yearning that I had had for some time. I checked on all the flights, allowed a day or two for delays, and celebrated my first Stratford opening by holidaying for six whole days in Australia. It seemed mad to everyone but for me it was the perfect way to put such an intense experience into perspective. The tonic of seeing friends and the brevity of my stay removed jet lag almost completely. Most of my Australian friends had only the faintest idea of what the Royal Shakespeare Company was, and by the time I returned I had the very healthy sensation that I'd just done a rather nice little play in the provinces which would be seen by few folk and was nothing to get hot and bothered about. By the time I finished at the RSC, I realised that I needed a trip to Australia every ten days.

On my return, there were plenty of things to keep me occupied. Kensington Palace had asked me to provide four seats for a performance of *Henry V* for Prince Charles and his guests. While I was about it, I booked three seats directly behind for my parents and sister who I knew would be thrilled if the great visit actually came to pass. I had sent the tickets off and was sworn to secrecy, but on the day before the magic date I was worried that I had heard nothing, and I decided to check with the House Manager. Perhaps security had been in touch with him. I asked him rather gingerly, 'I think we may have some VIPs coming tomorrow night. I wondered if you had heard anything?'

'Anyone in particular? The Prime Minister? The Queen?'

'Not exactly.' They clearly thought I was mad. Never mind. Early the next morning the phone rang and the shrieking voice of the House Manager announced, 'He's coming, he's coming. Oh God, oh God, the theatre's not clean. What'll we do?'

My parents informed me that the reactions of the audience when their Royal Highnesses took their seats were an entertainment in themselves. The visit was entirely private, so the surprise was great for everyone, and the news spread like wildfire front and backstage. At the beginning of the second half the stalls audience were waiting down at the front, staring up at the balcony to get a view of the Royal return, and in the upper balcony, people had crowded down to the front to do the same thing. Instead, they were faced with my mum and dad who seemed to take all this attention in their stride. Charles and Diana returned and the place was an uproar of cheering and whistling. One of the first speeches in the second half was Henry's 'Upon the King' soliloquy which deals, among other things, with the lack of privacy in royal life. From the audience that had just robbed Prince Charles of this very thing there was an almost audible shudder. The penetration of Shakespeare's lines was chilling.

I spoke to the Prince and his wife afterwards. He seemed much moved by the evening and said as much in a letter which he wrote some weeks later. Not only did he feel a very personal connection with the story, but both he and Princess Diana were both fascinated by the process of acting, by what you actually *feel* when you're being angry, sad, or whatever. It was a satisfying and all too brief conversation that confirmed our rapport and intensified my admiration for the man who was about to fight his way through the ten thousand-strong crowd that had gathered outside the theatre since news of the visit had swept round Stratford.

Golden Girls was a new play by Louise Page, which no one in the Company seemed to know very much about. The first actors conversations concerning such a project were always about what part we were playing, and jocular-modest was the dominant tone in these exchanges.

'So what are you playing?' I would ask.

'Well, the characters aren't fully developed yet. All I know is I'm playing the lead. What about you?'

'Well, actually I think *I'm* playing the lead.'

I asked around. Jimmy Yuill, Josette Simon, Polly James, Kate Bufferey. They were all playing the lead, and that made nine of us in total. I didn't know what the story was but it was supposed to be about athletics – clearly it concerned a nine-headed monster who'd been chosen to run for England.

The first day's rehearsal arrived and there was no script. It did make an appearance in unfinished bits which we all took away to digest, and for the rest of the day the Stratford phone lines were red hot. After the initial scouring of the text to assess the quantity of a character's lines, there were several irate telephone calls to Barry – it'll have to change, I'm not playing this. The usual stuff. Then there were the demure casual calls from folks who had enormous parts, saying, this is really very good, I'm so glad she sees me like this. I came very low in the lines count, but I could hardly complain after *Henry V*. I was looking forward to finding out about athletics and working with a group of really strong actresses. The play turned out to be the story of a British women's relay team and their Olympic adventures, and the plot was full of drug scandals, blackmail, and love affairs. The rehearsal period had begun and all of us got on with the often indulgent process of researching the part.

In this case, it meant athletics training. Jimmy Yuill and I were the male athletes, he the strangely named 'Laces', a trainer, and I, if you can believe it, a 100-metre sprint champion. The play was to be performed in Stratford's smaller theatre, the Other Place, and with seating for only 250 and the audience too close for comfort, vanity insisted that we get ourselves into a sufficiently impressive physical condition. Like myself, Jimmy enjoyed a pint and, unlike myself, smoked himself stupid. For both of us, measures had to be drastic. While the girls pursued sprint training, Jimmy and I enlisted the help of Brian Blessed, the Company's fitness fanatic, who agreed to take us through a training programme that would leave us looking like the young Olympians we needed to be. Cramped together in the front room of Brian's Stratford cottage, Jimmy and I wheezed our way through interminable press-ups and sit-ups and pull-ups and definitely no let-ups. Brian simply smiled all the way through these pre-rehearsal and lunchtime agonies.

A favourite torture was the end-of-work-out run. Brian's cottage was close to Stratford racecourse and strapping weights to our ankles and wrists he would send us off through the spring mud to run twice round the circuit. After these runs we would arrive back at Brian's cottage, me exhausted and panting, and Jimmy a hospital case, and despite the hot bath and sweet tea which Brian would provide, nothing could make us recover sufficiently to do anything other than fall fast asleep during any rehearsal that followed. From then on we decided that living the part had to stop and acting ought to take over. Arnold Schwarzenegger had nothing to fear from us.

Rehearsals were difficult. I felt very sorry for Barry Kyle, who made me aware for the first time of the pressures of the RSC timetable on its directors. On the Saturday before rehearsals started he had just finished a production and immediately after *Golden Girls* opened he would begin work in London on another. For Barry and for almost all his fellow directors, this was a familiar schedule. Although he worked like a Trojan he was quite clearly exhausted, and the behaviour of the cast didn't help matters. Louise's re-writes were arriving very slowly, and everyone was desperately throwing their weight around and implying that they might leave at any moment. The actors felt betrayed, Louise felt persecuted, and Barry, I'm sure, felt both; this combination of circumstances had contributed to exacerbating the already difficult task of bringing a new play to life. It was my first experience of an overtly combative rehearsal period, and although there was no malice in the air, there were very strong differences of opinion.

I wish that Barry and I had had a difference of opinion about my accent. In my attempts to give definition to what seemed an under-written part, I decided to use a Geordie brogue. I thought that the success of the many athletes from Gateshead would make this sound familiar, realistic and topical, and I convinced myself and Barry that I had a good ear for these things. It wasn't always totally under my control. In the night-time sequence of *Henry V* I had used a Welsh accent in order to underline the king's disguise. We had several real Welshmen in the Company, I did the research and became a real dyed-in-the-leek Welshman, although, as one reviewer pointed out, 'In the night-time sequence Mr Branagh is effortlessly a Geordie.'

It seemed that all I had to do was think I was playing my athlete Welsh and it would come out as the Gateshead hero. Sometimes, in truth, it did, but more often than not the accent would arrive at Gateshead via New Delhi and Australia. Well, athletics is an international language.

With only days to go we received the last scenes of the play, and many of us were still confused by the convolutions of the plot. I still don't know whether the leading athlete had taken the drugs or not, or whether the 'drug' was actually a placebo. Fortunately by the time we reached this point in the play my character was cracking up and it was quite conceivable that he had no idea what was going on. The breakdown I had to act was a tricky affair: I found it quite impossible to give the necessary emotional weight and retain any intelligibility in the accent – it veered all over the place – you either had Hamlet in tears, or what sounded like an inexplicable Peter Sellers mumbling 'Goodness gracious me.'

With confidence in our work at its lowest ebb we started to preview, and with the divine logic that operates in such cases, we realised immediately that we had a hit on our hands. Barry had provided an ingenious production that miraculously conveyed the smell and feel of a real athletics stadium, all in the confines of that tiny tin hut. The relay race finale, complete with strobe lighting and *musique concrète*, was a real theatrical coup. Audiences came away as excited as if they'd been to an Olympic meeting. In the course of our self-indulgent rehearsals we had lost all sense of the play's values, and while our reaction to the play's success was still tempered by these feelings, we were mightily relieved that it was a success and that we could work away at it as we played it through the year. I had learned a valuable lesson about not getting bogged down in re-hearsal, and that it was essential to be as honest about the play as possible. It had also left me genuinely worried about the welfare, spiritual and artistic, of Barry in particular and the RSC directorate

154

in general. I thought, quite simply, that they must all be knackered, and that good work was difficult under such conditions.

With *Henry V* and *Golden Girls* now both in the Stratford repertoire I was performing three or four nights a week. When *Golden Girls* opened, there was one day free before rehearsals started for *Hamlet*, and I had barely caught my breath from seeing Tony Sher's dazzling Richard III the night before when I found myself back in the Conference Hall with the five other *Hamlet* principals discussing our preliminary thoughts with Ron Daniels. This was the beginning of two or three days of advance rehearsal before the main six week block, and after that there would be a whole month of previews – a comparatively luxurious preparation time.

Roger Rees had returned to the RSC to play Hamlet, and it was his first major role with the Company since his huge success as Nicholas Nickleby. Brian Blessed was Claudius, Frank Middlemas was Polonius, and Frances Barber and Nicholas Farrell, who had both received great acclaim in that season's production of *Camille*, were joining the *Hamlet* company to play Ophelia and Horatio. The final member of this group was Virginia McKenna, who was joining the RSC to play Gertrude. I was particularly glad of Brian Blessed's presence in the group. A large man in every sense, he concealed a tremendous warmth and tranquillity under a surface gruffness and apparent coarseness designed to keep people at arm's length. He is totally without malice, and his outrageous humour would be a marvellous counterbalance as we set to work on this forbidding and complex tragedy.

It was a pleasantly informal way to start work on this great play. A director, sometimes faced with a full RSC company of perhaps thirty actors, can often feel that a lecture is required on the first day, a talk which will give a detailed analysis of the approach he or she is going to take. Often brilliant, this technique can be very dangerous, and I have seen it take up the whole of the day, when, however dazzling the analysis, the company tend to be more worried about costumes and sets and other apparently mundane matters. Ideas can also become too easily fixed at an early stage if rehearsals are forced to fit in with a rigidly preconceived idea of the play. Preparatory work and a view of the play is absolutely necessary but, as with actors, the degree of flexibility required is enormous.

This small group took all pressure away and it was one of the luxuries of RSC resources that this overtime session could take place.

Our first talks threw up some fascinating issues. At first we all listened dutifully to Ron, who talked with great passion (what else?) about the three levels of the play. I wasn't quite sure which levels they were or if there were only three but it seemed a useful way to start talking about it. Brian Blessed was determined to be less rarefied, he'd come to the RSC very humble about his relationship to the classics, and he was a mature, successful actor who still wanted very much to learn. He was always asking, in a very direct way, 'What are the rules of Shakespeare?' A big one that.

On our first morning he offered his first thoughts on Claudius. Up to this point everyone had been very timid in the face of Ron's intellect. Brian started to develop some of Ron's ideas about the character, but quickly reverted to a rather more dynamic and instinctive approach.

'The thing is Ron, I believe that . . . basically, when you look at this man and, you know, begin to wonder what makes him tick . . .'

'Yes?'

Brian was clearly burning to say it. He shot a quick glance at Virginia who sat beaming at him with her English rose fragility. He decided to plunge in.

'Well, the thing is . . . he just wants to fuck her.' I clenched my buttocks on Virginia's behalf. Although Virginia is not at all prudish, this was her first day at the RSC and her first experience of Brian's rehearsal style. I adored Brian, but I sensed this was perhaps not the best opening line, however true it might be about Claudius. 'He just can't keep his bloody hands off her. In the palace, in the garden, in the bloody kitchen. He's wild for her, she's in his blood and every time he sees her he wants to give her one.'

It seemed that Brian had finished. I looked for relief on Virginia's face. I thought we were over the worst.

'And the thing is . . .' – oh, Christ – 'she fucking *loves* it.'

I was ready to leap up and catch Virginia when she fell off her chair. Brian was unstoppable. 'Old Hamlet couldn't get it up. She hasn't had a decent fuck in years and here comes this bloke, her brother-in-law, who is a fucking stud and she cannot resist. She's just the same, she wants it every hour of the bloody day.'

By this time Ron Daniels had broken into a cold sweat. Brian's monologue had come out with his familiar all-embracing energy. This would not be a weak Claudius. Brian finally rounded off his character assessment. 'I mean, that's got to be it. A great big unstoppable plonker . . . I mean I think that's part of it . . .' He looked around amiably asking for agreement. 'I mean, I don't know what you feel, Virginia?'

'I think it's time for a cup of tea.'

Well done, Ron. It was a helpful break, and it helped to forge a very strong friendship between Brian and Virginia who, incidentally, were united in their advocacy of animals' rights. Brian's approach has its advantages.

The following Monday was the first full day's rehearsal with the entire company, and it revealed the curious advantages and disadvantages of the great RSC machine. Before us we had detailed costume designs, a set model, and an explanation from Ron about how everything would work. I was very happy with my Laertes costume but I couldn't help wondering whether this was the most effective production process. A part of me looked at the costume and thought, 'So that's how I have to play it.' Actors want it both ways: they'd like enough time to come up with ideas for costumes and props, but at the same time they resent providing the input for a director who has not arrived with sufficient ideas. The RSC had a huge staff, an enormous number of productions, and it simply wasn't practical or economic to make lots of last-minute decisions about production details. Advance work had to be done and that preparation could be constricting for the actors, who had to accept that certain decisions had already been made.

When I was playing Hamlet at RADA, the director was quoted as saying to the actor playing Claudius, who was rehearsing the Laertes plotting scene, 'We've really just got to get on with this as quickly as possible. All this stuff with Claudius and Laertes is where the audience are simply waiting for Hamlet to come back on again.' Well, not exactly, but I know what he means.

My Laertes, of course, would be different. The great idea arrived in week two: Laertes was mad. It was as simple as that, and I couldn't understand why no one had spotted it before. Nearly four hundred years of Shakespearian acting had gone by, and it was my revelation which would change the accepted view of Laertes.

It took three weeks of foaming, twitching and yelling to realise that this might perhaps not work. The play does deal with madness to a great extent, but so many of the other characters are so much madder, that poor old Laertes gets left behind. Nevertheless the flirtation with this idea did yield positive results. I wasn't mad but I did manage to get in cross, annoyed, perplexed and 'Blimey, all my family are dead – I'd better kill Hamlet'. This led me to the great discovery for the previews: Laertes was thick, as the proverbial plank, and that's why he was unstable, frightened, aggressive and finally vulnerable. He was a little man surrounded by great men and events that were way beyond his comprehension. With my typical leanings to excess, for a week or so Laertes resembled the Peter Sellers character in *Being There*.

Ron went along with all this, and showed remarkable patience, as did Virginia and Brian who never knew what was going to hit them when Laertes returned from Paris. For a while Frances Barber thought we should change parts: she could revenge her father and I could go and drown in the weeping brook. Silliness fell away as previews started. Roger was producing quite brilliant things as Hamlet and in its early stages the production had great clarity of narrative and tremendous commitment from the cast. My continuing experience of playing Henry was enormously helpful, it had increased my vocal power and my new confidence in playing the role was so marked that I had a few days of delayed shock and anxiety at the thought of how rough the performance must have been when we opened. Thank God we can't feel everything at once.

Hamlet opened to a divided press who ran the usual gamut of opinions about the production and performances. I had some good mentions and received further careers advice. 'Mr Branagh cannot speak the verse. He is a resolutely modern actor.' I rather liked the second bit. Traditional *and* contemporary, that's what I long to be.

Love's Labour's Lost started rehearsal before *Hamlet* had finished previewing – such was the increasingly frenetic pace of the Stratford season. The day began at 10, six days a week, and there would be rehearsal until 5.30, and at 7.30 most of the Company on any one night would have a show to do. At this stage my nights off – the nights *The Merchant of Venice* was playing – were increasingly rare. But not as rare as a visit from Trevor Nunn, with Terry Hands, the joint artistic director of the RSC.

The great day came in the middle of the season. The entire Company gathered in the Conference Hall. It was the first time I'd seen this man whose work I so admired, and I was desperate for him to see *Henry V*. Terry Hands had already made a visit and had been most kind and encouraging about the performance. I learnt a great deal from Trevor's performance that day. He is unquestionably a star. He sat leaning forward in his chair, speaking quietly in that warm, honeyed voice, and within five minutes the entire Company were leaning forward and straining to hear him. The impression was of a room of worshippers. Everyone was afraid to move in case they missed something in Trevor's address which took on more and more the feel of a quiet religious chant.

He spoke of this as a 'confessional'. He was well aware of his absence from the Company and knew that many of us felt hurt. Things would change. The whole speech was completely beguiling. He seemed, as they say, a regular guy. He talked of his hopes for the Company, his plans for the new musical *Les Miserables*, which he hoped very much would include some of us, and as far as his failure to see the work at Stratford was concerned, he was determined to put that right. His triumphant finale was pitched to the mesmerised audience in a tone of quiet, Martin Luther King intensity. Trevor 'had a dream', and that dream appeared to be to see all the Stratford shows within a fortnight. I imagine that subsequently he woke up and found other things to do. The next time I saw Trevor was twelve months later. Still dreaming, I presume.

The idealism I had felt on joining the RSC had been severely eroded, and many other actors felt the same way. Part of the problem was that the system raised expectations which were sure to be disappointed – the tone and substance of a Terry Hands speech, right at the beginning of the season in a London Company meeting, was built on the premise that we were one big family. This notion seemed to be the legacy of an RSC philosophy which began in the early sixties, based on the experience of a small, close-knit group of actors and other artists who came under very personal control and concern from the then artistic director, Peter Hall. It was an ideal situation in many ways: there was just the one Stratford theatre, and there was a much smaller number of productions played for a much shorter season. The tradition of artistic paternalism that Trevor and Terry wanted to continue was much easier in those days. Things were more manageable, and actors' commitments would be for periods of months, not years. When I joined the RSC there were four permanent theatres, a fifth about to start building and a sixth in preparation.

The physical growth of the Company reflected its success, and the highlights of this amazing development were the stuff of my student reading. However, the Company philosophy did not seem to have developed in the same way over the last ten years. It simply wasn't possible for Terry or Trevor to lead the Company in the way they had done – it was too big, it was dispersed geographically, creating major logistical problems, and laid a huge burden on the directors themselves. The system had become highly pressurised and enormous, and it struck me as wrong to encourage actors to expect an old-fashioned paternalism from joint artistic directors who did not have time to implement this.

Disenchanted RSC stalwarts talked with regret of the old days when you could talk to Trevor at any time about anything: the part, the play, or the rent you were paying on your cottage. The acting company seemed to require qualities from its leadership that could not be supplied. The directorship, by the same token, felt aggrieved, I think, at the lack of understanding on the part of the actors. In response to all this confusion the actors weren't exactly in a state of revolution, but they were, for better or worse during this time of intense change in the Company, beginning to assert themselves. At times it seemed closer to school with the actors as the stroppy sixth-formers and the directors as the misunderstood teachers, and both sides could assume these roles with depressing ease.

Next on the agenda was *Love's Labour's Lost* and, once again, Barry Kyle was being stretched to the limit. He did a magnificent job with a collection of increasingly argumentative actors, among whom I was chief. By this stage I had lost all perspective of the genuine advantages and luxuries that the RSC enjoyed, and I seemed to notice only the negative elements. My best interests were for the quality of the work, but the atmosphere resembled the claustrophobic self-obsessed world of drama school at its worst. Instead of assessing the quality of the excellent designs for *Love's Labour's Lost* I became exercised by the fact that everything had been decided beforehand. I did *not* want to wear a red waistcoat as the King of Navarre. To the management I must have seemed like a spoiled child.

This foot-stomping was partly induced by the particular atmosphere in Stratford at the end of the season. Like the directors, we too were absolutely knackered. The world began and ended in this strange, isolated town. There was no single person to talk to about the way things were, so we fought it out among ourselves. God knows what we expected of an artistic director: a nanny/psychiatric nurse/estate agent/mega-talent, that was all.

Love's Labour's Lost was warmly reviewed. It had the benefit of a wonderful Berowne from Roger Rees and a very strong group of women. I was way over the top as the King of Navarre – 'Benny Hill', said one fan, which was fair enough. I became very depressed by the whole thing, a feeling that was shared by many others in the company, although the reviews and the response of the audiences were very good. Many of us felt we could do much better. It wasn't just an end-of-season disillusionment, but it was a mixture of anger and sadness at our mutual complicity with a dangerous smugness that was developing in the Company. Somehow this big machine wasn't working.

All these confused reactions were poured into a one-act play called *Tell Me Honestly* which I wrote for the Company's innovative fringe season in Newcastle, and had its première in March, 1985.

David Parfitt, a Geordie himself, was in Newcastle and helped me with the show, and with the London transfers. We were building a small library of information about printing and posters, budgets and publicity, and we were gaining real satisfaction from this degree of connection to the work. It was referred to as an in-house satire, as I had based what loose structure there was on the end-of-year interviews that each actor had with Terry Hands. The piece was never meant to be malicious or accusatory, but I wanted to find through comedy a way of pointing out what seemed to be going wrong. The blame, such as it was, for Company uneasiness lay with everyone, but not everyone saw the joke. Luckily, this did not prevent the play from transferring to London or from transferring yet again for a limited season to the Donmar Warehouse Theatre. The very act of writing, directing and producing the piece with my fellow actors was in itself a way of understanding what it was we were rebelling against.

Tell Me Honestly described the desire, encouraged by the Company, to be more involved on every level and the frustration felt at not being able to achieve this in co-operation with the management. Many company members felt that they could offer more to the Company than just their basic skills as actors, but the system could not cope with their needs. My appetite for involvement, for real participation, was far stronger than any ambition simply to stay with the Company in order to play leading roles.

The Company management was perplexed by my attitude. Why couldn't I just shut up? Why couldn't we all just shut up and stop being ungrateful? This antagonism emerged in a protracted pay dispute distinguished by unreasonableness on both sides, with the RSC threatening to take *Henry V* out of the repertoire, making me certain that I was being singled out for special punishment. I threatened to resign, and finally the Company made an application to a special Trust Fund in order to find the nominal extra sum.

The whole episode depressed me no end. During the long months of this dispute the prospect of my leaving the Company at the end of the Newcastle season was both real and terrifying. I was not a fully established actor, and I was afraid that this new bolshiness would haunt me and stop me working ever again. My parents and friends begged me to give in, and I tortured myself about whether it was right to persist. In the end, when I got what I wanted, there was no sense of victory at all. Terry Hands' last minute farcical intervention over the Trust Fund was the final straw. I felt I was working for a Company that didn't really need me, and that if it weren't for the interruption it would have caused to the London performance schedules, I would have been out on my ear. To my great disappointment no single director had intervened in the dispute. I felt abandoned and it was clear that we were not agreed on the expectations of what the Company wanted from me and what I wanted from it.

The opportunist in me simply got on with things. I had the chance to play *Henry V* in London in a marvellous production, and it might establish me so that I would have enough weight to put my money where my grumbling mouth was. Through that Barbican season I was already planning a production of *Romeo and Juliet* in which I would play Romeo. I would have to direct it as well, as I was very interested in the play as a whole, and I would use the production to experiment with the size of company and working methods that my experience was telling me was necessary – an attempt to return, if you like, to the model of the early RSC. *When* I could do this was quite another matter.

Thanks to the RSC's regular employ I was able to meet a monthly mortgage payment, buy a flat, and protect myself forever from the north-west London underworld. I went dutifully through the Barbican season causing as little trouble as possible and observing the strange phenomenon of the RSC's London transfers. After the London first night of *Henry V* I compared the notices with those of the Stratford opening: despite the decidedly mixed tone of the original reviews the new set welcomed this as the 'acclaimed production'. They talked of it having already garnered 'raves'. In truth the production had grown enormously and my own performance was immeasurably improved. We played 139 performances in total, and only after 120 performances and fourteen months did I feel that I was actually beginning to embody the role in the fullest way. The quest to conquer Henry had been very difficult but very exhilarating, and like Hamlet, I wanted to return to it as soon as possible.

There were no improvements in my Laertes or King of Navarre – a good performance gets better, a bad performance gets worse. Laertes had been mad and then thick, now he was just boring. Against all my better judgement the King of Navarre did end up rather too often being a return to my gratuitous clowning.

Corpsing had not improved, and I let myself down repeatedly. A clutch of angry reprimands used to hound me out of the Barbican:

'I think it's *disgusting!*'

'It's *not* what we're here for.'

'Young man, it is simply not good enough, and neither are you.'

It was getting harder to laugh.

On performance 138 of *Henry V* at the Barbican the word went round: 'he' was in. I wondered who 'he' was? The Shah of Iran? Ronald Reagan? Donald Duck? No, Trevor. Trevor was in. I wasn't sure why. I knew that some of the Company had written to *Jim'll Fix It* asking to meet him, and perhaps this was his response. Well, my time was nearly up at the RSC and he wasn't going to get away with catching the penultimate performance of a show that had opened the previous Stratford season. No, not without a piece of my mind. I wasn't going to be 'Trev'd', the famous charm would not work with yours truly. No way.

Dressing Room One, Barbican. Two minutes after curtain down. I'm just taking a shirt off when there's a knock at the door – right, here I go. I turned round to vent my spleen, but I could no longer see or hear. I had been enveloped in Trevor's hair and beard and deafeningly loud in my right ear was an enormous vowel sound which turned out to be, 'Huuuuuuuuuuuuuuuuugely enjoyable.'

I tried to speak, but it was impossible. Eventually he let go of my hand, and stared intently at me as if I was a long lost brother. If it were possible he got more 'ooooo's into the next repetition: 'Really . . . huuuuuuuuuuuuuuuuuuuuugely enjoyable.'

I didn't dare speak. Despite the innocuous remark he looked as though he was going to cry. Oh. Hello. Here comes the big one. He was pumping my hand now as if he were leaving for the Front, definitely on the edge of a breakdown. The subtext was 'I'm worthless. I'm no one, but I will just try and say these things to you, a genius.' The body language was pure Uriah Heep. Martin Luther King returned for the closing lines. 'May I just say (pause. I thought he was going to fall over.) . . . may I just say that it is my very great ambition to work . . . with you (he started to move backwards) . . . really . . . (one hand on the door) . . . I really mean that . . . (fingers waving was all I could see) . . . Byeeee!!' The whole thing had taken a minute and a half.

Yes, I'd been 'Trev'd.'

In September 1985 I gave my last Laertes at the Barbican and took my leave of the Company. I felt some sadness but was certain of the wisdom of the move. Just before leaving, Terry Hands took me to lunch. He'd been to see *Tell Me Honestly* and I think had taken genuine note of all the actor-power that had manifested itself in this Company. He was also very perceptive about my performance of Henry V, and identified half a dozen things that would be tremendously useful to take into my next attempt at the role. There was no doubting the man's talent, and I regretted not having worked with him. He asked me straight out when I would like to rejoin the Company and what I would like to do.

'Direct and play in *Romeo and Juliet* with a company of my own choosing.'

He replied, 'Let me give you one piece of advice: don't. Firstly it'll ruin your own acting. Secondly, it'll never work. Ian McKellen's tried running actors' companies three times and still hasn't got it right. Thirdly, why don't you do it with us?'

'What?'

'We will give you your own company within the RSC, and you will have absolute choice over designers and directors, even stage management. What do you say?'

I tried not to look too shocked. 'Well, this is amazing, Terry. We must talk about it.'

I left the lunch table and never heard another word from Terry on the subject. If this was to be anything more than fantasy, I would have to do it on my own.

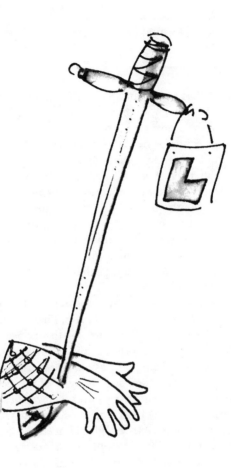

SEVEN

'O, brave new world'
THE TEMPEST

It seemed that I was not able to function well in large institutions. The RSC had given me marvellous opportunities, for which I was very grateful, and yet I left the Company with feelings of great frustration. I had enjoyed the excitements of rehearsals with Adrian, Barry and Ron, and the blaze of acting energy manifest in the fringe season had been exhilarating. However I felt that the size and merciless timetable of productions was working strongly against a consistently high quality in the work, and the burgeoning bureaucracy created tensions and fears among the members of the Company that were far from healthy. I had wanted so much to be a part of the RSC, but I was becoming increasingly unhappy, and decided to leave behind the impotent rage that had eaten me up for the last part of my time there.

There was no point in continuing to fight that system. I would go it alone. I knew the play I wanted to do. I had the energy and I had the passion, but what I didn't have was the money or the courage. On entering the big wide world I realised how much of my griping had been bolstered by being professionally secure; once the protection of the institution was gone so was most of my bottle. It would take something else to convert my natural cowardice and desire to work into a resolve sufficiently strong to achieve something.

In any case after all that raging, I needed something easier to do. Something quite different from the broader sense of responsibility that I felt at the RSC. I was also tired. I lacked the bravery of the McDiarmids. D. H. Lawrence came to the rescue. It was the centenary of his birth and Central Television had commissioned Alan Plater to write a ninety-minute television film about his early life.

I read the script and rediscovered my love for Lawrence the man. *Coming Through* covered the period up to his elopement with Frieda Weekley at the age of twenty-seven. This was the Lawrence I loved: young, passionate, brutally honest, intensely romantic and unafraid of the feminine side of his nature. In simple terms it was the story of a

166

bright lower-middle-class boy who had to come to terms with a talent that would cause him to leave his background, and his bewilderment and excitement at falling deeply and passionately in love with a married woman. I knew this period of Lawrence's life intimately. His letters are wonderfully honest and his literary work during this period reflects his emotional development. An immense amount of written material is available to flesh out the marvellous portrait provided by Alan, and for the first time in ages I could steep myself totally in a part. There was no worrying about designs or verse-speaking or the abuse of resources; I was simply being paid very well to play a part on film which offered me every opportunity for research into a subject which I loved.

During the two months of preparation for the part I lost two stone – I was determined to lose the look of a cubist cherub and produce the gaunt Lawrentian cheeks. It worked, and I looked as ill as Young Bert. I read everything that Lawrence wrote during this period, and I visited Eastwood where Lawrence lived and I explored the houses that his family had occupied. I went to the British Sound Archive and listened to recordings of Frieda Weekley talking about 'Lorenzo'. Contemporary accounts of Lawrence were invaluable: girlfriends, teachers, and colleagues all had impressions of the man which were often quite different from the image of the tortured intellectual. 'Bert', as they all called him, was wonderfully sunny, a great mimic, and marvellous company. I wanted, as Alan Plater did, to present *this* rather than the vituperative woman-hater.

The director, Peter Barber-Fleming, was highly sympathetic to this approach, which made the whole experience delightful. The cast included Alison Steadman, Norman Rodway, and Helen Mirren as Frieda. The scenes between the two lovers were quite beautifully written, and the final result was a very moving and informative film, of which I was very proud. We'd spent six weeks filming it, Peter had spent six months working on it. There was one showing, late at night on ITV, and it has never been heard of since.

TV was obviously what I was destined for. Two weeks after the Lawrence finished I began work on Ibsen's *Ghosts*, with a small cast made up of heroes: Judi Dench as Mrs Alving, Michael Gambon as Pastor Manders, Freddie Jones and Natasha Richardson, and they were all terrible gigglers. The rehearsals seemed to go in waves of intense creative work, followed by debilitating fits of giggles, usually initiated by Gambon or Dench who were always able to stop laughing long before me. Ibsen can be melodramatic at the best of times, but *Ghosts* had more than its fair share of semi-comic curtain lines. After a morning of going mad from syphilis it didn't take much to turn me into a hysterical wreck.

Judi's delight in this laughter seemed to be bound up in her greatness as an actress. She seemed able to embrace every emotion whole-heartedly. There is an amazing, child-like quality in her acting which allows her to cry or laugh with the full abandon of a child. She assumes nothing, doubts herself constantly, but without indulgence, and seemed often genuinely pained at what she regarded as her inadequacy for the part. Although she could be strong and commanding in life, she retains great humility and vulnerability. In a part that offered her marvellous scope for her extraordinary gifts I experienced great acting at first-hand.

Then there was Gambon. If it were possible, Michael is actually wickeder than Judi, a deadpan teddy-bear who is merciless in twinkling at other people while keeping a straight face himself. During the recording, Elijah Mojinsky, the director, wanted us to perform a short dinner sequence. A silent thirty second piece that showed the desolate supper in the Alving household. They would not be recording sound, but the later cut version would be accompanied by music and would be used to suggest the passage of time. All he wanted was for Natasha, as the maid, to serve each of us in turn while a tracking camera took a close up of each gloomy Ibsen face. Michael was served first while on his close-up. The difficulties of concentration for this scene that Ibsen hadn't written were considerable. It was the end of a long recording day. We were all tired. Tough.

'Action' was called, and we solemnly began our desultory improvised dialogue. Natasha began, leaning over Gambon.

'Would the Pastor like some potatoes?'

Gambon replied. 'Yes, I'll have eleven please.'

The face remained impassive. Then as the camera passed him he bent double over his soup and when he looked up at me the tears were rolling down his face. Judi's close-up was next and although the shot revealed only head and shoulders I could see that her hands were white, gripping the table-cloth for dear life. Once the camera passed her she threw her hands up to her face and stuffed a serviette in her mouth. By the time the camera reached me I was watching two Titans of the English theatre in silent convulsions. I was helpless and it was too late. I could no more have produced a straight face than

168

swim the Channel. They tried for several minutes drying my eyes and asking Judi and Michael to turn round. It was no use, every time the magic word 'Action' was called I could hear the tell-tale whimpers from Dench and Gambon and then I was lost. After five minutes the Floor Manager said, 'It's absolutely no use. Mr Branagh, the director has asked me to tell you that you must get down from the table and leave the studio. Goodnight.'

The air had turned chill. I started the long walk across the studio like the naughty dog in a Lassie film. This was it, the end of my career. We all met in the make-up room, Dench, Richardson, Gambon and me swathed in shame. The next day we were very good indeed.

I still felt compelled to be more than just an actor, and I felt almost guilty at the fun I had in making Coming Through and Ghosts. For some time I had had an idea about an Irish topic that I wanted to write about, and the experiment of Tell Me Honestly had encouraged me to write again. With Puritan zeal at its height I spent the evenings after rehearsals for Ghosts in the kitchen of my Camberwell flat writing the first draft of Public Enemy. A collection of different ideas had come together, and the play was an attempt to focus on several issues: the effects of long-term unemployment, the influence of the media, organised crime, religious fervour, the psychology of killers. All of this was channelled into a narrative concerning a Belfast lad with a Jimmy Cagney fixation. I knew it wasn't King Lear, but it was my first attempt at a serious bit of writing. I showed it to a few friends, confirmed for myself the amount of work required for a second draft and despatched it to my bottom drawer.

By the end of 1985 I was exhausted, and the New Year began with a month in Australia, for a holiday on which I intended to write. This time I set out to write an autobiographical love story for television, and once again it was banished to the bottom drawer. I obviously couldn't keep still. I felt guilty at working and guilty at not working. The problem was not the work itself, it was the nature of the work: I felt sure I should be doing something else and didn't have the courage to make the break. I wanted to form a company which tapped the imagination and energy of the actors involved, a company which placed the actors in a central position. If the actors wanted to direct or to write, then they would be encouraged to do this, and it need not be at the expense of full-time writers and directors. It would be a practical re-alignment of the collaborative process between writer, actor and director that would step up the contribution of the performer. I wanted to work on Shakespeare, but I wanted it to be accessible. There *was* an audience for Shakespeare – whether it was Newcastle, Belfast or Reading, and not just for people who knew about RSC. I knew it wouldn't be possible to do everything straight away and I didn't really have any master plan. I just knew that I wasn't doing the right thing.

The offers of freelance work came in with gratifying regularity. I completed *Billy IV* and even tried my hand at situation comedy, but I was still avoiding the real task that I saw in front of me and which David Parfitt and I talked about incessantly. The courage would still not come, and there were other temptations. Alan Plater's strong recommendation secured me an interview for the leading male in the BBC's *Fortunes of War*, their latest classic serial. Based on Olivia Manning's sextet of novels, there were locations in Yugoslavia, Greece and Egypt, Alan's adaptation was superb, the character of Guy Pringle intriguing, and the foreign travel very enticing. Stuff running a company.

I read all the novels, and went to the interview as Guy Pringle: bulky, teddy-bearish and distracted. Thank God the director, Jimmy Cellan-Jones, was taken in. It was early April, 1986, and after the lunchtime meeting he offered me the part there and then. I would start filming in September and continue for nine months. It was a great relief, and I already felt guilty about the delay it would mean to starting a company, but it meant money and possibly the kind of fame that would attract people to the shows that I was planning for the future. Anyway it was a bloody marvellous part.

I began to edge nearer to the kind of real involvement with the theatre that I needed; my writing continued its secret progress, and I flexed more directorial muscles. *John Sessions at the Eleventh Hour* was the latest of John's extraordinary one-man shows. David and I were producing and overseeing the bar, programmes and box office with another production company. I also directed, which was comparatively easy. John is a comic genius, but at that stage a little undisciplined in his approach to his material. I prevented him from assuming too much of his audience by playing the thick fourth former to John's PhD. The combination worked well and we thought seriously about planning another venture.

Moving from discipline to discipline, I enjoyed the learning process but was still restless. Now the film world beckoned. Clare

Peploe, the wife of Bernardo Bertolucci, was to direct a picture called *High Season*, a comedy thriller set on the island of Rhodes which took a light-hearted look at the clash between tourism and ancient culture in modern Greece. The script had had quite a history, and at one point Jack Nicholson had been lined up to play my part. I found it amusing to think that he and I could be up for the same role. Rik Mayall had been another star they had in mind, but eventually they had to use lesser mortals and so I was engaged to play the suburban James Bond character who stumbles his way through the story.

In prospect it seemed very exciting. Seven weeks on the island of Rhodes, living and filming in the village of Lindos. The script had its heart in the right place although it still seemed a little disjointed. I was sure this could all be sorted out and in any case, my part was funny. The people were nice – Jacqueline Bisset, James Fox, Irene Pappas, Sebastian Shaw and Robert Stephens – but there was no question that I was doing it for the money and for 'the crack'. The mercenary coward in full flow. But it didn't stop me moaning.

I'm hopeless in the sun. Why don't I ever realise? I'm a winter person. I had lots of time to kill, and the leisure nearly drove me mad. My ingratitude knew no bounds. The movie was an honest attempt to produce a charming light comedy, but there was a certain cheerful amateurism abroad which I found frustrating. Yes, I suppose I could have read *War and Peace*, but I've never had that kind of discipline. Instead I let my self-loathing and rage fire me in another way.

I sat down in my Lindos villa with a copy of *Romeo and Juliet*. I kept one with me most of the time, and I already had ideas for cuts in the text. Earlier in the year I'd made secret visits to the Shakespeare Centre in Stratford and read every prompt copy for each Stratford production since 1947, making copious notes and nicking everything that worked. I was convinced I could do the play with eleven actors. Hanging around in the Mediterranean sun I worked out which parts could be doubled and tried to construct a rough budget, basing my calculations on the time available between the end of the movie and the start of *Fortunes of War*. There were seven weeks exactly: three and a half weeks' rehearsal, three and a half weeks' playing. I made allowances for set and lighting and theatre rental, totted up the sums and worked out that we could do it for around £15,000. Good, *High Season* would pay for *Romeo and Juliet*.

The communication gods decided to plague me. From the tiny

telephone box in the post office at Lindos I rang David Parfitt to put the scheme to him, and after two days and numerous attempts I got through. He was free, and he would do it. We were off. The first problem was the venue. David rang the various fringe theatres we fancied – most were booked, or not interested in a show for which some queeny actor was going to be the director. Especially not a cocky little shit like me. It was obvious that I couldn't direct the operation from a Greek telephone box, and that I would somehow have to get back to London. This was an elaborate procedure: there were sufficient gaps in my filming schedule, but the production company was understandably reluctant to let me disappear in case disasters occurred in filming or indeed on my flights. I behaved appallingly and managed to make three trips home, on one occasion simply ignoring the orders of the producer who, very sweetly, didn't take me to court. They knew I was mad keen to do *Romeo and Juliet*, and not even the difficulties of obtaining a holiday charter flight could deter me. These return trips could only be booked from London, but I cajoled and bribed my way into getting hold of the magic tickets. The show had to go on.

On the first trip back I got nowhere. All the problems of the venture raised their head, and very few of the solutions. David had received resistance from almost every theatre owner – it was all very short notice and everyone needed to talk it through. This was no use to me, as I was on the tourist special back to Rhodes on Monday morning. Then Peter James, artistic director of the Lyric Theatre, Hammersmith, expressed interest. The 110-seat Studio theatre was available for our dates, but Peter most definitely wanted to talk to me first. Like a gent, he was prepared to come at the crack of dawn on Monday morning so that I could get to Gatwick for the eleven o'clock flight.

Peter set out all the sensible arguments against the venture: he was very happy to see the Studio used at a time when it would normally be closed but he was also genuinely concerned for me. Three and a half weeks was not a long time to rehearse the first Shakespeare you'd ever directed, and playing in it as well would compound the problem. Did I know what I was taking on? This would be my first appearance on stage since finishing as Henry V. There was likely to be a very close scrutiny of me in a part which I had never played before. I myself knew how much the great parts benefited from a period of playing in, and because of the limited run, we could give ourselves only one preview before the performance would be judged by the national press. I still wanted to do it.

I put my reasons as cogently as I could. The first and very necessary one was my passion for the play and the part. My reading had taught me that Romeo had always been a difficult part. Some of the greatest poetry in the play is given to Juliet and to Mercutio, and Romeo can often seem very limp. Conveying his virility and youthful energy as well as the gradual access to true poetic feeling is a difficult process. Both the leading roles provided an eternal problem: they require technical accomplishment and maturity of a kind that is rare in actors who are the right age to play them. I felt that there was probably a possibility that over the next couple of years I might be asked to play the part somewhere, but it seemed to me that with every month and year that passed I would have less chance of conveying Romeo's very youth. I might act it better but I would feel it less, and I wanted to take a risk on my own rawness. The apparent impetuousness that characterised the mounting of the production had in itself the kind of energy that Romeo would need.

Rehearsal time was short, but I had seen six-week rehearsal periods yield two weeks' work. The discipline which was needed to get through the play in three and a half weeks galvanised rather than depressed me. I ran through my insurance policies. I had already made contact with Hugh Cruttwell, who had agreed to join the production as an artistic consultant, and he would be there to monitor my performance and to offer regular comments about the production. Russell Jackson, from the Shakespeare Institute in Stratford, agreed to act as text advisor. Both men were available to the cast at all times on a private basis, so that despite the lack of time there was a back-up system comparable with that of a large company.

As I explained finally to Peter, I hoped that all this would free me sufficiently so that I could attack the directing of the whole play, which was my chief motivation. I wanted as young a production as possible: a young Lord and Lady Capulet, a younger nurse. I wanted to implement cuts that really could create, with the appropriately fiery playing, the 'two hours' traffic of our stage', rather than the usual acting time of over three hours. I'd often seen productions of the play drag, and wanted to create the effect of fate *rushing* the lives of these two people to their tragic ends.

I was doing it for a new kind of audience, an audience that I felt would respond to such a gesture. I received letters from people who had seen me on television and who wrote of their desire to take a risk on Shakespeare, or even on just going to the theatre. They would talk of their feelings of intimidation, and there were accounts of deadly evenings at productions which had confirmed their worst fears. I wanted to reach a large group of potential Shakespeare-lovers, beyond the obvious range of RSC die-hards, and I knew that although we couldn't do everything in a limited London run, and although it might be rough and raw, at least it would be different, cheaper, and, I believe, never boring.

The financial side of independent production is fraught, since so many things are being attempted at once. We were clearly in no position to seek subsidy, but this was fair enough given the circumstances of the production. We wanted seat prices to be low enough to be available to a greater audience, and yet we were dependent on box office revenue. The actors would all be paid £100 a week, on top of which we had to pay National Insurance, and there were fees for design, publicity, lighting, and printing. With a sell-out run, I would still lose nearly £7,000 of the £15,000 that the show would cost. I invested the cash gladly and David Parfitt worked for nothing during the remaining weeks of my Greek tragedy until rehearsals began. I was still utterly determined to do it and Peter James shook my hand and smiled. If nothing else, he was convinced that I couldn't be stopped.

Back in Lindos I worked very hard on the text of the play. Now that the deal was done, I was terrified, as there was no turning back, and I worried about everything – the directing, the acting, and the producing, and when I finished worrying about that I started worrying about the money. I wasn't in a position to be a one-man Arts Council. Pat Marmont rang up with a rescue plan: Pat O'Connor was directing a film *A Month in the Country*, based on a beautiful novel by J. L. Carr. I'd met Pat O'Connor earlier in the spring, when he'd indicated that he would like me to play the part of Moon in the piece. Since then the money had fallen through and I'd given up on the project, but now it was back on, only it was filming right across the *Romeo and Juliet* playing dates. They'd worked out a way of compressing my scenes into two weeks of shooting, and it would begin the morning after *Romeo and Juliet* opened. They would provide a car to get me back to the theatre in the evening, but would I be prepared to take on that kind of work-load?

174

I asked Pat what the money was like. She told me, and I thought of the budget for *Romeo and Juliet*. 'Tell them I'll ride to the set on a bike, just send the cheque.'

I managed two more trips back to London over weekends, and with days to go managed to cast the entire piece. I was so grateful to the actors who bothered to come to the interviews that I seemed to spend the time apologising for the lack of time and for the fact that I was directing. Many people turned us down, but we did produce an exciting cast – a refreshing mixture of people I'd worked with, people I admired and people I didn't know.

When rehearsals did start, their brevity was a positive advantage for the terrified novice director. There wasn't time to argue about silly things, lots of homework had to be done in advance, lines had to be learned early and things got on with, and the pace helped me. I didn't have to provide half-hour lectures after each scene, and I used a form of actors' shorthand to make many of my points. The cast didn't expect a highly intellectual approach, although the presence of Hugh and Russell ensured that this was available.

The pressure was immense. I would stay up late at night or arrive very early in order to do my director's homework, and at lunchtimes there would be meetings about design or costume. There were also fight rehearsals and publicity to do in the evenings, usually in the form of interviews. That done, there would be a trip to David's flat, where we talked about VAT, budget expenses, publicity and box office. Because of the short run in a tiny theatre we were already a hot ticket, and we eventually sold out even before we opened. That was a worry – what if it was dreadful?

Several critics thought it was, and the Branagh-bashing that I'd expected took place to a certain extent, but there were some good reviews, especially for the other actors, which delighted me. However none of this bore any particular relation to the quality of the work itself – I had my own clear opinions about what we had achieved but it did seem very important that we weren't publicly dismissed if we were to develop this company idea further. I was thrilled now to give opportunities to people who were clearly destined to be important actors: Samantha Bond as Juliet was singled out for taking the play's greatest role with such tremendous conviction. Andrew Jarvis, as Capulet, gave a highly charismatic and dynamic reading, and both these actors have gone on to produce really marvellous work in the classics. Simon Shepherd, Mark

Hadfield, Anne Carroll, and all the cast provided very exciting things. As part of the very necessary seedbed for this kind of work I regarded the production as a total success.

Gielgud has described the process of 'catching up' that is involved when an actor is both playing a role and directing. This is far less of a problem if you've played the part before, but in creating my Romeo for the first time I really had set myself an enormous task. But not impossible. With the help of Hugh and Russell and audience feedback I felt certain that by the third week I was far from letting Samantha or any of the others down.

The 6 am drive to location for filming was tough. Pat O'Connor and Colin Firth, who played the leading role in *A Month in the Country*, made the filming itself most fulfilling. Colin is a supremely generous actor and he was very kind when it came to allowing my shots to be taken first in order to let me get to the theatre at the end of the day. There were some very hairy journeys, and I'm not sure who it took most out of: Romeo, arriving pale and wan, or the anxious cast of clockwatchers who thought that Juliet was going to have to *scream* 'Wherefore art thou, Romeo?' But this nerve-wracked schedule seemed the only thing capable of producing the kind of work I believed in and calming my die-hard Protestant worries about getting into debt.

Lots of actors came to see the show, and Peter James remarked that there was a marked difference in the rest of the audience, which he identified as predominantly young and new to Shakespeare. Several people walked out, and an equal number regaled me in the bar afterwards with their disappointments in the production, but lots of people loved it. I was most impressed when Terry Hands paid us a visit, and stayed behind to talk. He was very generous about the production, although he did say that it lacked a context, some identifiable place or country within which the feud in the play would have extra weight. The play could, for instance, be set in Israel with the Montagues and Capulets as Jews and Arabs, or in Belfast with a Protestant/Catholic conflict – an analogy that had already crossed my mind. I explained to Terry that this seemed to me not context but distraction. The feud in the play was a domestic one, not a religious one, and in altering this, you disguise a central issue in the play. In this production, and in any others I might tackle, I wanted to see whether fine performances from excellent acting imaginations could actually provide as much illumination for a play as a single dominating design or production concept. I had no particular antagonism to strong directorial ideas, but I wanted the actors' contribution to seem more than just a facet of the production.

For hundreds of years, for good and ill, the actor has been acknowledged as the chief vessel through which the play is understood. In recent times the emphasis has moved dangerously far from this principle. The kind of theatre which had emerged in the late forties and early fifties, and which had been pre-eminent ever since, had produced excellent results, but, in my brief experience, one of its chief failings was a frequent underestimation of the role of the actor. This change stemmed from a healthy suspicion of a star system often ruled by destructive egotism, of everything that had helped the theatre to stagnate in the way that it had. It seemed to me that things had moved too far, and that it was time to re-establish proper balance in regard to the actor's part in the process of putting on a play. Not every actor wanted the situation to change, and the director-as-guru mentality was convenient for the masochistic tendencies in some and, for others, it often provided a convenient shift in responsibility. The greater degreee of responsibility that my work was beginning to advocate was a potential threat to both kinds of actor, and, of course, there might be many who believed that everything was designed for the greater glory of Kenneth Branagh.

Terry inevitably suspected a degree of fickleness. His own experience told him that the rigours of mounting this production would have taken a heavy toll on me, and he said as much after the show.

'Well, have you got this out of your system now? When are you going to come back and join us?'

He knew it was a lost cause. I had my own masochistic tendencies. Despite the remarkable privilege, it seemed too easy to waltz back into a glorious organisation which I knew perpetuated conditions that I felt militated against a sustained quality of work. Striving in the commercial world simply to become rich and famous was also not an option – clocking up money and parts, manically cashing in on the temporary kudos I had received. No. I was *compelled* to pursue the idea of a semi-permanent company, and to attempt a balance between running the company and managing what was also selfishly important to me, a successful freelance career. In a way, the one was impossible without the other. If I believed in the potential of this work I wanted it to be seen by a lot of people. For this kind of work to be truly popular the public would need to know who I was, I would have no qualms about extensive press coverage, and I had to build as far as I could on my commercial possibilities. It was unrealistic to think that you could eventually reach large numbers of people in the theatre if they hadn't seen you on television or on film.

I came to the end of *Romeo and Juliet* and realised that when *Fortunes of War* was completed, nearly a year from then, I might have this commercial credit. If I was to capitalise on what *Romeo and Juliet* had taught me, and if I was to attempt a semi-permanent footing for this company, then now was the time to act. I had plays that I was keen to direct, there were actors I wanted to work with, and there was an increasing network of contacts within the theatrical establishment that made it simpler to deal with the practical realities of finding theatres. David and I had found a way of working that divided responsibility clearly and with complete trust, and I knew that together there would be sufficiently strenuous scrutiny of our plans to make them both realistic and possible. I needed to make a commitment to continue putting (quite literally) my money where my mouth was, and would have to deal with the fear and doubt that would constantly attend. I certainly did not feel sure of the success of such a venture, but, by the time my feet touched the tarmac in Yugoslavia for the first day's filming of *Fortunes of War*, I knew I had no choice but to go ahead.

Adventure

EIGHT

'Company, at what expense?'
HAMLET

After the excitement of London theatricals, it was not surprising to find Ljubljana a little dull. The place itself seemed strangely devoid of character, and our hotel, the east European version of a Holiday Inn, carried all the same scars of modern comfortlessness. But Ljubljana was certainly a convincing backdrop to our show, which was proceeding well under the jaunty and enthusiastic leadership of Jimmy Cellan-Jones. I had quickly built up a rapport with the leading actress, Emma Thompson. The heart of the series was the story of the marriage between Harriet and Guy Pringle, a young, stumbling union full of misunderstandings and anxieties set against huge international events which gave greater intensity to the domestic difficulties. Emma's understanding of the role of Harriet Pringle was complete, and it was enormously enjoyable to work with her.

Emma's character was on screen much more than mine, so Yugoslavia provided me with valuable time to think about the

formation of a company. David and I had already left practical plans in motion. Peter James had a copy of *Public Enemy* which he was reading with a view to a possible co-production the following year. During the whole period of *Romeo and Juliet* he had been particularly impressed by David's administrative acumen and much encouraged by the new and large audiences that we seemed capable of drawing, and I hoped that these things might encourage him to take a risk with the play.

I was asking other people to take risks. Earlier that summer I had visited Chichester to see *The Relapse*, in which John Sessions was appearing. Lord Foppington, my old audition character, was being played by Richard Briers. Although the production was in some ways uneven, it confirmed to me what a superb actor Richard Briers could be. With remarkable good taste, Richard and his family came to see *Romeo and Juliet*, we chatted in the bar afterwards and, as he was leaving, I accosted him with an idea that had struck me with extraordinary force as I sat in the stalls at Chichester. The next Shakespeare that I wanted to direct was *Twelfth Night*, but there would be no point in attempting a production unless a piece of anchor casting were achieved. In the Vanbrugh Richard seemed to be an actor bursting to explore a great role. I grabbed him on the stairs.

'I hope to do another Shakespeare next year. Wondered if you were in the market?'

He looked rather surprised. I had obviously had too many pints – this was hardly the place for job offers. 'Oh! Fire away.'

'Well, I want to do *Twelfth Night*, and I'd love you to consider playing Malvolio.'

'Blimey! You serious?'

'Yes. I'll tell you what, if you'll seriously consider it then we'll talk about it when I come back from Yugoslavia. I don't know yet where or how we're going to do it, but it will happen.'

'You're on.'

I could tell that Richard had meant what he said. He'd admired *Romeo and Juliet* and I felt sure that if we could come up with the practical details, then he would play the role. So far, so good.

John Sessions had spent his Chichester season and beyond producing the first draft of a massively ambitious one-man show about Napoleon. It was to contain immense amounts of factual detail about Napoleon's life, which would be presented through the medium of

John's comic genius. The characters in Napoleon's life were to be 'played' by the enormous gallery of actors and politicians that John could mimic with such savage accuracy. He wanted the show to be 'total' theatre, a combination of high and low culture that was visually exciting, fast and intellectually stimulating. John's aim was to convey the shape of this fascinating life, but above all, he wanted to entertain. He also wanted me to direct it, and it seemed that yet another piece for a potential first season was falling into place.

As I Guy Pringled my way through Yugoslavia (which was standing in for Romania) I kept in constant touch with David Parfitt about all these developments. I also bored my fellow actors rigid with the preliminary working-out of my ideas for the company's first season. Emma showed immense patience with the Garrick of Eastern Europe, who would spend time between takes saying, 'And what if we did . . . ?' Or, '*I* know a marvellous play . . .' Or, 'Have you ever seen . . . ?'

I was particularly prone to plan-making on the days off when the actors would get together for a trip. It was on one such trip that the final part of an opening season began to take shape. We'd 'gone over the wall' from Yugoslavia into Italy and had spent the day in Trieste trying to find out where James Joyce had lived, and searching for pasta to relieve us of the Yugoslav obsession with Schnitzels. It was tea-time in the main square, and Richard Clifford and I were sipping a cocktail while waiting for the bus back to the camp. 'Don't you think,' I said, 'that it would be incredibly useful for really fine actors who've played in the great Shakespearian plays to direct young actors in the same roles? I don't just necessarily mean stars. Nor do I mean a sort of piecemeal experiment. But if you had a real season where these novice directors could have the comfort of each other and where the conditions were controlled enough to reduce their worries over the technical aspects, don't you think one could make great developments in one's acting?'

Richard nodded. There was no stopping me now. I was well into my stride and well into my third Martini. 'A season that could develop new Shakespearian actors and directors, and which would consequently have a special quality. And it wouldn't be done in London, in a glare of publicity, but it would be protected and performed, at least to begin with, in a place that's deprived of such work. Then there's a risk for both parties . . .'

Richard tried to chip in with his approval but I was already miles away thinking of people, places and plays. It really was possible, I thought.

Over the following weeks in Yugoslavia I developed the idea. There were senior actors I knew or had some contact with whom I was sure would at least listen to me. One that I knew slightly and admired hugely was Anthony Hopkins. After endless drunken evenings, Emma persuaded me that I should stop talking and simply write to him with my idea that he should direct me in a role that I suspected would never necessarily be mine, Macbeth. I wrote to him and he wrote back. Yes, he was interested and he would talk, and he agreed with my thoughts about the state of things in the theatre. Bloody hell. If this went on I really was going to have to form a company.

The Yugoslavian leg ended and *Fortunes of War* took up residence in the old Ealing studios newly acquired by the BBC. Tim Harvey, the designer, had produced a magnificent interior for the Athenée Palace Hotel, which gave a perfect impression of old Romania. I liked and admired Tim very much, and something told me that we would work together again.

Now that there was the semblance of over a year's work in prospect, David Parfitt and I attempted to face the financial realities of producing such a vast amount of work. We made preparations to visit the Arts Council and the British Council and developed our own ideas for luring 'angels' to finance the various ventures. Peter James had agreed to do *Public Enemy*. It would cost £50,000, we would have to provide £25,000 and any profit would be split down the middle. A date was set for an opening in July, 1987. After this we would present *Napoleon* somewhere, this time financed by John and myself.

Christmas 1987 was the playing period for *Twelfth Night*, but where we did it and how was up for grabs. Financially it would be affected for good or ill by the success of the previous shows, but we weren't in any position to hang around. Richard Briers needed to know soon if it was on, before committing himself to an unknown company. At the beginning of 1988 I had decided we would attempt a Shakespeare season of four plays, all directed by actors. We were talking about eighteen months' work built on promises, passions and hopes. We had no definite finance, only one confirmed venue, two actors (me and John Sessions), a lot of bull-shitting to do and no name.

At least, we did have a name, but it took some getting used to. I liked it, but David wasn't keen – he wanted to call the company 'Compendium', which reminded me of the boxes of assorted board games that you get at Christmas. While in Yugoslavia I had woken up in the middle of the night, some time after the Trieste adventure, with a name that I was certain about. It seemed to reflect our youthfulness and express some sense of rebirth that was going on in the British theatre. I wrote it down on my Holiday Inn easy-by-the-bed notebook and looked again in the morning. It still seemed good. Later that morning in a break, I made my umpteenth trip up the rather useless tower which constituted the one tourist attraction in Ljubljana. I tried it out on Richard Clifford who, in company with Ronald Pickup, was fighting the Ljub-jub blues.

'What about "Renaissance"?'

'Brilliant,' they said.

Done.

Judi Dench sent me a birthday card. I hadn't seen her since *Ghosts* but wasn't surprised to be a beneficiary of her famous ability to remember everything. She'd been in my thoughts, and fate was lending a hand. Everything about the way Judi had rehearsed as an actress for the Ibsen had convinced me that she could direct. She questioned not only the motivations of her own character but of all the other parts, and at all times wanted to know how the play was shaping up as a whole. We'd had chats about the instinctive feeling actors had that they could do just as well as the director, and we had also agreed that fear would always defeat such feelings. Not any more. I got in touch with Judi straight away and suggested lunch.

Behind the scenes things were moving swiftly. John Adams, who had directed me at RADA, was leaving his job as artistic director of the Octagon Theatre, Bolton, and was in a strong position to land the job of running the Birmingham Repertory Theatre. As part of his pitch to the board he wanted an artistic package to present, and he approached me in late '86 to join him as an associate director. I refused, but I did tell him about plans for the Shakespeare season. By this stage I was also talking to Geraldine McEwan and Derek Jacobi and although nothing was certain, John appreciated that this could be a strong part of his package. As part of my desire for controlled conditions, I very much wanted to use the Birmingham Rep Studio where the productions could have the right kind of simplicity to calm our novice directors. It would also be cheaper. John and I struck a deal where he could include Renaissance as part of his already impressive plan for the sadly neglected Rep Studio, and he guaranteed that if he got the job we would at least have a venue and a sympathetic landlord. Money did not come into it. Our season would be an expensive business and with all John's good intentions it would not be possible for Birmingham to help finance it. But at least, in prospect, we had a theatre, and the perfect spot from which to launch a tour which might or might not end up in London.

The plan was to rehearse and open all the plays consecutively in Birmingham, where they would remain in repertory for a short season before touring to Belfast, Dublin, Bath, Brighton, Manchester, Newcastle and Leeds, before a final – and we hoped, triumphant – three-month season in London.

Judi was shocked but delighted when I put the offer to her. She confessed with a shiver that only two weeks earlier she had admitted to herself for the first time that she felt able and wanted to direct. Which play, I wondered? I asked the question, and then, by an extraordinary coincidence, we both said at the same time, '*Much Ado About Nothing.*'

But Judi wasn't going to agree straight away. The prospect was still full of terrors, and her own humility made her quail at the prospect of actually auditioning or giving orders to actors. And anyway what was this new company, Renaissance? She was having to put all her faith in me. What if the money fell through? What if the previous productions were all terrible? How would that affect the reputation of these Titans? She knew I meant what I said, but I was still only twenty-six and a stranger in a strange land. She was impressed, excited and terrified. It had been a lovely lunch, and she said she would think about it.

I approached Anthony Hopkins with the idea of his directing *Macbeth*, and he agreed immediately. He was passionately opposed to bad directors and felt it was about time that actors had a go, and he recalled a particularly unhappy production of this play at the National Theatre, where everything seemed to have gone wrong, even the costumes. At our breakfast meeting he was still venting volcanic Welsh spleen. 'I looked like a fucking armadillo.'

It was taking a while to gather this group. I was very much in awe of them and would spend several days staring at the telephone, trying to find the courage to ring up and present these schemes, which I knew to be subject to all sorts of circumstances.

It was particularly odd to be facing Derek Jacobi across the lunch table. One of my original acting heroes, he had also encouraged me early on, and here I was attempting to offer him a job. The play I had in mind was *Richard II*. A brilliant young actor I knew was desperate to play the part and I remembered that Derek had done it on television. I wanted to bring another strong young leading actor into the company and I felt the combination of him and Derek would work well and give the casting more balance. Although realistic about commercial considerations, I did not want Renaissance to be the 'Kenneth-Branagh-gets-all-the-big-parts Company'. I remembered a conversation I'd heard in relation to Ian McKellen and the Actors' Company:

'Isn't it marvellous about Ian McKellen and the Actors' Company. This week he's playing Hamlet, and last week he was in something where he just played the footman.'

'What was the play called?'

'*The Footman.*'

A little cruel, I think, but it reveals the difficulty of balance when a leading actor and personality is the driving force behind such an enterprise. Often the personality is the factor which makes the theatre decide to take the shows, and the matter becomes purely commercial. If the personality then plays a very small part in a production, it can both confuse and disappoint the audience, and it can even upset the balance of the play, an accusation levelled at Olivier when he took the small role of a butler in a play during the latter stages of his reign at the National Theatre.

Derek did not jump at my idea. He felt that *Richard II* was far too demanding a role for the sort of young actor I was thinking of, and, an important consideration in this case, it was not a 'company' play – the women's parts were poor and there was a lot of standing around for the other men. Although I felt strongly that this rarely performed piece should be seen in the provinces, I took his point about the potential tensions it could create. What, then? Was there a Shakespeare that he did feel strongly about? There was, but he would only direct it if I played the title role. It was the play that he knew best of all, and the play that he had most to say about.

'You must be able to guess,' he said.

'No.'

'*Hamlet.*'

Christ. I really hadn't bargained on that one. I wanted to play the part again but somehow hadn't imagined it coming up so soon. Was

I ready, and were these the right circumstances? Would I be in awe of Derek to the point where I would be merely impersonating him? I thought about these things for all of three minutes before shaking Derek's hand and saying, 'Great idea. Let's do it.'

Anything to get him into Renaissance. It was Christmas '86, and according to our plans *Hamlet* wouldn't start rehearsing until April '88. I could worry about it then.

Before flying to Egypt in early '87 for the next leg of *Fortunes of War*, I had a few days in which to net Geraldine McEwan as the last of this potential quartet. The wife of Hugh Cruttwell, Geraldine, I knew, was able to convey a tremendous delicacy and lightness which seemed appropriate for the play that I wanted to include in our season, *As You Like It*. It was the only Shakespearian comedy that Geraldine had not appeared in, and Rosalind was one of the few Shakespearian heroines that she had not played. The piece had always fascinated her and, like Judi, it seemed that this association with a particular play was meant to be. Although Geraldine appeared the quietest and shyest of the four actors I had approached, she was also the one who accepted the challenge both immediately and whole-heartedly.

I left for Egypt knowing that I had their interest and provisional commitment, but many other things had to fall into place before it could all work out. And I had no idea how we were going to pay for it all.

Egypt was a revelation. Through the hallowed portals of the Cairo Hilton, the Giza Ramada and the Luxor Movenpick, we had a very

privileged view of the land of the pharaohs, and an army of seventy BBC technicians and cast followed the Pringles on their travels. I visited the Valley of the Kings, and felt impressively solitary as I walked down the narrow steps to the eerie tomb of Tutankhamun. About halfway down the mysterious stairwell, I heard a familiar voice declaring theatrically,

'And so Larry told Zeffirelli to get lost . . .'

It was Robert Stephens, a member of the cast, telling an anecdote to a confused Egyptian guide. And there were many other incongruities as we balanced work with tourism – I shall long remember the sight of Alan Bennett bouncing along on a camel en route to Saqquara, the Peter O'Toole of Blackburn.

Work provided a combination of some marvellous acting scenes as well as the chance to actually climb, in the line of duty, one of the great Pyramids at Giza. Best of all, I had a week off in the middle. Any sensible thespian would have done some exploring, instead I rushed back to West London where there was a chance of a venue for *Napoleon* and *Twelfth Night*. The Riverside Studios were available if we could do the right deal. In five manic days, David and I booked in both shows and managed to convince Richard Briers that performing at this unconventional venue would not destroy his reputation. I told him in any case that this was the Titanic Theatre Company. If he went down, he would take us all with him.

John Adams now looked closer to getting the job at Birmingham and this allowed us to start committing all these details to paper. With my accountant we worked out a scheme for raising the first £25,000 for *Public Enemy* which would allow a punter some chance of a return on an investment of £500. Also in a moment of madness we persuaded the artistic director of Riverside to give us a weekend festival called 'Renaissance Nights' to play when *Napoleon* was on. This was yet another one of my aims for the Company: the promotion of new writing and acting. 'Renaissance Nights' was an opportunity for the Company to read and perform full length and one-act plays along the lines of the festival work I'd done while at the RSC. Although it was going to be our first full season, I was convinced of the need for this volume of work: we had to arrive with a vengeance, and I wanted to be sure that there would always be something new to do, so that the mistakes we would inevitably make could be rectified at another stage. At the end of that cold January week, I flew back to steaming Alexandria with deals done for our first three shows, venues confirmed and the 1988 Shakespeare season several steps nearer to being realised.

Malcolm McKay was to direct *Public Enemy*, and he made it my task on the second Egyptian leg of *Fortunes of War* to do a second draft. This was completed on my return but while we were in Giza I was helped by having the play read by both Alan Bennett and Emma Thompson. Alan was very encouraging, and made lots of specific suggestions, particularly about characters' names and their particular tastes, and Emma challenged the political content of the play.

The central character of Tommy Black – which Peter James wanted me to play and which I had written with myself in mind – had particular requirements. The piece opened with a complete re-creation of the famous 'Yankee Doodle Dandy' dance routine from the James Cagney film of the same name. Cagney had performed it in short sequences for the film camera, and I would have to do this difficult and unfamiliar routine in one burst. At Christmas I had met up with Julie Fell, an assistant choreographer on the West End Show *Me and My Girl*. She'd been recommended by Emma, who'd been in the show, and Gillian Gregory, the choreographer, who helped to take me through my initial paces. Despite the fact that it was a complicated tap dance, Gillian and Julie were convinced I could do it. I learnt the basics of the number in early January and in breaks from filming on the Pyramids found myself practising taps and jumps and twirls much to the bemusement of the Arab extras.

Back in England push was rapidly coming to shove. John Adams had got the job as Artistic Director at Birmingham. We confirmed dates with him, and we now had a full season starting in June '87 with *Public Enemy* and finishing in October '88, at the end of the Shakespeare season. We now had obligations and commitments to several people, but we still had no money. Between Egypt and Athens there was a fortnight in which to finance everything *and* get confirmations from Hopkins, Dench, and Jacobi, who now had a problem with availability.

Stage One. The Arts Council. David and I nervously entered the impressive building in Piccadilly, and waited patiently in a corridor until we were shown into an office and were introduced to two very amiable women. We explained our programme for the first season, but there was a problem in that we had not consulted them in advance, before certain commitments and decisions had been made. They made it clear that this was not how they operated, and that official procedures did not allow for any great flexibility on their part, in spite of the high quality of our programme and personnel. The answer was a firm 'no'.

We decided that going it alone need not turn us into capitalist monsters. The financial principles of the company were based on keeping afloat, and not on making a profit – David and I took no management salary, and any profit we did make would be shared out among actors and production staff whenever possible, as indeed happened after *Twelfth Night* and after the successful London Shakespeare season. It was a reasonably simple and honest approach, and general company accounts have always been available to anyone working for Renaissance. David and I were both disappointed that the Arts Council were not prepared to back us, but we wanted to stick to our original conception of Renaissance. How the outside world would view our enforced freelance status remained to be seen; for the moment, we had to get on with plans for the season, and there was much to be consolidated.

Phone calls to Judi, who was in the middle of rehearsals for *Antony and Cleopatra*, revealed a much greater fear of the project than I had suspected – she would still not commit herself. Hopkins was also now undecided. The night before I left for Athens I was rushing up and down the Euston Road from meetings, first with my accountant and then with John Adams, trying to find a phone box that worked. When I got through to Judi, and pleaded for a decision about *Much Ado* before planning a press conference, she was still unsure. The rain was pouring down and David Parfitt was outside getting drenched searching for more coins and clutching a soggy prototype of the investors' letter with which we hoped to lure the first moneys. The Lyric Hammersmith were insisting that we have a press launch soon in order to give *Public Enemy* a chance. I was about to go away for a month. Everything was getting too close for comfort. I told Judi I'd come and see her.

My bags were packed ready to rush to the airport, but I squeezed in some time to cajole Judi over the lunch table at the National. It felt like Joe Allen's all over again, with familiar faces walking past, smiling, saying hello, and 'Wonder what they're up to?' written all over their faces. Judi was now in previews for *Antony and Cleopatra*, and she had been thinking about *Much Ado* for four months. After a difficult few performances, she had thought about the work in progress and decided that she knew what was wrong, and put her

190

thoughts to Sir Peter Hall, who accepted them gratefully. They were real directorial points, and she had had the courage of her convictions. A day or two later she had asked Sir Peter whether she should direct *Much Ado*. 'Of course,' was his answer.

And now, at last, I had mine. Judi is famous for what one might describe as creative vacillation, but I was glad that she had thought so long about it because I knew that once committed, she would devote herself heart and soul to the job.

Derek's availability was now certain. He was so convinced by the idea of *Hamlet*, and of directing the boy who had thrilled to his performance in the same role ten years before, that he had gone out of his way to make the American engagement for his West End hit, *Breaking the Code*, fit into our schedules. Geraldine was also confirmed. My only lingering doubts concerned Tony Hopkins, whose confidence about the project was shaky. None of them were doing it for the money, which was minimal. When another brick was placed in the wall, I would pass on the information to David who was rapidly producing a press release so that the whole impressive season might create the right bums-on-seats interest for *Public Enemy*, which would be in rehearsal with frightening speed.

A glorious Greek spring made the final foreign location for *Fortunes of War* sheer bliss. We filmed at the Acropolis and other ancient sites, and there were marvellous day trips. We even went to Delphi where we heard the first cuckoo of spring, but not even the oracle to whom I silently prayed could tell me whether the whole Renaissance thing was going to work out. Our commitments were firmer than ever. An art gallery had been booked for late April in order to hold a press launch, and David was now using a fax machine to send copies of possible letterheads and Company logos. Across the dinner table of the InterContinental, Athens, these roughs would be discussed and voted on by the cast and crew. We decided on a simple classical design by Shaun Webb, who was to become an integral member of the Renaissance Company.

We were gradually building up a strong team. Our stage manager for *Public Enemy* had worked on *Romeo and Juliet*, as had other members of the production staff, and, although David and I still took no salary (there was no account to take it from), we did realise that we needed some help. A secretary/assistant/Person Friday was chronically necessary, as the paperwork, which was increasing daily, was too much for the two of us alone. Loot from *Fortunes of War* paid for office equipment and the salary of just such a person. We were very fortunate to net Marilyn Eardley, who had worked closely with us on *Romeo and Juliet* when she was at the Lyric. We also searched for premises, but had no money to pay rent. There was no choice: the room in my flat, which I had always ear-marked as a study for the time when I would become a great man of letters, was converted into the Renaissance nerve centre over a weekend of frantic activity. The following Monday, with borrowed filing cabinet, desk and typewriter, Marilyn took possession and I said goodbye for a possible eighteen months to any possibility of escape from Renaissance. We had an office, headed notepaper, a full season's programme, and *still* no money. Pushing our luck wasn't in it.

We drew up a list of prospective investors which included friends, colleagues, actors and directors who might be sympathetic to financing the first show. The deal reduced itself to a simple flutter, but needed pages of accompanying text in order to explain everything to our and their accountants for tax purposes. A week before the press launch, we sent off over a hundred of these original requests. By now we were back at Ealing finishing off *Fortunes of War* and with deadlines expiring all round, Emma Thompson, David Parfitt and myself were on the floor in my dressing-room between takes stuffing envelopes with pleading letters. Emma took her own invitation, walked next door, wrote a cheque and brought it straight back. Money in the bank. We were off.

So was Tony Hopkins. With a week to go before our public launch he decided that now was not the time to commit to such a new and frightening experience. I was pretty frightened of him and had no intention of trying to persuade him out of it. There was some sense of relief: three plays seemed easier than four, and the balance of *Hamlet*, *Much Ado* and *As You Like It* felt right.

With the press conference almost upon us we'd attracted around £12,000 from friends and family, and there was no turning back. The *Fortunes of War* production gave me the day off in order to worry myself stupid and I walked into the Covent Garden Gallery in trepidation. Peter Thompson, the press representative we'd first met on *Another Country* and who had worked with us on *Romeo and Juliet*, had produced a marvellously impressive turn-out. The place was packed with journalists. We'd also managed to coerce Judi Dench, Geraldine McEwan, Richard Briers, Derek Jacobi, John Adams, Peter James and everybody's mum and dad. The logo was unveiled, the letterheads were there to read, there were information packs and later on there was me standing on a table, feeling very silly, but trying to explain in a short speech the idea behind the whole thing. If nothing else, the assembled members of the press had to admit that we had produced a very weighty programme of work. In fact one of the many questions I answered afterwards was whether I was trying to provide something for everyone.

The answer was yes – the appeal was intended to be very broad. We wanted to present popular art. Not poor art or thin art or even 'arty' art, but popular art that would expand the mind and the senses and really entertain. Fuelled by the passion and commitment that we felt to each particular project.

We got through it, and the press coverage was certainly impressive enough to create interest in investment for the *Public Enemy* account. However as the rehearsal date neared we were still short, and I was happy to dig into my own pocket to make up the slight difference, but it was a worrying precedent not to have a full subscription for the first production, and it would put more pressure on the need for *Public Enemy* to be successful in order to produce more finance for *Twelfth Night* and the Shakespeare season. Without Arts Council or private money, those productions would remain dreams, and our imaginations had already outstripped the financial realities. The budget for the Shakespeare season was based on reasonable estimates for sets, costume and lighting and the attempt to pay everyone at least £200 per week made a depressing equation with potential box-office revenue. Our decision to stay in the 150-seat Studio meant that seat prices and the actual volume of tickets sold could not possibly recover the overall budget which was standing at a frightening £250,000. Assuming that we could possibly raise this, which seemed almost impossible, it was becoming clear that we would have to tour the shows to much bigger theatres in order to recover the deficit of even a sold-out run.

What had we started? My involvement with Renaissance meant that I was unable to do any freelance work in order to subsidise it. I knew that we had to complete the season at all costs, and kept in my mind a last resort of selling the flat and then, perhaps, borrowing the rest. One thing at a time. Perhaps *Public Enemy* would be a huge success – West End transfer, film rights, who knows?

If directing and acting is difficult, then writing and performing in a new play is even more taxing. Although the second draft had made great strides, the piece required constant work. In a six-week rehearsal period, I spent evenings and weekends on rewrites, and then came in at 8.30 every morning to practise dancing for an hour and a half. There was also the part itself, which was immensely tough: part schizophrenic, highly energised, dangerous and very hard to place. And then there was the work-load of future Renaissance plans. I really was at full stretch and became irritable with the director, despite excellent help from him on both text and performance. I was also assisted by Hugh Cruttwell, who had agreed to continue his unpaid role as artistic consultant. I was and am still far too close to it to judge how good or bad the play and production were, but I also had to confess to being hoisted by my own petard in having written a great vehicle for myself. To give the play a real chance I really should have cast someone else in the central role, but there was some really fine acting, particularly from Ethna Roddy, an actress straight out of the Webber-Douglas Academy to whom we were able to give an Equity card. A week of previews revealed, as *Francis* had done, the need for time, but audiences were loving what was being variously described as a thriller, a modern melodrama, a political play and a star vehicle.

The critics, on the whole, dismissed it, and audiences dropped as the wave of indifference took hold. There seemed no attempt to see the piece as a serious play. I came in for an inevitable bashing over my presumption in having both written and performed in the play, and then there were others who indulged what they saw as my act of folly. The general feeling from the press was one of disappointment in a Company about which there had been high hopes. None of it really mattered; the Company remained happy and *Public Enemy* improved as time went on, but it was a blow to know that these first knocks would threaten the financial viability of the rest of our season. I responded to this by grabbing whatever freelance work I could. During the run I managed a week on a television adaptation of O'Neill's *Strange Interlude* with Glenda Jackson, and managed to land the part of Thomas Mendip in Christopher Fry's *The Lady's not for Burning*, which I could sandwich in between *Napoleon* and *Twelfth Night*. None of this was very good for my health or my private life, both of which were suffering. I felt out of control – it was as if I believed my enormous work-load gave me licence to behave exactly as I wanted. I would tell lies to all and sundry in order to explain absences which I deemed necessary because 'I was so tired'; I ate and drank immoderately, and didn't give a moment's thought to anyone but myself. I was unreliable to work with, and felt pretty miserable.

I had little enough time to worry about these things. The morning after the opening of *Public Enemy* I started to rehearse Napoleon with John Sessions, and realised that as much energy is required from the director as from the performer in rehearsals for a one-man show. John was kindness itself and worked around my erratic fatigue but all work and little play made Ken a very dull boy indeed. I didn't look at a newspaper, I never dreamed of asking after anyone's welfare – not while there was even more pressure on this show to succeed. Tension was increased by the necessary publicity for the show generated brilliantly by Peter Thompson and which centred inevitably on me. The imminent screening of *Fortunes of War* and the release of *A Month in the Country* meant that I was particularly hot property, and I was besieged. I was also attracting various sorts of nutters who badgered me for advice, money and jobs – understandable, but impossible for me to deal with in the circumstances, and quite often I wanted to avoid even answering the phone.

During the final stages of *Napoleon* rehearsals I received repeated messages from the Riverside box-office to call a stranger named Stephen Evans. I didn't bother – there was no information about what he wanted and I suspected the worst. In an unguarded moment going to the loo, the vague reception staff told me there was a phone call for me. For some reason I thought it was my agent and so picked up the phone. An intelligent, gravelly voice rumbled down the phone, 'Ah, got you at last. My name's Stephen Evans and I think I can help you.'

Oh Christ, I knew it was going to be another nutcase.

'I've read about you and your Company, and I think that I might have access to certain funds that might make your life easier.' Oh, really. I see, a City gangster who's trying to off-load some Panamanian slush-fund. Why do I talk to these people? 'Obviously, it would be good if we could talk. What about Monday morning? Say eleven o'clock?'

Yes, yes, yes. Anything just get him off the bloody phone. I put down the receiver and didn't give it another moment's thought.

At about five to eleven on the following Monday morning I was escaping from the Riverside auditorium where a disastrous technical rehearsal was in progress. The only thing in my mind was a coffee, which meant waiting for a quarter of an hour while the Coffee Bar assistant worked out whether they sold any of the stuff. Waiting at the counter with increasing frustration, I was joined in the queue by an attractive forty-year-old man of medium build who leant across the counter and attempted to communicate with the space cadet assistant. 'Hello, I've got an appointment with Kenneth Branagh.'

Bloody hell, I'd been nabbed. I introduced myself and made profuse apologies, although I was in no mood to talk even to this fairly innocuous looking customer. With deadly rudeness I passed Stephen on to David Parfitt and returned to the nightmare rehearsal where I really was needed. During the course of the next half hour I saw them wander in to have a look at the set being painted, but my mind couldn't have been further away. In another break I managed to shake his hand distractedly, and apologised for not having had a proper chat.

At lunch, David explained that the man to whom I had been so rude had agreed to find the £60,000 that we would need to finance *Twelfth Night*. I was now even more convinced of the Panamanian slush-fund, but David insisted that he seemed absolutely genuine and would send the first cheque in the following week. Understandably and ungraciously, I was suspicious, and remained so until my first proper meeting with Stephen when he visited *Napoleon* with his wife, Lyn. This time I was a pathetic Uriah Heep, grovelling with shame at my earlier behaviour. He chose not to remind me of that but instead enthused about the show, which was a tremendous tour-de-force for John.

It had not been easy. Technically, *Napoleon* was massively ambitious. There were over 150 lighting and sound cues, smoke, snow – you name it and we tried to do it, and all with one stage manager and one director, who were both working on *Public Enemy* up to the Saturday before Monday's technical rehearsal at Riverside. The technical week was a disaster, and the first preview was the most appallingly jinxed performance of anything I've ever been involved with. Nothing went right. There was no choice but to cancel the second preview and for me to get my act together. John remained remarkably calm. The day's break worked and on Saturday night we played to a full and appreciative house who showed us how the evening could take off if John's talent was supported by a reliable production.

By the time Stephen Evans saw it, John was hugely impressive and the show fulfilled all the Renaissance creeds of life-enhancing populism – at least that was my story and I was sticking to it. Stephen and I developed an instant rapport: he was a shrewd businessman, something of a maverick, a stockbroker with a strong freelance strain who was also genuinely interested in the arts. He had already dabbled in what he described as 'helping' opera and dance organisations, but none of them had satisfied his desire for greater involvement. He didn't want to interfere artistically, but he was seeking a realistic collaboration between the worlds of commerce and art. I told him of our plans and decided on the spur of the moment to outline a totally outrageous proposal which I felt could capitalise on what I hoped would be a triumphantly successful Shakespeare season. I had no facts or figures with which to support this idea, but I had my usual combination of vision and cheek, and two bottles of Lambrusco. I wanted the Renaissance Company to feed into other mediums. I felt that one shouldn't be limited by conventional patterns of work, or by the methods of other companies; healthy ambition, in this instance, should not limit itself. In any case, he asked for it.

'So what will you do after the Shakespeares?'

Pause. Here we go. 'I want to make a film of *Henry V*.' I checked his face. The colour hadn't drained, and he was still looking me in the eye. 'I will direct and play the leading role.'

He still hadn't flinched.

'Have you directed a film before?'

'No.'

'How many films have you acted in?'

'Two.'

A longer pause. He still hadn't backed down. 'Do you think it's possible for you to do it?'

The longest pause. 'Absolutely . . .' – another brief pause as I looked him in the eye and raised my glass '. . . with your help.'

His face broke into a smile and we clinked glasses. There was a lot of talk about, and the film was a distant prospect, but we were in business.

The reviews for John's *Napoleon* were marvellous, and made the job of organising 'Renaissance Nights' slightly less daunting. It fell to David to do a Herculean job in arranging favours left, right and centre for actor friends to perform what turned out to be a very wide selection of new work. I had pushed off to Leeds where I was having a delightful time on the Fry play and trying to cast *Twelfth Night* over the phone. The pace was increasing by the day. Stephen Evans' entry onto the scene was hotly followed by Howard Panter, a West End producer, who wished to transfer *Napoleon* for a limited season. The Albery Theatre looked as though it would be available, and Stephen and Howard combined to produce a financial deal that made a six-week season possible. Mounting it in the West End would mean a two-day absence from *Twelfth Night* rehearsals for me, but I was beginning to get used to this kind of manic scheduling. The effects of all this were beginning to show: when my mother saw me at a performance of *Napoleon* in the West End, she let out a gasp of horror at the spotty, scruffy, stubbly tramp before her.

As I had suspected, the presence of Richard Briers in the production attracted a very strong team of actors. Rehearsing the play gave me great pleasure, and my instinct that a production set in the winter, with snow covering a mysterious Victorian garden, would bring out the brooding melancholy of the play seemed to be justified. It is undoubtedly a comedy, but the dark undertow of rejection and loneliness and cruelty experienced by many of the characters was beautifully brought out by the cast. At the centre of this production was a definitive Malvolio from Richard, who proved that a great comic actor can be a great tragic actor. There was fine work from all the cast, but this was a very special performance, funny and, in the end, deeply moving. Hugh Cruttwell had advised me and had ensured that my instincts about the play were translated early into a production that attempted to reach as many people as possible. I took my parents as a touchstone, and they loved it.

This production was also the first occasion on which our Royal Patron could be present. I had had the gall to invite Prince Charles to become Patron, making my initial approach in a letter typed from a hotel bedroom in Egypt. The long and delicate process of Royal assent had given us his acceptance just before the press launch, and we were delighted that despite a frantic schedule he could attend a Royal Gala Preview of *Twelfth Night*. This was the first of a number of occasions on which David and I mercilessly dropped Stephen in it. The idea had seemed brilliant at the time, a wonderful way of benefiting one of the Prince's Trust's charities, an element of our work that we wanted to develop. But selling 350 seats at £50 a ticket is easier said than done, however worthy the cause, and especially if you are still a relatively unknown theatre company. Stephen came to the rescue by blackmailing and cajoling numerous City colleagues into attending what turned out to be an uproariously enjoyable evening.

The Prince was on fine form and left everyone in the building aglow. He had effortlessly made meaningful contact with anyone he met, and the euphoria of having encountered a genuine star was felt by everyone in the Company. We all went on to have a very late night indeed at a marvellous party provided by Stephen Evans, with not a slush-fund in sight. The excesses of the Royal Gala meant that the following evening's press performance was performed in an atmosphere that was relatively free of the hysteria normally associated with such events. I don't know if hangovers are the perfect cure for press night nerves, but it certainly worked in this case: the performance went smoothly, and after a week of previews was developing beautifully. The press reception was unanimous – straight raves. I couldn't believe it, they were the best notices I'd seen for anything and suddenly, despite the shaky start, we were the Company who could do no wrong.

Both Judi Dench and Geraldine McEwan saw the show and loved it, and it was a great relief to know that these risk-taking directors had seen a successful production. Derek Jacobi was already in America, where *Breaking the Code* was a huge success on Broadway. The busy lives of this trio had meant that casting the Shakespeare season was almost more difficult than my InterContinental Company negotiations with David. We had had one meeting in July which they were all able to attend, and since then Derek had seen as many actors as he could before leaving for America. Now it was Judi and Geraldine's turn. David and I co-ordinated reactions between the three directors over the telephone to New York. When Geraldine and Judi plumped for someone, a photograph would wing its way across the Atlantic for Derek's approval – his Horatio had to be someone else's Don Pedro, and it needed give and take all round. Time was short, and pressure increased when Thames Television took up the option to film *Twelfth Night* for television. The Renaissance cup was running over, and it became very important to keep things in control and to guard against the very dangerous increases in scale that we had always tried to avoid.

The financing of the Shakespeare season progressed with relative ease, with Stephen Evans and Howard Panter combining under David's direction to make the quarter million gamble possible. I made a quick trip to New York with Jenny Tiramani, our designer, and spent a week with Derek working on *Hamlet*. On my return to England I went up to Birmingham to discuss programming with John Adams – when to have matinées? How many performances? How much rehearsal time? We also agreed that Renaissance could be the subject of a television documentary, with a camera crew filming various stages of our work over the year ahead. This, with the success of *Twelfth Night*, was generating enormous interest.

I managed one quick break in Scotland before Christmas and then spent three days in Los Angeles in January '88 promoting *Fortunes of War*, a visit which allowed Emma Thompson and I to fulfil a lifelong ambition and visit Disneyland. Both of us were nearly sick on 'The Matterhorn', but we thrilled to the new 'Star Tours' ride, which was a mechanical but completely convincing trip on a space ship straight out of *Star Wars*. We emerged like wide-eyed six-year-olds, yelping through our candy floss, and heading for 'Pirates of the Caribbean', 'Wild West Land', and as many rides as we could fit in.

Emma and I were now established as a couple. It was a real pleasure to work together on her television show, *Thompson*, on our return to England. I thought it brilliantly original and innovative television. There was an excellent cast, and it was great fun to do.

Meantime, I approached the 1 February rehearsal date with trepidation, but also with some relief. After endless organising, it seemed that for a time I would go back to being simply an actor, and I had three marvellous parts – Benedick, Touchstone and Hamlet. These were thrilling opportunities, but difficult ones, too, and the old fears returned. Once again, I found it very hard to enjoy my professional achievement, and I was already torturing myself with visions of potential disaster. I decided to follow Olivier's advice, have a bash and hope for the best.

NINE

'Go travel for a while'
PERICLES

We were all feeling very nervous about the Shakespeare season, and throughout the casting sessions Geraldine and Judi had been modest and hesitant, with everyone straining to be nice to each other. It was a pleasant fault, but Judi saw the need for an ice-breaker, and once the Company had been finalised she had the inspired idea of holding a Company party in her country home, a beautiful Elizabethan house in Surrey, on the Sunday before rehearsals started. It was a chance for this young group to actually see each other once before embarking on nine months' work together. Riotous company photographs were taken, large quantities of champagne were consumed, and I ended up playing football in Judi's garden, with my godson, Calum Yuill.

The party had relaxed everyone but the following Monday morning, which started with rehearsals for *Much Ado*, was still a very tense occasion. Judi was visibly frightened, and grabbed me at once, telling me to stick close. It was plain that she wasn't keen to give a directorial lecture, and she declared immediately that she didn't have 'a concept' of the play. What she did have was a very clear idea of how the play might look, and convictions about certain aspects of *Much Ado* which she felt were important. Throughout our discussions she had been very humble about her own ideas, all of which were strong, and on this first morning she was touchingly vulnerable as she spoke to us about the dark side of *Much Ado*, about its strange treatment of sex, and its often sinister quality, which was an aspect she wanted to underline. She also stressed the lightness of touch which the play demanded. During the first week of rehearsals Judi's tone of voice and manner suggested that people might not take her seriously or do what she said, a nervousness that was quite unnecessary, as the whole Company was more in awe of her than she was of us. Although Judi had made very sensible cuts in the play, she was terrified of giving them to the actors, who she plainly thought might mutiny. But laughter began to break down the barriers, and amid general hilarity the cuts were noted, moaned about noisily, and the read-through proceeded with first-day nerves starting to disappear.

Relieved and slightly hysterical actors broke for lunch and I went to a meeting with a film lawyer. Stephen had decided to go ahead with *Henry V* and had crazily agreed to the timetable which I had put forward. With the airy certainty of the blissfully ignorant, I had told him that the film would cost £2½ million. I don't know where I produced this figure from, but I reckoned that at least it would frighten him. He had managed miraculously to produce £250,000 for the Shakespeare season, and I was hoping he might respond to the challenge. He'd insisted nevertheless that I produce a screenplay on which a full budget might be based. I had no choice – if I really did believe in a film version of *Henry V*, then I had to do something about it. All through January I slaved over a hot typewriter to produce a text and detailed stage directions which would allow my conception of the piece to be visualised by others, and to be broken down into budgetable scenes.

I delivered the script, and with it the virtual ultimatum that I would not do it unless filming began at the end of October, immediately after the Shakespeare season finished. God knows where this chutzpah came from, but I had very strong instincts about the whole project. The pace of events at Renaissance had developed so rapidly that I think my mind and ambition were racing ahead. Anything seemed possible: the Shakespeare season, which had once seemed impossible, was shaping itself into a nationwide tour with a London season; we were moving from a 150-seat Studio auditorium into large theatres up and down the country, and would be playing (we hoped) to up to 2,000 people each evening. I had a blind and ridiculous faith in the venture. We were still in control, and my instincts told me that, if Judi's first comments were anything to go by, then *Much Ado* had the potential to be very special, and I was sure that the other two productions would at least be exciting. We were on the verge of finalising a West End season that took us to the end of October, and, again, I had a hunch that the possibly triumphant arrival of Renaissance in London for a three-month season could be the showcase which might produce the final bits of finance for the movie. Money men, distributors, anyone could come and see us in the flesh providing the 'popular' Shakespeare which the company and all three directors would be trying to create.

At this point film plans were highly fanciful, and yet Stephen and I both knew that if they had any chance of being realised then, all through the nine months of the Renaissance tour, we would have to be arranging meetings, fixing studios, sorting out designs and organising everything as if shooting really was set to start on 31 October 1988.

In early February we had a screenplay, an actor/director, and the goodwill of Judi and Derek, who had already agreed to be in the imaginary movie as Mistress Quickly and Chorus respectively, making an impressive start for the cast. We'd *have* to make it. The film lawyer did not agree, and asked many of the questions which would plague us over the coming months – it's been done before, why do it again? How do you know Shakespeare will work on film in the eighties? How do you know you can direct? In short, he produced a number of very sensible responses to what seemed like a pie-in-the-sky project. I reported back to Stephen and then lost myself in *Much Ado*, where I was simply an actor doing a job, and not a film mogul.

Judi felt her way carefully through the first week. She didn't enjoy the initial 'blocking', but far preferred the work on character that she was starting with each of us, and on the speaking of the text, which she was determined should obey strict rhythmic rules. By the second week she was firmly into her stride and the laughter in rehearsal was almost as great as the discipline with which she conducted each session. She was particularly savage with my Benedick. She had not wanted to cast me in the role originally but as several actors turned it down and as I made a good pair with her preferred Beatrice, Samantha Bond, I got the part. I found it extremely difficult to get to grips with the role and, though striving for the opposite effect, I was making him very broadly comic. Judi jumped on this immediately. A great comic actress, she was not going to have Branagh's vaudeville act disturb the balance of her production, and she led me very much in the direction of the heartfelt warmth and naturalism of Samantha's Beatrice.

Watching Judi at rehearsals was marvellous. She was like a clear glass through which one could see the mood of the piece ebb and flow. Her instinct was infallible: like an orchestral conductor she knew exactly where to place each pause, each rest, and each acceleration. As the weeks went by her directorial gifts blossomed, and she always resisted the urge to act the scene out for you, searching instead for the words and the imaginative suggestions which would release the actor further into the part.

Judi's ideas for the design of the set and costumes developed and in look and tone she was catching a delightful Mediterranean quality which could convey the light and shade in the play. Confidence was growing all the time, right through the Company – Judi could really direct and the Company responded vigorously. We were already discovering a gold mine in Pat Doyle, who had provided a marvellous score for *Twelfth Night* and was now producing some beautiful tunes for *Much Ado*. The music would be performed entirely by the actors, which was another element that bonded the Company together and reinforced our sense of commitment. We really were all in it together, and there was a sense of something very special in the air. As the month's rehearsal in London drew to a close we looked forward to the opening in Birmingham with real anticipation.

It was impossible not to be excited. Judi had informed me before rehearsals started that she'd just got 'a marvellous job for the panto season', which was a delightful way of announcing herself as a Dame of the British Empire. The newspapers were full of Judi, and I was doing endless publicity myself. There was no choice. Birmingham Rep wanted to celebrate our arrival and we were concerned about the box-office: even with a sold-out run at the Studio, Renaissance would be left with a deficit of £80,000. This was serious money, and I was aware of the danger involved. We were in a financial corner, and forced to draw as much attention as possible to a project that we had hoped to initiate quietly in order to protect the delicate conditions of this new actor/director experiment.

We arrived in Birmingham to receive the joyful news that we had indeed sold out, and were now faced with a flood of letters of complaint from people who couldn't get in. *Hamlet* had sold out its fifteen Birmingham performances on the morning that booking opened. Although we were worried about its effect on the quality of the shows, I was relieved to think that by taking the shows to larger theatres on tour, more people would be able to see the plays than at Birmingham. I hoped that one day we might find the right balance – studio Shakespeare is great, but only for the 150 people who manage to get in. How is intimate acting in Shakespeare shared by lots of people? By making a film of *Henry V*. But more of that later.

We began the technical rehearsals for *Much Ado*, the most unfamiliar area for our novice directors. The studio setting helped, as the smaller stage seemed fairly manageable and Jenny Tiramani's set of an elegant Sicilian Villa could be lit relatively easily by Judi, who was working with her long-time colleague and lighting designer, 'Basher' Harris. Judi remained a stickler for detail in this technical area. She hated sloppiness in production or acting, and the actors and stage managers rallied, with everyone in the eighteen-strong team making themselves available for scene changes. There was a tremendous sense of togetherness – everyone knew the precariousness of our financial position and everyone had access to Company accounts. This openness produced the sense of goodwill that creates that hard-to-define quality of a marvellous 'Company feeling'.

It doesn't always follow that this produces a marvellous performance. Although friends who were in loved it, the first preview of *Much Ado* was a tense affair. The first performance of a comedy is always difficult: people never laugh when you expect them to, and it is very difficult to find a playing rhythm. For our first-time director it was a harrowing experience. The actors are occupied with the play and at this stage are simply concerned with their own performance, but Judi was discovering the unfamiliar feelings of directorial helplessness and a tense concern which embraces every aspect of the production. She walked slowly into the large communal dressing-room after the show, looking white and shell-shocked. I had seen her in the tiny auditorium where everyone was frighteningly visible, hunched over her director's notebook and suffering with every stumbling attempt by her inexperienced cast to get it right first time. Now it was all over and her voice was hoarse with anxiety. 'It was like watching a pile-up on the M1.'

There was laughter all round but it was clear that she was quite shaken. As everyone disappeared to a local Indian restaurant to mull over the lost laughs, Judi stayed behind and took me by the arm. 'Oh, Kenny – it was like giving birth to a baby that isn't breathing properly. You watch it trying to walk and then it falls over and can't get up, and you can't *do* anything. It's agony.'

Judi went back to her hotel and came in the next day with new resolve and an armful of notes. The next performance picked up enormously, as we relaxed and allowed the audience to relax as well which – surprise, surprise – allowed them to laugh. On the Sunday I spent my day off in Manchester, where I danced on a giant record player as my last contribution to Emma Thompson's new show. The change was as good as a rest and Emma, who had seen the first preview, was very encouraging.

I left for Birmingham on the Monday morning which was the

Company morning off. This allowed them a slightly longer weekend away from an increasingly frenetic work schedule. The local press night for *Much Ado* was Tuesday, but before that on Monday afternoon we had our first rehearsal for *As You Like It*. There really was no stopping: note sessions with Judi had to be fitted in after *As You Like It* rehearsals, or grabbed over beans on toast in the Rep canteen. Financial dictates had forced us to contract the rehearsal periods like this, and I was already wondering whether I would be able to stand the pace.

With a shaky Benedick in performance and a Touchstone about to start rehearsal, I still had far too many other things to think about. Stephen Evans had secured Elstree Studios for our hypothetical production of *Henry V* and I was needed in London for meetings with a producer who seemed to be the next step towards realising the project. Bruce Sharman was an experienced film man with an impressive list of credits, and over another precious free Sunday we talked about the production, its difficulties and the budget. With an accountant he had produced an accurate figure to confound my fly-by-night fancies: we would need £4.5 million, and more if we went on location. I had talked idly about putting the battle scenes on Dartmoor, but this was out of the question – it would add weeks to the schedule, go across Christmas and add millions to the budget. No. Turn again Whittington. I returned to Birmingham and put my feet on another step of what was at least an exciting treadmill.

The Tuesday press night for *Much Ado* went well, and afterwards Judi, who was now much more relaxed, was already reluctant to say goodbye to the Company of which she was becoming very fond. She had come through with flying colours and the local press concurred by saying all the right things, bar one critic who made the cardinal error of saying I was rotund. I am still looking for her.

The weeks were flying by but the rhythm changed dramatically with Geraldine McEwan whose much slower, more methodical approach to *As You Like It* was in sharp contrast to the swift and breezy atmosphere which Judi created for *Much Ado*. Both had judged the moods of the plays perfectly and rehearsed them in just the right way. The seeming fragility and breathtaking honesty of Geraldine's personality defined the delicacy of this play – a beautiful discourse on love. She was extremely patient with a young cast and produced marvellous things from Tam Hoskyns and James Larkin as Rosalind and Orlando. The Company were all helping each other, and on this production in particular there was a good level of mutual help and support. Company feeling had not diminished – we were united in exhaustion, if nothing else.

With confidence growing in my Benedick, I was encouraged by Geraldine to take great risks with Touchstone. She had chosen an Edwardian setting for her *As You Like It* and this allowed the Fool to emerge from the music hall. I didn't have to be asked twice, and armed with a marvellous arrangement of 'It was a lover and his lass' from Pat Doyle I set to work on developing a Touchstone that borrowed from Max Miller, Archie Rice and about every professional comedian I'd ever seen. It was a loud performance, but was just about legitimate, and it was borne with great patience by my fellow actors who had every sympathy with a comedian who has to make the following joke on his first entrance:

ROSALIND   Where learned you that oath, fool?
TOUCHSTONE   Of a certain knight that swore by his honour they were good pancakes, and swore by his honour the mustard was naught. Now I'll stand to it, the pancakes were naught and the mustard was good, and yet was not the knight forsworn.

Boo-boom. You try making that funny. Shakespeare might have been amused by it for a week in 1599, but in Birmingham in 1988 it provides certain difficulties. Archie Rice it was. Forgive me, father.

The candle continued to be burned at both ends. Monday mornings meant film meetings in London where the salesman in me would try to persuade the latest contact of Stephen's to part with a million pounds. This time it was the Completion Guarantors, who were, in effect, the film's insurers, and without whose approval the film could not be financed. Their main concern was my directing as well as acting. Thinking on my feet, I produced Hugh Cruttwell out of the air. He was already advising in Birmingham, and without permission I instantly unveiled him as artistic advisor on the movie and in so doing proved to them that I had a sufficiently strong insurance policy. They were satisfied. Yes, they would guarantee the film. *And* I could direct.

Phew!

If we found the 4½ million.

Ah. Back to Touchstone.

Bold though my performance was, I was not rising sufficiently to he challenge of Touchstone. As Hugh pointed out at a preview I imply wasn't on top of the text. Of my three roles in the season, I ound Touchstone the most difficult to learn with the famously :omplex and unfunny 'lie' speech being a particular pill. It was the irst sign of the work-load taking its toll. I bought some vitamins and went back to the text. Since *Romeo and Juliet*, it had been eighteen months of solid hard work, and I really was going to have to be careful. *Hamlet* hadn't even started.

As You Like It opened to enthusiastic local press and audiences. Like *Much Ado*, the plaudits were for its freshness and wit and lack of pretension. Both shows were elegant and simple, allowing the plays to breathe through, and placed great emphasis on the acting itself which was developing in confidence all the time. As well as the two principals here, there was a fine Jacques from Richard Easton and a lovely Celia from Sophie Thompson. We were developing new talents, which fulfilled an essential aim of the Company. The only drawback was the pressure on everyone who, by the time *Hamlet* opened, would have been rehearsing and playing solidly for three months.

My own pressure was, of course, self-imposed. As Derek arrived from a triumphant Broadway season, we began *Hamlet* rehearsals, were playing *As You Like It* and *Much Ado*, and Tim Harvey, the designer for *Henry V*, came to stay with me in Birmingham to work on plans for the film. By this stage so much time, effort and now money had gone into *Henry V* that we didn't dare let it drop. In that first crazy week with the moody Dane, I was rehearsing from 10 am, breaking at 5.30 pm, playing one of the comedies, then having design meetings over a late supper for a movie that might or might not happen. Was I doing too much? Yes. Was it any good for Hamlet? God knows.

Derek started rehearsals at high speed. He wanted a dramatic and highly theatrical production that acknowledged the rich store of theatrical imagery in *Hamlet*. He worked amazingly fast and knew every single word of the text, so that when anyone dried he was ahead of the stage management in prompting them. At first I resisted his suggestions, and I was determined not to be hurried or over-awed. There were a couple of days' wariness, and then we both began to trust each other and went to it with a vengeance. The play was blocked in a week. He had marvellous ideas for the women: there

209

were extra entrances and even re-allocated lines to help produce a truly heart-rending Ophelia from Sophie Thompson and a very strong Gertrude from Dearbhla Molloy.

Derek directed my Hamlet with amazing sensitivity – I had my own instincts and he shaped them. There wasn't an acting problem in the part that he hadn't already faced and analysed himself, and the alternatives that he offered me were fascinating. He was also of tremendous help in colouring speeches and knowing when to rest on the lines, which was particularly useful for the closet scene, which seems to me the Becher's Brook for Hamlets. At Drama School I had fallen into the trap of ranting through it and running out of steam early on, but Derek showed me how to pace myself and find enough breath and energy to get through *and* to make sense of the lines. He seemed to take to directing like a duck to water.

Derek and I developed a form of telepathic shorthand where short phrases and words would take the place of long explanations. Hugh balanced this by watching run-throughs and following up with typed notes which charted my development in the role. Everything Hugh said was aimed at deepening my performance, for my propensity for superficial energy was at points betraying the intellectual content that Derek sought to illuminate. But between Hugh and Derek I made great strides.

The first performance was electric. There was a packed house and a large returns queue, and I had the strange sensation of being followed right up to my very first entrance by an American TV documentary crew who had been filming throughout rehearsals. During the performance the time passed in a whirl of worrying about getting on and off, but there was undoubtedly something in the air. At the end of the play we had taken several curtain calls and were back downstairs in the dressing-room shrieking with relief when people started commenting on the ferocious banging noise which came from above us. The audience was stamping its feet and still cheering. The cry went round, 'We've got to go back. We've got to go back.'

Exit fifteen hysterical actors who stumbled and fell across the tiny Studio stage where they were greeted by a magnificent standing ovation. People occasionally rose to their feet at RSC shows I'd been in, but it was the first time I'd experienced the full-blown version. We dragged Derek down onto the stage and eventually made our tearful exit, looking forward to a long and strong drink.

Over the following weeks I learned about the uncomfortable phenomenon of playing Hamlet twice on Saturdays. The stomach-wrenching sick feeling that overtakes one as the first soliloquy begins is truly terrifying and it's impossible not to be aware of quite how far you have to go in this Everest of a role. But at that point we'd stopped rehearsing full time and whatever the controversial response might be to Derek's production, it was a very honourable addition to a trio of excellent shows. A local press night was followed swiftly by a national press night. The major critics had already visited the comedies and been warmly enthusiastic. With the usual cavils, we seemed to get away with Hamlet, too. There were raves, and, as always, there were those for whom I could never be Hamlet in a million years and who found the production an offence to their sensibilities. The daily tide of congratulatory mail confirmed that the general public response as well as that of the critics had been very positive.

There was certainly no opportunity to rest on any laurels. As soon as *Hamlet* had opened, David and I were forced to ask the Company to agree to understudy each other, as a cover system was necessary for the big theatres that we would play in. At Birmingham we had simply taken a risk on everyone staying in good health. If an actor had been off, then the performance would probably have been cancelled and 150 people would have been disappointed. Touring to large houses, a guarantee of performance was required in order to fulfil insurance obligations. The result was a very complicated cover system where people in smaller roles could cover the larger ones and still manage to play their own part if an emergency arose. The logistics of this meant that almost everyone had extra parts to squeeze into their already heavily taxed Shakespearian memory banks. It was not an ideal situation, but the Company responded magnificently with people actually volunteering for particular roles that interested them. It meant extra work all round for stage management and an impingement on the actor's precious free time while on tour. I felt extremely guilty, as I had watched the pressure on the understudy system at the RSC and had always wanted to improve such a difficult area. We had clearly not thought this one through sufficiently. Things would be different next time.

Towards the end of our stay in Birmingham, Prince Charles asked if Renaissance could provide a Shakespearian entertainment for a private party at Windsor. Judi Dench, Derek Jacobi, Emma Thompson were all available to perform in this 'Miscellany', and we rehearsed some of the Bard's greatest scenes in the Patron's Bar at the Birmingham Rep. I directed the show, which was excellent practice for *Henry V*. It was terrifying to be directing great actors, but I was relieved and delighted to find that they were prepared to listen to me. They all headed south with their fifty-minute programme, while the rest of us set off across the water.

On with the shocks. The Opera House, Belfast, and we went from 150 people to 1000 people. There was a full house. I'd spent all day doing 'local boy makes good' publicity, and in the late afternoon, when I saw our Studio set seemingly adrift in the expanse of the great stage, my heart sank. I was learning quickly that being a small-time impresario and playing Hamlet four times a week was an uneasy mixture. For various reasons, Derek had not been available to see his show transfer to a big house, and by the time I arrived, David and the stage management and design teams had been working for hours to do an instant conversion. The cast turned up, and although we had attempted rough re-blockings in the last week at Birmingham, we were faced with immediate adjustments which dealt with sight-line problems that had been impossible to predict in advance. We did what we could on the spot and at seven o'clock I retired to the dressing-room/office I was sharing with David. Peace seemed very

hard to find and this seemed the very best or the very worst preparation for an evening as the moody Dane.

The warm reception from our Belfast audience resolved most of the problems of tiredness and adjustment. They were just plain delighted to see us. After the performance we attended the first of the many parties that would be a feature of the tour, and which were often provided by one of the local sponsors that Stephen had encouraged to support our week in a particular town. The reaction of our Belfast hosts was ecstatic, and there, in full glorious loyalty, were my parents, who had flown over especially to see the great home-coming. They were in danger of expiring with pride.

The bookings for the week ahead were near capacity, there was a great deal of publicity. Walking into town from Uncle Jim and Aunt Kathleen's house, where I was staying during the Belfast run, I was often recognised and stopped. Local people were no longer sus-picious about Billy's English accent – they'd read the papers, they'd seen *Fortunes of War*, and they now seemed to accept that I was an Ulster one-off. There was a funny sort of inverted snobbery and pride about my involvement with Shakespeare. They liked the idea of one of their lads showing the English how to do it and they were delighted that Belfast was first stop on the tour. The recurring uneasiness that I felt about my Irishness was beginning to disappear. Suddenly I was being accepted for what I was and not what people thought I should be. I left Belfast with more peace of mind than I was used to experiencing in my home town, and it was a feeling that would thankfully remain with me.

The towns rolled by, and I felt as if I was in a montage sequence from one of those American movies where the train steams across the plain and those whirling place names rush up into the frame. Only this time it wasn't the Cohan family from Yankee Doodle Dandy steaming through Ohio and Nebraska. It was Dublin and Bath and Brighton. Up and down reviews, up and down sponsors and, thank God, packed houses – it looked as though we might recover the £80,000. David Parfitt's anxious gaze at the weekly figures became slightly less manic. In between advance publicity for the towns ahead and the dreaded understudy rehearsals, Stephen would grab me for work on the film, and likely punters would be brought along to see the show when we were within shouting distance of London. During the week in Brighton, I commuted and found time to deal with the latest film crisis.

After detailed planning with Tim Harvey about how to produce Agincourt in a car park, Elstree Studios was sold overnight in a mysterious deal which left us without a place to shoot. It seemed like the death of the project. Pinewood and Shepperton both had problems with our dates, but we almost managed to complete a deal with Pinewood who then had to pull out and go ahead with a more definite offer from another movie. It seemed unlikely that Shepperton would be available. We were forced to wait for a cancellation and to carry on raising money, although no studio had been booked.

Manchester, Newcastle and Richmond. It was all travel, and Sundays passed in a haze. Although I tried to keep one day free every week, Renaissance activities continued to impinge. Most extreme was a trip to Denmark. After months of detailed negotiation, we had produced a wonderful bonus trip in the shape of a visit to Krönberg Castle, Elsinore, to perform *Hamlet* in its actual home for a two-week season. The green spires of this Renaissance palace were an impressive sight. The place had extraordinary majesty, and once across the moat and inside the inner castle with its sea-facing battlements, we all felt an undeniable frisson – one could imagine sea battles and ghosts of all kinds. Several months in advance of our August trip

David, Derek, Sophie and I gave up yet another Sunday to drum up publicity for the Danish run. They knew and loved Derek who had already played there, but they didn't know me from a bar of soap.

Tiring though it was, the trip did confirm the marvellous atmosphere that could breathe out of this strange Renaissance castle, where a troop of Shakespeare's actors were reported to have played in the 1590s. It was impossible not to be affected by their ghosts or those illustrious actors who had played the Prince at Elsinore in the current century – Gielgud, Olivier, Burton. Heady stuff.

Theatrical romance does not a movie make. Bruce Sharman needed a second draft of the script. On the Monday of our appearance in Newcastle I found myself in Teddington practically manacled to his desk and doing the re-writes which were necessary for rebudgeting. Bruce dropped me at Heathrow airport so that I could catch the 4.30 plane, and on checking in I found that there was an unspecified delay. It was our opening night of *Hamlet* in Newcastle, and I was stuck in the Departure lounge at Heathrow. At 5.45 we took off, David met me at Newcastle airport, and I arrived in the theatre at five past seven. I must never play Hamlet under these conditions again.

It was difficult to resist the intoxicating momentum of the movie. It still seemed like a crazy notion but we now had a detailed budget, designs, a pencil booking at Shepperton (it looked like there would be a cancellation), a business expansion scheme which looked as if producing £1½ million, and now there was interest from the BBC who were prepared to consider an investment in this unmade film in return for the television rights.

In the latter stages of the tour I found myself on planes and trains commuting from the North in order to attend the latest vital meeting. We were just about to start official pre-production, that is, have offices, a skeleton staff, and begin the long-term preparation that was necessary if the movie were to start shooting on 31 October. With the last-minute preparations for Elsinore taking up more and more time and the tour fatigue at its most extreme, Stephen Evans called a two man council-of-war in Manchester after the midweek *Much Ado*. He had grafted relentlessly on the project and had maintained enthusiasm and belief at a time when many others were expressing doubts. How could I possibly prepare for the first movie I had ever directed if I was playing eight shows a week in the West End?

The objection was fair, but I reckoned it could be done, and something told me that if we didn't strike while this particular iron was hot the movie would never be made. The spectacular and surprising success of the Renaissance tour seemed to make anything possible, or at least, that's what I thought.

On a bleak rainy night in Manchester, Stephen did his utmost to persuade me otherwise. He could have pulled out there and then, and without him the project had no chance. I could persuade as many people as possible over lunches and dinners but he was the one with the contacts, the introductions and the financial know-how to make it work. Instead of threatening me, he tried to make me see sense. It was surely wiser to start in the New Year, to have a rest after the Renaissance season and then have a completely clear period in which to prepare the film. It all made total sense, but I was also sure that in the weird world of movies, it would ensure that once people had enough time to think about its drawbacks, the film would never be made. I said as much and left it to him to make up his mind. I took a cab back through a miserable Manchester night to the digs I was sharing with David and his wife, Sue, and wondered what would happen.

And then there was David Puttnam. A rescue plan seemed ready to dispel Stephen's doubts and renew my belief in the whole thing. Through Brian Wenham, whom Stephen had inveigled onto the Board of the newly formed Renaissance Films PLC, and through the recommendation of Prince Charles, David rang our office. He spoke to our brilliant new miracle-working administrator, Iona Price, and arranged a meeting. At his mews office in Kensington he and his partner, Colin Vaines, quizzed me in great detail about the usual things: directing/acting, what crew I wanted, the tight schedule, my physical condition. I'd faced this kind of questioning before and was ready for anything. David was cautious about the project, but was interested in helping us. He had a deal with Warner Brothers who had distributed all of his Enigma movies, and we now had £2½ million. He suggested that he go to Warner Brothers to see whether on his recommendation they might be prepared to put some money up front in order to buy the American distribution rights and allow us to make the movie. It was an exciting move. Quite what David's involvement would be wasn't clear, but we would work that out if and when Warner Brothers showed an interest.

This was giddy news to take into the last week of the tour in Leeds, and it coincided with confirmation that the BBC would make an

216

investment in the film. The week ended in a flurry of phone calls as I pursued the busy David Puttnam for news of the Warner Brothers' response. The silence was deafening, and it reinforced another harsh lesson of the movie world – if you're supposed to hear on Tuesday, you'll hear on Friday; if something is definitely going to happen on Monday week, then it happens on Wednesday fortnight.

Stephen and I were finding ourselves in this uncomfortable position halfway through the Elsinore stay and with pre-production dates winging towards us. Action was necessary. On my one day off from twelve consecutive Danish *Hamlets*, I flew to London for a meeting between David, Stephen and me. It was at least a respite from the relentless Danish glamour that had already produced two Royal visits in our first week at Krönberg, including one from our own Patron, Prince Charles, and one from the Queen of Denmark.

As David appreciated, time was not on our side. Warner Brothers were hedging over the project, and Stephen suggested that we forget their involvement. He was confident of raising the rest of the money in this country, but we needed to know if David would definitely become involved. David confirmed that he would take on the position of Executive Producer, providing this was acceptable to Bruce Sharman and as long as Stephen could convince him of the strength of the money. Stephen was sure he could and was even more convinced that with David's name and the BBC's attached to this quintessentially English project, that the other £2 million could be found easily. Proof of David's direct style and commitment had been given by his instant decision to fly to Elsinore the following Saturday to see *Hamlet* and to discuss some of the details of the film production.

The international airline timetables had been kind to me once more, and I arrived back at the Castle with an hour to spare. All of the male members of the Company had been assigned roles in the movie and they were relieved that my mission appeared to have been so successful. The proof of the pudding was David's appearance the following Saturday. If I had any doubts about his interest they were swept aside by the candour with which he answered all of my post-show questions about crew, schedules and his involvement. With his extremely able assistant, Lindsay Posner, he seemed ready and willing to make the whole thing work. On his return to England he met up with Bruce Sharman and the two of them planned a way forward for the movie on the existing schedule and at Shepperton.

At last it seemed I could relax about the financing of the movie and take a breather before the full horror of working out how to direct it. This was accompanied by a delicious week's break in which I experienced all too rare moments of utter happiness in the front room at Camberwell, with the summer sun pouring in through the window and all seeming well with the world. Then the phone would ring – it was definitely Shepperton, so could I go and see the studio and plan Agincourt for the third time? It really did seem to be coming together. Not only was there Tim Harvey as designer, but we now had a production supervisor, Vincent Winter, and a director of photography, Ken MacMillan, who had shot *A Month in the Country*. It was late August and we traipsed round the Thames Water Authority's field opposite Shepperton Studios, still a million pounds short, but with David Puttnam on board and the world's longest tracking shot developing in the mind of Camberwell's Orson Welles. The next three weeks would be nerve-racking. If we pulled the plug on the project at the end of this period, then Stephen would lose £80,000, and for every week after that the total would rise. Turning back would be an expensive process.

The West End openings of our Shakespeare season were set for late August and early September 1988, and the plays were launched over consecutive weeks with relative ease. Not only had the performances grown enormously through theatres large and small, indoors and out, but the directors themselves had visited the plays regularly to service the productions and to curb my worst excesses in the comic roles. By this stage we were ready for anything. Our experience in Denmark of playing sometimes obscure Shakespearian comedy to a largely foreign audience had stiffened the sinews. West End first nights lost a little of their oppressive tension when one remembered a rain-soaked Danish matinée of *Much Ado* where Benedick's first soliloquy was accompanied by an air-sea rescue taking place at the back of the sea-front auditorium. When the Danish Queen saw the production, the rain was so insistent that Gertrude played the closet scene in an oil-skin in order to protect her nightgown. There really were worse things than opening nights, and since the season began we had had our fair share of them.

With the plays open to yet more good press, with the usual reservations about my Hamlet, and with queues round the block at the Phoenix, attention turned full time on the film. We had no choice but to start intensive pre-production. Actors were ringing me daily asking whether it was on or off, and technicians and specialist crew were being lined up by Vincent and Bruce. We all sat like greyhounds in the slips hoping that the combination of Stephen's financial acumen and David Puttnam's film experience would secure the last million pounds. There had been an ominous silence from David's office since the Elsinore visit, and I was uneasy when summoned to a special meeting with him which turned out to be on the afternoon of the press night for *Hamlet*. I seemed destined never to let this performance have the benefit of a clear day's rest.

David's news was bleak. 'I'm sorry to have to say this, Ken, but it is my absolute belief that this film will not be made.' Oh fuck. 'I've been in this situation before. Every warning signal is flashing. I believe totally in you, and I believe totally in Stephen. What I don't believe is that you have enough time. With the best will in the world, and with the best skills in the world, it just will not be possible to do the paperwork in order to get this money into place.'

'But . . .' He was unshiftable. He would continue to act as advisor and could not actually stop us from going ahead, but his feeling was absolute. The potential damage to my career was enormous and unnecessary.

'I am convinced that this film will collapse either two weeks before or two weeks after shooting begins.'

That was that. Exit David Puttnam from Renaissance film world and enter Kenneth Branagh as the gloomiest gloomy Dane the West End had ever seen. I found myself between scenes and during the interval sharing my misery and fear with Stephen and with Emma and managing to stop ringing people like Judi and Geraldine and everyone else to whom I felt morally obligated. Stephen refused to be down-hearted, and still felt the film was possible. He believed Puttnam was referring to finance that came from more usual sources. The great strength of Stephen's contacts was their relative lack of cynicism, and their basic unfamiliarity with the film business. Like me, he was also alarmed but encouraged that down at Shepperton necessary work was already proceeding on some of the larger sets, which had to happen if we were to start on time. The enormous wall that I had asked Tim to design for the 'Once more unto the breach' section was already being constructed and there was also a fiercely impressive plaster model. This was exactly Puttnam's point. We must not be wooed by the excitements of these apparent signs of the film being a reality. Everybody was subject to two weeks' notice. If we stopped the next day, it would cost us *three* weeks' money for everyone, apart from the materials and other costs. Bruce was keeping a beady eye on all of this but it was clearly not good for film morale that the increasing numbers of staff should be living under the threat of collapse.

Now it was Stephen's turn to convince me to carry on. There were still key areas of casting to finalise. We talked about mortgaging our various properties to keep it alive for another few weeks while he and his associate, John Wilson, had a chance to do the paper work on the last million. It never came to that but it was with trembling heart that I sat opposite the tea table with Paul Scofield and Ian Holm in an attempt to persuade them to join up. Both were kind, courteous, asked sensible questions and believed totally in my ability to make the film happen. The fear which attended the whole venture had focused the mind wonderfully and if I didn't have a movie confirmed, then I did have a dazzling clarity about the movie that I would one day make. Ideas for colours, costumes and storyboards spilled out. The nearer it got, the surer I was about the gritty realistic approach that was necessary to make it the truly popular film I had in mind.

My enthusiasm was fitful, and alternated with bouts of extreme fatigue and utter depression and doubt about the whole project. Each day meant that we were further committed. Pat Doyle, who I knew instinctively would be the right composer for the piece, had been engaged to produce a demo tape. More money. I was at Shepperton every day, meeting with actors, casting directors, construction managers. The sets were growing at an alarming rate. There were three weeks to go and we still didn't know whether we had all the money in place. As I continued to grab between-show meetings with Stephen, and David held the theatre company together my mind was full of every cinema hardluck story from Zanuck, Welles and onwards. The final stumbling block was a bank guarantee for half the money. I still don't quite know what that involves but we couldn't proceed without it, and nor could we keep the actors hanging on indefinitely. All the deals had been done, but we had asked everyone to wait patiently for 'confirmation'.

After yet another late-night sponsors' event where I had said a million thank-you's and drunk too much cheap white wine, I found myself at midnight in Joe Allen's with Stephen over a dinner where I gave way to my overpowering depression about the film's fate.

'We've done it, mate. I'm relaxed on that.'

'Relaxed?' I said wanly, my face hardly emerging from the black bean soup. 'Then can I confirm with all the actors?'

'Give it another forty-eight hours.'

'Oh Christ, Stephen.' The face went back into the soup. The end. I could take no more. I had no more enthusiasm with which to stall the increasing number of apprehensive actors who were desperately seeking reassurance. Nor could I continue to run from the equally understandable curiosity of the numerous backstage visitors that came to see the Phoenix shows.

'But I'm telling you we've done it.'

It was useless. I'd now got to the stage where I would believe we'd done it when I was watching it in a cinema in 1989. And I was forced to realise that there would be no perfect, golden moment when an individual or a company would say wholeheartedly, 'Yes, it will all work out, the film will be made.' The film industry doesn't operate in that way.

Stephen was right. Although I went through the following days like an automaton, it was clear that we were going to make it. I was summoned to the latest high powered meeting of Renaissance Films PLC where I signed anything that was put in front of me. The consequent paper work made up a volume the size of a telephone directory which catalogued the deal by which the £4½ million would be produced and released in time for us to start shooting on 31 October. My scepticism remained. If it did fall through at this late stage I wanted to be able to get up in the morning. Things went on happening – the actors were confirmed, and a full construction crew was engaged. I had to have conversations about camera equipment with Ken MacMillan and, with ten days to go, we had a full read-through of the piece with the entire cast.

Of all the dreams that this scheme had included, this had seemed the most unlikely. There, under one roof, in a film to be directed by me, were gathered the entire Renaissance Theatre Company, actors from *Public Enemy* and *Twelfth Night*, as well as Paul Scofield, Ian Holm, Derek Jacobi, Geraldine McEwan, Alec McCowen, Brian Blessed, Judi Dench, Richard Briers, and Emma Thompson, in short, one of the greatest casts which could be assembled for such a venture. A mixture of young and old, and all hugely talented. If I discovered that I couldn't direct on film I would still have to go a long way to obscure the talents of this remarkable group. I took a deep breath as I looked around the great table at which we were all nervously sitting. Debilitating nerves were one thing I could no longer afford. I plunged into my directorial address. This was the one time they would all be together, and I wanted this to be a 'Company' picture. Here was the one opportunity to establish the tone and taste of the movie so that we all understood. Everyone listened. I played Pat's marvellous demo and the atmosphere was thick with a sense of rare occasion. A disaster it might be, but a singular one. Everyone was glad to be there. We few, we happy few.

And few were the days of movie rehearsal that followed. Actor availability and my commitments to both film and theatre meant that there was one chance to go through each scene before the actors disappeared. Paul Scofield would rehearse all his French Court scenes in one day before returning some six weeks later to film them, by which time we would hopefully have completed three quarters of the movie. In these brief walk-throughs of the scenes I found myself being dangerously dogmatic. I simply trusted that the people involved would challenge me on my worst excesses. There was no time to do anything else. Again not an ideal situation but the only one in which to get this particular thing done. I had to believe I was right.

The Friday afternoon before shooting. I'm sitting on a strange piece of camera equipment actually practising for the opening shot on Charles Kay. Trying to get used to people calling me 'Governor'. Back to the theatre for the weekend marathon. Two final Hamlets. All the thank-yous and well dones were over. We'd had our end-of-season parties and tearful last performances. I felt very proud of what the whole season had achieved and although there was effort of a different kind ahead, my chief feeling as I vacated my dressing-room was one of relief that the undeniable slog of eight shows a week in demanding roles was over. There was a lot of Hamlet in Henry V but I would only have to produce it in short bursts and not in front of a thousand people between 7.30 and 11 pm. One of the things I looked forward to most was having the evenings to myself.

I had a quiet restful Sunday, part of a delightful and important habit that I was developing. At this stage dread seemed pointless. I'd done everything I could to prepare. I owed it to myself to enjoy the following seven weeks as best I could. Otherwise what was the point? The chief joy of that day was the continued sense of being unshackled from the gloomy Dane and the relentless pressure of the theatre. *Henry V* seemed a much lighter affair by comparison. I said a short prayer, took a rare sleeping pill and continued to hope for the best.

Good night, sweet Prince.

TEN

In the maelstrom of thoughts and activities that made up the filming of *Henry V* it was very hard to keep a grip on reality. Very soon days began to blur into one another, and the only way to assess how one was feeling and how it was going, was to try and record things as they happened. The following is a rough diary account of this highly charged period, on which I have imposed some kind of retrospective order.

Monday 31 October
Day One. The first scene of the piece, and a scene which is vitally important for establishing through the clerics – Ely and Canterbury – the tone of the whole first section of the film. A conspiratorial political mood; an unfriendly palace and a dark world beyond. Ken MacMillan responded to my request for some very atmospheric lighting. At the same time I wanted not to be aware of it, and wanted this scene to feel like a documentary. For all sorts of reasons I'd made the shooting of it extremely simple. It made the business of the first morning easier and somehow I quelled the paranoia that this hugely experienced crew would suspect me of filming the entire film in the same way. Other elements helped to make life easier. When I rolled up on set to munch on the obligatory bacon roll I was mightily relieved to see the reassuring and smiling faces of Charles Kay and Alec McCowen, who were playing the clerics.

My chief concern with the first shot was not to repeat the experience of a short test that we had made on St Crispin's Day, 25 October. The purpose of this had been to experiment with hair, make-up and costume, and allowed me the first chance to direct Colin Hurley, a young actor who had learned the part and who would stand in for me as Henry V. Despite the propitiousness of that date, I had still been certain that the fates were against me. I could remember clearly David Tringham, the first assistant, shouting for quiet, calling for the camera to turn over. Nothing was happening. It wasn't until I received a friendly dig in the ribs that I barked, 'Action'. I was determined that this should not happen on my first official day. Indeed, the reverse happened, and I found myself mumbling 'Action' before we'd even rehearsed. Calm down, Branagh. Charlie and Alec were brilliant, absolute pros who knew their lines backwards and were giving me the benefit of every doubt. The set began to give out the necessary atmosphere of trust that I needed in order to work.

By midday the seven set-ups were complete and the scene was finished. I couldn't believe it. A morning gone and we were on schedule.

The afternoon was tougher. Because of the speed, what I had dreaded had come to pass – I would be required to act on my first day. It was a baptism of fire. The entire English Court was required to be present for my opening speech, which meant twelve actors and behind them, in this vast medieval hall set, literally dozens and dozens of crew all thinking (as I imagined) 'Come on then, let's see what you can do'.

I did get on with it, even though my voice went up an octave. Despite Hugh's already excellent help I sensed I'd be doing this one again. Six o'clock arrived, and with it a huge sigh of relief.

Tuesday 1 November
Still in the English Court, and most of the pressure off me as actor, thank God. Instead the pleasure of watching Charles Kay make brilliant sense of the difficult Salic Law speech, Brian Blessed acting superbly, and providing a wild anarchic presence to relieve any potential tension.

'You can't direct for toffee, you big pouf.' He yelled this at the top of his voice, and the whole studio was in uproar. I laughed loudest and decided I loved the man to death.

Once a large number of important characters are gathered together and facing each other on a set, technical problems begin. I wanted to capture the paranoid atmosphere among these politicians, and this meant a great deal of coverage. I needed many different set-ups to record the reactions of all these important characters who figure throughout the film, and wanted the audience to be very familiar with them from the start. Unless one is extremely careful it's very easy to lose track of who's looking at who, and when. If you don't get it right, then it can make editing impossible. This whole

224

concept of what is known as 'crossing the line', of actors appearing to look one way and sometimes looking quite the other, was an unfathomable mystery to me. I understood the principle of it but no element of its practice. I was saved, as I would be continually, by Annie Wotton, the script supervisor, who not only kept me right on this, but with David Tringham, suggested valuable shots and adjustments that I hadn't even thought of. Though it was early days, a sense of team work was developing. I was being supported.

And we were still on schedule.

Wednesday 2 November

A slight sweat on today. Alec McCowen had to be released by lunchtime in order to get to Chipping Campden for an evening performance of his latest one-man show. Deadlines like this seem to guarantee delays, but we got away with it, if only by the skin of our teeth.

Lighting this picture would be difficult. I wanted a smoky, fire-lit, medieval darkness in which we could still see people's faces and which was not too dour. Possible, but very time-consuming. Already I was unreasonably impatient about delays, and I reckoned that I had about a week in which to prove myself as a director. I had an unwritten agreement with Stephen that if things started to go wrong early on, he would take me off the picture. There was far too much at stake. I resolved not to get behind schedule through any fault of my own but I finished Wednesday by re-shooting my opening speech which was considerably butcher after the disappearance of my first day nerves.

Thursday 3 November

A new set for the conspirators' scene. It was very cramped and exactly what I wanted for the Hitchcockian underbelly of this sequence but, try as I had, homework had not yielded up the right way to shoot it. There was a dangerous rehearsal in which I was sure people would rumble my indecision. But as I was to learn on a daily basis it is not possible, or even healthy, to plan every move and set-up in complete detail. Things can occur on the day which change any preparation you might have made and, with helpful advice coming from actors and crew, there are often improvements. So it proved with this scene, which I wished to make fast-moving, tense and violent. Once the set was properly lit, we were able to shoot the scene quite fast and bring something of that quality to our actual working methods. Once again the professionalism and discipline of the actors was a fundamental element in keeping us on course. No one dried. No one misbehaved, and Blessed's encouragement continued unabashed.

'Your direction's crap, Ken. Do you understand? *Crap*.'

I really couldn't take myself seriously.

Friday 4 November

By lunchtime it was clear that we were going to finish this scene by the end of the day, which put us a whole day ahead. Bruce and Vincent called me off the set to discuss this unexpected contingency. I had naively thought that we would have the day off. Not a chance. Another set was ready – the English Camp at night, but I hadn't done my full homework on that one. It was an exterior sequence, shot inside and I hadn't a clue what to do, or how to use the large number of actors who would be appearing for the first time and out of sequence.

'Well, we could always do your long speech, Ken.'

I understood the practical elements of Vincent's suggestion but 'Upon the King'? I wasn't ready to do that. My whole system was geared to the schedule. I didn't believe I could cope with this kind of change. Perhaps I could make up some new shots for the conspirators' scene?

Saturday 5 November

'Upon the King' it was, and all in one glorious set-up. Whether it turned out to be any good or not remained to be seen. At least there had been a psychological advantage in gaining a day, and I think the crew seemed genuinely impressed that their baby director could remember all of this four-minute speech in one go. Unusual in films. We celebrated by finishing early. I went home relieved but now newly apprehensive for the week ahead of night shooting on the 'Once more unto the breach' sequence.

Sunday 6 November

A recce for an opening sequence shot on the south coast which would later be cut. With divine wisdom we had chosen the day of the London to Brighton car rally and spent the hour-long journey either way in three-hour traffic jams. It did offer a lot of time to think, and I

226

was able to mull over the rushes that I had seen that week. They were screened during lunch and provided me with the extremely difficult task of monitoring performances and trying to find my chicken salad in the dark. Mike Bradsell, the editor, had already produced a rough assembly of the first sequence. It was impressive enough to be shown to Stephen and some of the money folk who were beginning to make their appearances on set. The week ahead would draw them even more strongly. The Harfleur set was a magnificent epic structure – dark and brooding. And bloody difficult to shoot.

Monday 7 November
Arrived at 4 pm to examine the chaos, which looked as though it would never be converted into a highly disciplined and dramatic battle sequence. Everyone was called at around 5, but I knew that we'd be lucky to have anything on film by 9 pm. I had a quick canter on my horse. Vic Armstrong, the brilliant stunt director, had patiently encouraged me with lesson after lesson during the pre-production weeks to revive the Roy Rogers of old. He'd provided a magnificent white horse that felt as easy and safe to drive as a tricycle, but looked much more butch.

The weather was on our side, although it was amusing to see the high fashion eccentricities of a film crew preparing for the cold. David Tringham was moon-booted up to his armpits. David Crozier, the sound mixer, was in a jump suit, redolent of Pussy Galore, and Annie Wotton was encased in what seemed like a blue eiderdown warehouse. I worried about how we were going to talk to all these people. They had so many clothes on I was convinced they wouldn't hear me.

I spent the first two hours saying, 'What's happening, David?' to the crazed first assistant who, with his two deputies, was trying to marshal our 100-strong English siege force into the positions that I wanted. The complicated tracking shots that I required were not only difficult to light on the back lot at Shepperton, but they also required complicated camera equipment and cranes.

We had a go at last, and the atmosphere of friendly chaos seemed to work for the mood of the scene and the famous speech. Henry's words became passionate, almost desperate pleas of persuasion to a confused army who had been driven out of Harfleur for the umpteenth time. Things were going slowly but it was undeniably exciting to see Ian Wingrove's special effects lighting the Shepperton sky and giving the convincing effect of Harfleur in flames. The only problem was it all took so bloody long. Maintaining energy and concentration as the night wore on was difficult. Even the midnight supper break for stodge intake could not prevent the onset of fatigue.

Tuesday 8 November
Home at 7 am. Up at 3 pm, and on the set at 5 pm. More of the same, and more difficult with each passing night to rally all our troops and persuade them that spending another cold night in an increasingly muddy field would be exciting and fun. As the nights wore on there were less people available, and the shooting schedule had to be planned so that we covered as much large-scale action as possible early in the week, before it really was a case of we few, we very, very few. Keeping track of what we'd shot was difficult. Annie was a genius, and David Tringham also helped in my instant education about film grammar. The weather gods continued to smile on us and no time was lost through rain or snow, an extraordinary achievement in the middle of an English November.

Wednesday 9 November
The English army principals had behaved remarkably all week. They were all there in the cold, John Sessions, Ian Holm, Richard Briers, and Robert Stephens. No complaints and all the hallmarks of really fine performers: total concentration on a scene when they were off camera, and everyone helping each other out. The unit was beginning to take on the aspect of an army under pressure, led by an inexperienced director who nevertheless wasn't losing his bottle. The camaraderie helped us deal with our first stroke of bad luck. Malcolm Vinson, the camera operator, with whom I had already formed an excellent working relationship, was injured when a piece of camera equipment sheared and the crane he was sitting on threw him to the ground, fracturing his pelvis. Rapid diagnosis confirmed that he was fine and would recover comfortably but would not be able to complete the picture. We stopped shooting early and went home to think.

Thursday 10 November
One of the more bizarre things to deal with that week was having a second camera unit. I hardly knew what to say to the first one. When

Trevor Coop, the main operator, would ask the familiar question about a set-up, 'What would you like here, guv'nor?' I found myself answering, more often than not, 'Anything you like, love. As long as it's exciting.'

My incompetence had endeared me to Trevor who saw us through this last night of the Harfleur sequence while the second camera unit doubled for him. With a television documentary crew also following us around the set, I wasn't sure at times what camera I was supposed to look at.

Friday 11 November
The rushes for Harfleur looked great. Much to my surprise, there was sufficient scale and drama, and in the scene between the four national captains, a marvellous sense of impending danger in the British ranks. As I had hoped the whole sequence at times resembled other kinds of conflict, most notably the First World War and its trenches. I was convinced the material could combine to make a truly exciting sequence, but I was relieved that I didn't have the nightmare job of Mike Bradsell, the editor. Harfleur would be a challenge, to say the least.

The English night-time sequence would be a great challenge for me, and the change of rhythm a great shock after the chaos of Harfleur. It felt as though one was hardly doing anything and that this was the point where the audience would leave the cinema. But my instinct had told me that this sequence was the very heart of the play – the reflective, melancholic, sombre pause before the battle seemed to fascinate Shakespeare. My hopes for the sequence were confirmed on shooting Robert Stephens' definitive performance as Pistol, which managed to retain the feeling of despair that we had caught in the rehearsals for the Boar's Head scenes. Really fine acting.

Saturday & Sunday 12–13 November
At last a weekend off to sleep and recover from having actually filmed one of the great set pieces that people would be inspecting with such scrutiny.

En avant.

Monday 14 November
We do the Outside English Camp at Night, inside during the day. My senses were becoming very confused. Mike Bradsell had worked slavishly to produce a rough assembly of what we'd shot to date, and it included my version of 'Upon the King'. I could see it wasn't right and, with the omnipotence of a director who's a day ahead, I decided to do it again. David Tringham had made valuable suggestions as to how it might be shot and I knew that Ken MacMillan was delighted to have another crack at lighting this very difficult set. I revelled in this unexpected luxury and planned it for the next day, and settled back to enjoy a superb performance from Michael Williams, who brought great compassion and intelligence to his Shakespearian namesake.

Tuesday 15 November
With a peculiar irony I embarked on the second shot of 'Upon the King' as Prince Charles came onto the set as part of a visit to Shepperton. He'd been shown round the design department and some of the other sets, had seen some footage and was now faced with Henry's very personal soliloquy on kingship. With his customary patience and tact he waited until I had, in my view, got it right and then chatted to me about his continuing support and interest in the project. He certainly was a Patron, and a great supporter. He'd even turned up in Bath, informally, to see our *As You Like It*, and his reaction to my Touchstone had been identical to my grandmother's in Belfast: both of them did an instant dressing-room impression. It is delightfully disconcerting to see either your aged grandmother or the heir to the throne flicking their cuffs, bending their knees and mimicking my classical Tommy Cooper.

He left me to get on with it, and told me that he really would be looking forward to this film premiere. There was one convert. Another 4½ million, and we'd get Stephen's money back.

Wednesday 16 November
The system has finally adjusted to being back on days. The English Camp sequence is finished. Stephen and Bruce are still pleased with the rushes. Something must be wrong. Disaster is obviously round the corner.

230

Thursday 17 November
Back outside and time to hang Richard Briers. Shakespeare kills Bardolph off-stage, but I wanted to show the effect on Henry and on the army. And of course I wanted it to rain. During the Agincourt campaign it had rained for eleven days and nights on the long march from Harfleur. It had been disastrous for the English army, and the man-made precipitation that we arranged was far from welcome with our film crew. Everyone gets wet, of course. Permanently. Equipment has to be covered, the sound is difficult to record, and the special effects people need time to control the flow of water through their numerous hoses. It was time-consuming and difficult. But rain it was.

Friday 18 November
A certain campaign weariness began to show itself. Teddy Jewesbury, our Old Sir Thomas Erpingham, had suspected shingles, and I feared that he would take me to court for having brought them on. And, despite the brilliance of Peter Frampton's prosthetic nose for Richard Briers, the artificial appendage had a limited life-span under the effects of continual rain. In addition, the weather was mucking us about. Sun, would you believe – sun in mid-November. We had to crack on with this scene before the clouds parted completely, Richard's nose fell off, and we suddenly found ourselves shooting *Carry On Agincourt*. The absurdities of the situation, and the fact that the light went at 4 pm, put a spring in our step. To my utter amazement, we'd gained another day. This was a tremendous boon, as I had felt more and more strongly that the film itself, and the Boar's Head sequences in particular, needed the help of a more direct reference to the character of Falstaff. Not only would Judi Dench describe the man's death in heart-rending detail, but I wanted the audience to be aware of his tremendous influence on the young Hal. I assumed no previous knowledge of the other plays on the part of the wide audience I wished to reach and had resolved to insert a flashback scene which would give the film more emotional weight. I scoured the *Henry IV* plays and constructed a scene that described Falstaff's relationship with Hal and with all the low-lifers. What I needed urgently was a fine actor to play this flamboyant, life-loving character. It required instant, full-blooded acting that could be sad and funny in the space of one short scene.
The gods decreed that Robbie Coltrane was available to take his

first swipe at a part which must be his birthright. A brief telephone conversation to this extraordinary Scotsman confirmed for us both that he could and should do it.

Saturday 19 November
First day on the splendidly filthy, spew-ridden Boar's Head set. Judi Dench's first appearance. She was nervous and vulnerable but, as always, ready to plunge in and trust her director and fellow actors. There were problems in trying to judge the exact mood and tone for the first appearance of each character, but the main problem was in controlling the giggling that went on, chiefly occasioned by Richard Briers' transformation into a lewd, gross Bardolph. With the Neanderthal Nym of Geoff Hutchings, the spit-spurting Pistol of Robert Stephens and Judi's own filthy Mistress Quickly, the incongruity was powerful and often comically infectious. The scenes needed to be funny, but we tried to keep the sense of underlying danger.

Sunday 20 November
Rest. Sunday had now become an oasis of calm and peace that was supremely important to me, the only day in which I seemed to live in the present. On the film, and throughout my work with Renaissance, I seemed to be preoccupied with the past or, more often, with the future, and consumed by an obsessive anxiety that allowed me very little real or lasting satisfaction as I went along. This sense of achievement was something I almost consciously denied myself, a complex debt being paid for feelings of guilt about my success. It is not a condition designed to produce happiness, or which allows you to consider alternative ways of life.

Monday 21 November
Proof, if it were needed, that Robbie Coltrane had the potential to be the definitive Falstaff. He was funny, melancholy, alive and deeply moving. I was delighted.

Tuesday 22 November
Rushes confirmed my on-set opinion. The flashback sequence seemed to work marvellously. And as we moved into the scene which recounts the death of Falstaff, it was clear that Judi, having played the scenes with Robbie, could infuse her lament for the dead knight with even greater feeling. The play is so infinitely varied that these

232

scenes felt as though they belonged to a quite different movie, so marked was the change in tone. It augured well for the finished piece.

In the meantime, I was revelling in not acting through the tavern sequences, and the mounting irritability that I was expressing about delays, the amount of smoke, and anything else that seemed to be in my way, was accepted with good humour by the cast and crew who, I suspect, put it down to fatigue.

Wednesday 23 November
Back outside for some mopping up on the Bardolph sequence, and the first appearance of Derek Jacobi. Securing Derek's availability for the film had involved Houdini-like escapes from previous commitments on his part. As it was, we could only call on him for brief periods, as he was about to open in London as Richard I I and had already started rehearsing *Richard III*. If scrambled Shakespeare was whirring through his brain, he gave no indication with his first speech as Chorus, the difficult 'Now entertain conjecture'. The lunchtime rushes were a blow, as they presented numerous technical imperfections on what had been a glorious take of Judi with the death of Falstaff speech. We had no choice but to do it again.

Thursday 24 November
More smoke, more delays, more irritation. But against all the odds, an even better performance from the ever-patient Dame. It was 7.30 in the evening before we had cracked it. I'd insisted on the whole thing being done in one, a five-minute take where many things could go wrong. The tension on set as we attempted the umpteenth take was almost unbearable. Only Judi's example prevented me from flying into an impotent rage against someone or something. Not worth it, love.

Friday 25 November
Patience had proved to be the right course. The rushes were superb. Just as well, as we were now back outside with a vengeance: the English Camp before the battle, and, for me, the hurdle of the St Crispin's Day speech. This needed a tremendous epic setting and we were back on the famous Thames Water Field. Behind us were pylons, to one side was a modern housing estate and on the other side was a reservoir. This called for great ingenuity on my part, and as many trees as we could use to disguise the modern world. As if this

wasn't enough, the religious calm of the speech was regularly punctuated by the sonic horrors of the Heathrow flight path.

Saturday 26 November

More air traffic, but miraculously the weather remained constant. There were no breaks for rain or sun, just pauses while we waited for the noise to die down. It was well worth it. Attempting to re-record this kind of dialogue in a studio was very difficult, and from my own point of view as an actor, almost always less successful. We had to have as much live sound as possible. We stayed on schedule and headed off for the weekend with our toughest week ahead of us.

Sunday 27 November

Panic.

Monday 28 November

We were off. 8 am on a frighteningly empty field in Shepperton. Annie Wotton and David Tringham looked at me with nervous anticipation: how do you start filming the battle of Agincourt? They weren't the only ones who wanted to know. We had 150 extras, thirty horses, numerous carts, actors and stuntmen. Fuck it. Bring 'em all on.

The numbers might be small, although they seemed pretty bloody enormous to me, but I knew that somehow we could achieve the effect I wanted – the brutal, savage scrum of Agincourt. It was important to fill the frame with as much activity as possible. There was a basic story-line which involved most of the principals, but with so many people and animals milling around in apparent pandemonium, and two camera crews, it was very hard to keep control of the narrative. It would have been very easy to get carried away and forget the basic colour coding that we'd employed and actually let the French win.

Tuesday 29 November

Having spent most of Monday in the saddle, I was megaphoning my way around the field as a bow-legged arthritic wreck. Reports of rushes were good. A relief.

Wednesday 30 November

We started on the slow motion stuff, which would be used to cover

234

the middle and end sections of the battle. With seventy-two frames per second whizzing through the camera, it meant that rushes' sessions stretched to over an hour at the end of a battle-weary day. The mud was getting deeper and each day was merging in with the rest. We needed a computer to work out who'd fought who.

Thursday 1 December
Not content with the time-consuming demands of slow motion, I now wanted rain again. Brian Blessed and the rest of the English army were getting used to this sadistic approach from their director. At this end of the week, they really did feel as though they'd been in a battle.

Friday 2 December
With the second unit starting to look after the residual stunts of horses falling, people being shot by arrows and everything else that was nasty, we moved back into the English Camp to film the aftermath of the battle. This scene which involves the death of the boys and the listing of the dead, is extremely affecting and was beautifully played by Ian Holm, who caught Fluellen's Welsh sentimentality exactly. Acting with him was like playing a racket game with someone very much more skilled. One was never sure how the ball would come back, but it would always be exciting and unexpected. He is a master of film technique. I'd heard the Ian Holm School of Acting described as follows: 'Anything you can do, I can do less of.'

Saturday 3 December
It was a funny sensation to read the list of the French dead while Europe's holidaymakers were whizzing overhead. I felt so much heavier and older after the experience of directing the battle, and of fighting in a great deal of it, that it was not hard to convey the immense relief at seeing light at the end of our particular tunnel.

Sunday 4 December
Rest. Calm and contentment.

Monday 5 December
The greatest tracking shot in the world. That was my theory, anyway. It was certainly bloody long. After the close-up carnage of

our Agincourt, I wanted to reveal as much of the devastation as possible. On our limited location we had not only built a 500 foot tracking platform, but Tim Harvey and his team had constructed a terrifying battlefield, where our 300 extras would mingle, wounded and dead, with horses and large numbers of dummy horses and people. To the accompaniment of a single voice starting the *Non Nobis* hymn, the exhausted monarch and his men would march the entire length of the battlefield to clear the place of the dead. As they marched, the music (provided on playback by Pat Doyle) swelled to produce a tremendous climax. There would be no question about the statement this movie was making about war.

David Tringham made this chaos work, and with our massive crowd and our remote control camera on its strange electronic arm, we began by 12.30 on that long day to start on the amazing shot. It was the last instance of my taking an inexperienced risk. Everyone had been suspicious that the shot would not work. We needed more coverage. Well, we did at least put another camera on the same track to gather close-up material, but I was convinced that the whole thing needed the sweep that the main tracking shot could give it. After each take, during which I carried Christian Bale the length of the field, we would watch nervously the video playback facility which we had specially employed for the day. The quality was poor and we had no alternative but to keep going. The visibility on Trevor Coop's monitor set was so poor that it was impossible to know what the remote control camera was picking up. Live, the action looked marvellous. As for the finished product, we would have to sweat.

I arrived home exhausted and somehow defeated and, for no good reason, burst into tears.

I felt as if I had come back from the war.

Tuesday 6 December
No acting. Hurrah! There were the French scenes to do now, and first on the list was the 'Comanchees coming over the hill' shot which I envisaged for the French generals pre-battle. I was delighted that our French seemed properly civilised and elegant, quite distinct from the rough English, but just as military. In the Olivier film they had been dangerously effete, which for me undermined the whole story. You had to believe before the battle that the English had no chance. With Richard Easton as the Constable and Michael Maloney a wonderfully fiery Dauphin, the French were a formidable force.

Wednesday 7 December
Back in the warm at last. I was glad not to have the wind whistling round my cod-piece any more. After the gory detail of the battle, it was a relief to direct the tense but still comic scene in the Constable's tent on the night before the battle. Derek came into this scene briefly and it was a comfort not to have the life-or-death dash to the theatre that had accompanied his filming during the battle period. We needed him for night shots and so had to wait until the light had dropped at 4.30 pm. We then had to take the scenes very quickly in order to rush him into a car and back to the Phoenix Theatre in time for *Richard II*. I would look at his haunted face, remember myself in that position and think, never again.

Thursday 8 December
Calm arrived with the appearance of Emma Thompson and Geraldine McEwan, both brilliant comediennes who transformed the French lesson scene into a beautiful, tenderly comic affair which manages in brief to show the woman's role in this depressingly male piece. She and Geraldine – fresh from her success in *Lettice and Lovage* – worked a treat together.

Friday 9 December
Enter Paul Scofield. If ever anyone was born to play kings, then it was this Titan, with his regal frame and haunted majestic face. I was more in awe of him than of any of the other legends working on the film, and yet he was the shyest of them all. He had no choice. Brian Blessed broke up any potential for undue reverence with his midday yell across the floor after I had given him some notes as Exeter. 'You never give Paul Scofield any fucking notes. You're just a bloody arse-licker. You've destroyed my performance.'

Scofield helpless under his crown.

Saturday and Sunday 10–11 December
Twenty-eight today. Bloody hell. The props boys made a surprise attack on me at the surprise birthday party while I was cutting the surprise cake which was in the surprising shape of the Harfleur wall. Wes and Gary's surprise involved two plates of shaving foam and much loss of dignity on my part. I licked my wounds on the Saturday night at the nicest birthday dinner I've ever had. Quiet, among

friends, and the whole delicious rare feeling lasting through Sunday.

Monday 12 December
Once more unto the breach, and it was the last week of filming. Signing the treaty. Scofield, me, Blessed, everyone. Hysteria. When the greatest seriousness was required, the greatest giggles started. I saw Scofield with the tears pouring down his face, pointing to Blessed and grabbing hold of Emma to say, 'Keep me away from that man.'

A VIP arrived on the set in the shape of the great director, Fred Zimmerman, who had directed Scofield in *A Man for all Seasons*, a marvellous film in which Scofield had given one of the all-time great screen performances. During breaks I listened in on their friendly gossip. About how Orson Welles had turned up on the set of that movie to play Wolsey and didn't know a line. Blimey.

Tuesday 13 December
The nobles disappear and leave Emma, Geraldine and me to get on with the wooing scene. It's a strange episode to place at the end of such a play and needs playing of the utmost delicacy if it is to tell us any more about this troubled monarch, and this strangely sensitive princess. The scene is both funny and tremendously sad. The princess has no choice, but she is spirited and intelligent, and subtly challenges Henry, who is unusually vulnerable in the scene. At the read-through, Judi had told me how much she had enjoyed playing this small role on three separate occasions in her early career. It is brief but beautifully written, even in broken French.

Wednesday 14 December
Hugh continued to be an enormous help. My insides were screaming out, 'only a few days to go', but I also felt a growing sadness that this marvellous family atmosphere on the set was about to be broken up.

Thursday 15 December
The very last lines of the play and most of the English and French armies were on set, with Derek, who was taking yet another break from *Richard III* to deliver the final Chorus speech. From Derek and

Paul the wonderful gravitas of the last movement of the piece is beautifully clear. All the lines seemed to be about resolution, with peace and hope emerging through the terrible experience of the play. As we waited for the last take to be checked, the atmosphere in the studio was thick with emotion. A brief moment of hysteria while the unit photograph was taken gave way to a moving scene where we said goodbye to all the actors. Only Derek had scenes left to do. For everyone else, it was the end. From Paul, Brian, Emma, Michael and everyone who had been part of this remarkable seven-week period, there was a tearful pride in the parting. It had been a glorious job and these last days had been among the happiest I had ever known, either personally or professionally. I shook as many hands as I could without giving in to sobs and reserved my warmest hugs for Brian, and for Emma.

The rest of the day was spent catching up on what are laughingly called 'inserts'. Shots of maps, feet passing, anything that we needed to help Mike edit. The mood on set was melancholy. I became irritable and found myself arguing with Annie Wotton for the first time in seven weeks about the way a map should be folded. What had happened to me?

Friday 16 December
A fresh breeze blew away the nostalgia of the previous day with our one location trip to Beachy Head where the Shakespeare-stuffed Derek would be required to deliver a Chorus speech while looking out at the French coastline. I arrived at the spot ridiculously early and found the place eerily quiet. We were on a deserted National Trust clifftop where the birds had decided to shut up temporarily to allow some Hamletian reflection on what had passed in the previous two months. Derek came and went, performing the speech beautifully. We tried unsuccessfully to get another shot which I had felt at one stage could open the movie – a pan across the French coastline eventually taking in the White Cliffs of England and ending on the contemplative face of yours truly. The whole thing was accompanied by the hollow crown soliloquy from *Richard II*, which seemed to express something of the message of our *Henry V*. The shot did not work and I decided to drop the Richard anyway. It simply didn't belong.

Saturday 17 December
A gesture towards Christmas shopping.

Sunday 18 December
The last day. In true cinema tradition, the last shot we filmed was the first shot of the movie. Derek was exhausted, but recovered after lunch, which is about as long as it takes us to get the tracking shot right. Stephen arrived for the last take and when the gate was checked we realised that we had actually finished filming a new version of *Henry V* in 1988, in seven weeks, one day ahead of schedule and amazingly under budget. I poured champagne into my dazed frame. We had done it.

Monday 19 December
Tidying up. Rushes good. Mike Bradsell confident that we can see a rough cut of the whole movie on Friday. Strewth. Meanwhile the wrap party. I went through in a state of high intoxication and endless thank-yous. I must have thanked everyone twice and when I started on the third circuit it was time to go home.

Friday 23 December
The week had passed in a blur of Renaissance meetings. Now it was time to look at the topic of our meetings. This first rough cut ran for two hours and forty minutes. Far too long. I knew that I would take at least twenty-five minutes out. That was OK. It was a little bare without the music but the potential for sound and orchestra was enormous. We'd invited heads of departments from the movie team to see it, as well as a selected group of close friends. They were all astonished at what we'd achieved so quickly. The possibilities for the film seemed limitless. As we sat over a late breakfast (the showing had been at 7.30 am) there were about thirty people in the room.

Several bacon rolls later I returned, exhausted, to my office and mulled over the enormous task ahead. There was a quote from *A Midsummer Night's Dream* which someone had scribbled on the noticeboard. It seemed an appropriate line for the months of post-production which loomed before us: 'Take pains, be perfect'. Fair enough. Here we go.

PRODUCTION HENRY V
CAM: K.MacMillan DIR Henry V
SLATE   TAKE
END LAST
DATE DEC 18 1988

POSTSCRIPT

'Sit down and rest'
THE TEMPEST

And what then? Well, there's been lots of 'then'.

A brief holiday and then a whirlwind introduction to the world of film post-production, where the director seems to have a frightening power. Supported by a brilliant editing team, headed by Mike Bradsell, and with a consultative rather than interventionist policy from Bruce Sharman and Stephen Evans, I have enjoyed this very demanding job. And thanks to the miracles of cinema technology, I have been able to produce exactly the film I wanted. It will not be to everyone's taste, but for me it succeeds in realising what we set out to do. The ensemble acting is superb, the work of each department is excellent, and an indefinable element of commitment and heart shines through the picture. It *is* a popular, accessible and yet serious view of an underrated play.

At least, that's what *I* think. For the moment. In whatever way time, distance, objectivity and the judgements of others affect my view of the film in the future, it seems essential to be able to enjoy the results of all that work in the here-and-now. It is not something I have always been capable of doing, but it's an attitude towards my work that I shall try to maintain.

What effect will this have on Renaissance? I hope that it means we lose some of the frenetic energy which seemed necessary in the early days – the nightmare timetables, the constant fatigue, and the incessant drive towards the future, while the very reasons for the formation of Renaissance were neglected. With inevitable compromises over working conditions, occasional thoughtlessness about Company welfare, an unsatisfactory understudy system, and other teething troubles, we have fallen at times into every trap that I had set out to avoid.

Having had time to reflect, it is clear now that an enormous amount has been learned. Slowly but surely the moves to create and protect our chosen conditions of work are becoming more effective. The manic autumn of '88 showed us the dangers of stretching ourselves beyond reasonable limits. At the same time the success of Renaissance has allowed us to carve a theatrical future that is no less exciting, but less unrelenting in its demands on the Company.

A world tour is now being planned where, nevertheless, continued financial pressure will make rehearsal time relatively tight, and will force us to make a number of compromises. But even then, the administrative structure, understudy system and workload will have improved as a result of the lessons learned over the first two years of the Company's life. Of course there will continue to be tensions for the young theatrical puritans, but they will resolve themselves. In time.

Time. One thing that I can at last enjoy – it has been mercilessly overstretched during the last two years, and it has been my greatest personal loss. Things are changing. David and Stephen are developing their own strong ideas for the Company, both on paper and in practice, and I am very happy to share responsibility, and to allow the Company to develop a character which is distinct from me as an individual, and which can stand on its own as a positive force in the theatre. This is happening in many ways: the success of the London season has allowed Renaissance to buy back the offices which the book originally helped to pay for, and its financial independence is complete.

Now that this book is finished, there is time for me to have a break. A great deal of *Beginning* was written at the same time as editing *Henry V*, and the self-imposed restrictions of time created enormous pressure. Now, at least, that way of working can change, both through desire and circumstance. The final cathartic thrust of finishing the movie has quenched the roaring ambition of a young man in a hurry, although it has not stopped me from wanting to realise particular projects in the future. I feel as passionate about certain plays and parts as I have ever done, but it is clear to me in retrospect that my success has not been accompanied by any real sense of sustained enjoyment or achievement. I have never given myself the chance to make any serious assessment of my work, and I have thus denied myself many chances to improve as an actor, which now stands as my primary concern. I shall continue to write and direct, and I shall also revel in the chance to see other work of all kinds. Yet another casualty of the last two years has been the lack of opportunity to see other actors' work in current theatre and films – a very dangerous situation.

It seems to me that a profound change has occurred, a shift of perspective which I welcome. At last I can see that a balance between professional and personal life can be achieved, and I hope that I continue to keep it in view.

Here's to it.

The readiness is all.

London, May 1989.